Catching
Ricebirds

Catching Ricebirds

A Story of Letting Vengeance Go

MARCUS DOE

HENDRICKSON
PUBLISHERS

Catching Ricebirds: A Story of Letting Vengeance Go

Hendrickson Publishers Marketing, LLC
P. O. Box 3473
Peabody, Massachusetts 01961-3473

ISBN 978-1-61970-825-9

Printed in the United States of America

First Printing — May 2016

Front cover photograph of the author by Shannon Lankford of Real Life Photography (www.reallifephotography.net).

The village weaver photograph used on the cover spine was taken by Adam Riley of Rockjumper Birding Tours (www.rockjumperbirding.com). It is used with his permission.

Library of Congress Cataloging in Publication Data

A catalog record for this book is available
from the Library of Congress
Hendrickson Publishers Marketing, LLC ISBN 978-1-61970-665-1

I live in memory of Lue Klayenneh Wisner Doe

Mother, all the sweet things you did for me
were not in vain. Thank you for everything
you taught me in the short time that I knew
you. I will never forget how kind you were.

I have learned throughout my life that sometimes
our deepest disappointments and darkest days are
when God speaks to us most clearly. In times of
great and desperate confusion, God taps on our
hearts. In our loneliest nights He whispers clearly.
During our quietest walks, God pulls aside the
curtains of our hidden hearts. He says, "Come
ye faithful servant and I will give you rest, cast
your burdens unto me and I will lift you up."

West Africa

Monrovia and vicinity

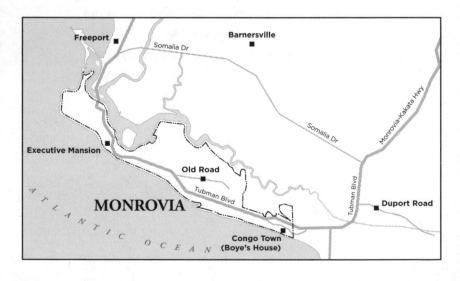

Contents

Acknowledgments   ix

Prologue: Jonah Speaks   1

Chapter 1: Land of Liberty   11

Chapter 2: Family Life   25

Chapter 3: Through a Child's Eyes   36

Chapter 4: Death Enters   53

Chapter 5: A Family Falling Apart   62

Chapter 6: A Country Falling Apart   72

Chapter 7: The War Arrives   84

Chapter 8: Entrenched in War   96

Chapter 9: Life behind Rebel Lines   108

Chapter 10: Imperfect Liberation   123

Chapter 11: The Decision to Get Out   132

Chapter 12: The Refugee Boat   145

Chapter 13: Freedom's Sky   153

Chapter 14: Assimilating in Ghana   169

Chapter 15: News from Home   183

Chapter 16: Going to America   190

Chapter 17: Drifting Alone   201

Chapter 18: Jolted Awake 215

Chapter 19: Facing Home 226

Chapter 20: What the Years Took Away 241

Chapter 21: Jonah to Joseph 248

Acknowledgments

It feels like I have lived three different lives. There are hundreds of people to whom I owe great debts and I would like to acknowledge their contributions and shout out to them publicly. God is sovereign and he ultimately plans our lives, but he used people to guide me along the way. First, my beloved parents, to whom the book is dedicated, the late Roosevelt T. Doe Sr. and Mrs. Lue K. Doe; these two did their best to raise me and made a courageous decision in their last days to make sure I was left in good hands. Roosevelt T. Doe Jr. and Mildred W. Doe took me into their home after just six months of marriage and became my parents. My brothers and sister, who encouraged me to complete this project. Thank you for your keen insight, wisdom, and the incredible love and encouragement you have shown me. Mark and Martha Wenzel, I love watching you live out the gospel in your marriage. To the beautiful woman who read the manuscript as many times as I did, my biggest supporter, my beloved wife, Annie, thank you for encouraging me through the process of writing a book. I love you.

There were many people who believed in me before I had any idea what was to come. I would be remiss if I didn't mention my teachers at J. L. Gibson Memorial School, where I began my education. Aunty Steffi Benjamin, thank you for encouraging me and praying for me. When I told you I was moving to Colorado to begin writing you told me to pursue it. Ms. Jarsea Burphy, thank you for the positive encouragement. You were one of the voices that first told me I was indeed smart enough to go to college. Mrs. Federline, you helped me through the final two years at Seneca Valley. I appreciate our lifelong friendship. My uncles Nat and Mac, thank you for your advice and prayers and spirited debates over the years.

When you are an orphan you get "adopted" by so many families along the way. Grace Swan, thank you for hosting all of us hungry high school kids and encouraging us to keep pursuing our dreams. Mrs. Toni Morris, thank you for walking me through those first years of adult life. You took me under your wing and made me your son during those years when I wasn't sure what professional adult life was really like.

Some of my most treasured lifelong friendships were formed in Naples, Maine. My dear friends at Camp Skylemar gave me the opportunity to make cross-cultural friendships and exercise my gifts of coaching, teaching, and leadership. Shep, Arleen, and George are some of the best people to work for. I will forever be indebted to Pastor Jim Marstaller, his wife Myra, and the friendly folks in Naples for encouraging me and first giving me a platform from which to speak and tell this story.

Thank you to my church families over the years: Bethel World Outreach Ministries, all the members there who poured into my life in so many ways; Church of the Redeemer, Gaithersburg, where I grew exponentially in my faith, thank you; Fellowship Denver, a church that welcomed me to a new city with new opportunities for friendships and fellowship. Tom Nylin and the guys in our men's group—you guys were my family in Denver. To the teachers and staff at CORCS, thanks to all of you for walking with me through those first two years of teaching. KaRon Coleman and his great family, for investing in my leadership abilities and encouraging me to pursue a seminary degree, thank you, brother. To my friends in Denver and coworkers at High Point Academy, you encouraged me to take the trip to Liberia and explore forgiveness.

To my friends who didn't think it was crazy that I was writing a book: Desmond Osei- Acheampong, Ronnie Grant, Paul "Shake" Rodgers, Onyibo Illochi, Wale Akanni, Tyque McCarthy, Evans Mensah, Billy Burch, Chuck Domenie, C. LeMar McLean, Angela Cummins, Katie Brown, Nick Stachokus, Jacqui Carter and so many others, thank you for pushing me to complete the draft. Joel and Lauren Steidl, Annie and I treasure your friendship. Thanks for your encouragement and incredible help along the way. To my encouraging new sisters, Katie, Heidi, and Holly, thanks for welcoming me into your family.

I owe a huge debt of gratitude to all of my professors at Gordon-Conwell Theological Seminary who encouraged me to keep on pursuing what God had planned for me. Dr. Matthew Kim, thank you for looking through the paperwork with me and for answering my emails about publishing. Dr. Patrick Smith, whom I served as a Byington Scholar, every time I sat in your office I left with new ideas about how to view the world. There are a few close people whose friendships and prayers have kept me going through seminary. Andrew James, thanks for connecting me to everyone. My soul care group, Ben Ruyack, John Whang, Cody Zuiderveen, and Alexander Lee, thanks for praying with me and listening to my book updates over the last two years. My great friend and brother, David Hines, thank you for a great honest friendship.

There are two people who worked closely with me, who now know more about Liberia than they ever thought possible, my editors Melissa Wuske and Carl Nellis. Thank you for shaping the early drafts of my manuscript into something that was worth reading. I appreciate the hours that you put into turning my thoughts and words and life into this book.

Lastly, this book is dedicated to the memory of those who lost their lives in the civil war and all the people of Liberia. We share each other's suffering, and our lasting grief. Let us never forget those whose lives were taken from them in the violence and chaos. It was an enormous emotional journey to write this account.

Thank you again to all who helped along the way.

Jonah Speaks

"Tell me about yourself," Mrs. Burke said.

I had evaded various forms of this question for more than a decade. I was scared to break down and cry in front of friends, acquaintances, teachers, coaches, and colleagues. I used mantras to keep myself quiet: *My story is just too painful to tell. No one will understand.*

I had long avoided the truth about my life, but this time I was ready. Here, in my first professional job interview, I would tell my story.

I could feel the weight of this act approaching just moments before as I arrived at the school for the interview. I'd attended services many times at the church where the school was held, but as I pulled open the glass doors, I knew today was special—and not just because it was a job interview. I fought to keep my nervousness at bay.

The receptionist looked up when I entered.

"Good morning! May I help you?" I shook her hand.

"Hi, my name is Marcus Doe. I'm here to see Jennifer Burke?" My response was intoned like a question, making me sound timid and unsure. In the car on the way, I'd coached myself: *Always articulate firmly.* I'd missed that objective, but I wouldn't let that stop me. The receptionist spoke into the phone.

"Please let Mrs. Burke know . . ."

My anxious mind blurred the rest of her words. *What are you doing here, Marcus?* I thought. I was twenty-four years old, just out of college. I had no professional experience to lean on. I was unsure of myself, but I was certain I did not want to start a new job—a new life—shrouded in lies. I was finally ready to be proud of my origins. *God, please help me answer these questions truthfully*, I prayed silently.

I wiped nervous sweat from my palms onto my pants as Mrs. Burke walked toward me. She greeted me with a warm smile and a delicate handshake. I tried not to envelop her hand, but the result was a very feeble handshake—another blow to my plan, to my confidence. The walk down the hall was longer than I remembered. Once in her office, Mrs. Burke sat adjacent to me, not behind her desk as I had pictured in my mind. *Stay calm.*

Mrs. Burke opened the interview with a quick prayer. I do not remember what she prayed for or for how long. I could feel a swamp developing in my shoes. All I could think of were anxiety and sweat—my goodness, the sweat.

I could feel the question looming closer. I knew I'd have to override my instincts if I wanted to tell the truth. Sidestepping was my well-developed reflex. Lying was a habit I was determined to end today. I didn't care if tears came streaming down my face. Maybe I wouldn't get the job, but I would be free. I'd been a slave to my own untruths for too long.

My faith, my urgency, my desperate honesty surged, and Mrs. Burke asked her opening question, the one I'd been waiting for.

"Tell me about yourself, Marcus."

"I was born in Liberia, West Africa," I began.

✳ ✳ ✳

I'd almost had to tell my story the summer before. I was a counselor at a camp in Maine where I'd worked for several summers. My friend George, a few other counselors, and I were returning from a camping trip to Quebec with about fifteen campers. Upon returning to the United States, the routine trip turned to distress for me, the campers, and counselors. The border officials deemed my place of birth abnormal—Liberia was still a country at war and had been for many years. I was pulled out for questioning. I tried to stay calm as I answered the questions. *I moved to the United States nearly a decade ago; I have nothing to worry about,* I told myself. My friends were worried. Their knowledge of me didn't extend past our summers at camp, so they had no idea what the problem could be. After about thirty minutes, I was allowed to re-enter the US. I ignored the group's quizzical looks. *They won't understand.*

After the Canada trip, I kept a tighter hold on my identity, if that were even possible. After I shared my story with Mrs. Burke, though, I knew the freedom that comes from letting another person know my past. I knew the feeling that came from connecting with another person and letting that person connect with me, and I knew it wouldn't be the last time I felt it.

But change is a slow process. Lying and avoidance had deep roots in my life. I was still haunted by the pain of my past, still uncertain how people would handle knowing the real me. So I stayed quiet.

Though I wouldn't have admitted it then, my life was like the biblical story of Jonah. He was famously swallowed by a fish, but it's really a story about his heart. God had given him a message for the people of Nineveh, but Jonah chose not to follow God's command. He thought by boarding a ship in the opposite direction he could avoid God's plan. God gave me a message too. Strange as it seems now, I too thought I could outrun God.

* * *

In 2006, when I was twenty-seven, I left my friends and my comfortable surroundings in the United States for a teaching assistant program in Le Havre, France. I had been teaching for two years already, and I was glad to continue. I was even more excited about living on the European continent for nearly a year—something I'd always wanted to do.

Madame Campion, whom I'd been corresponding with for a few months, picked me up at the bus station—La Gare on Cours de la Republique. She drove me through town, and after a short dinner at her place, she showed me my housing: a tiny third-floor apartment in a poorly lit building seemingly overwhelmed by the smell of stale cigarettes and extra furniture—the rooms and hallways were cramped with extra bed frames and dressers. The floor had concrete tiles, which reminded me of a world I hadn't seen or spoken of in years. Madame Campion told me where to find the nearest pay phone and supermarket, and, of course, the school.

"Whenever you wake up tomorrow, take a walk around the city," she said. "But now I will let you sleep. You must be very tired."

No sooner had Madame Campion's footsteps faded down the hall and staircase than there was a gentle knock on my door. It was my new neighbor Cristina. She'd awoken as I dragged my suitcase up the stairs, so she came over to say hello. She was from Chile. She and I would be working at the same school; she would be teaching Spanish, and I would teach English. I arrived in France anxious to make friends, and Cristina seemed to have done the same. At the moment, though, I was in no mood to talk, but I was courteous and exchanged pleasantries. We made a plan to check out the city in the morning.

Beginning with our walk the next day, Cristina and I struck up a friendship thanks to her linguistic dexterity. She spoke Spanish and English. My French was average at best. I relied heavily on my English, because I was shy and afraid to look stupid. She had a clear way of explaining things and a positive attitude about everything. She was absolutely fun to be around, and we rarely left the building without one another.

As we started to explore our new city, we headed first to the pebbly beach. The city of Le Havre sits at the mouth of the Seine River, which empties into the English Channel. The water was choppy and very cold. Le Havre natives and visitors strolled up and down the promenade that ran alongside the beach. The local merchants had set up small makeshift kiosks: restaurants, snack stands, and places for tourists and vacationers to sit.

As Cristina and I sat on the edge of the water, we saw cargo ships going in and out of Le Havre. We talked about our friends and school, what we were excited about for our year in France, and the aspects of French culture we were learning.

During the year, we often walked through the empty streets after dark. Le Havre was a quiet town at night. But even though we were becoming close friends, even though I didn't have to be nervous about my French when I spoke to her, I could never quite overcome the urge to hide my past. Though I knew from talking to Mrs. Burke that sharing brought freedom, I stuck to what was familiar: the silent shadows. I was like Jonah on the ship, hiding out while the storms welled up around me.

One night I sat alone at the top of a hill overlooking Le Havre. I was frustrated with myself: *Why can't I tell my story? What am I really afraid of?* I could see the whole city and the ships coming and going in the harbor. I wondered where all that cargo was going.

I remembered the cargo ship I'd escaped on sixteen years before. My homesickness and sense of adventure beckoned me: perhaps I could get on a ship headed for Africa, retreat to my past rather than face the future God had for me. Though my plan to avoid God wasn't working, I clung to it, landing myself in the dark belly of a fish, a shadowy place in my soul. But that's where I started to seek God.

Eventually, my year in France ended, but my silence did not. One thing had changed, though: I was fed up with my lies, my avoidance. I wanted to speak.

* * *

In 2008, after years of avoidance, after years of prompting from God during my daily prayer time, I spoke.

For eight summers, I'd worked with George Simeon, Patrick "Shep" Sheperd, and Arleen Sheperd at camp. I loved and trusted them, and they trusted me. They had hired me to coach basketball and soccer. What they ended up with was all of me, a wide-smiling young man who loved children and even answered to the nickname Cookie. Arleen often described me as a gift. George had been a spectator many times around camp as I displayed my athletic talents on the fields and courts.

It was time for them to know who I was. Sitting in Arleen's office early in the summer, I unburdened my heart to them for about thirty minutes.

I began by telling them about the losses I'd endured so early in life. I told them about a world far away. I told them about people they would never meet and emotions they would never feel. I crumbled that morning as I opened my life to them. The pain that I carried suddenly became visible and tangible to my friends.

The atmosphere in the room was filled with sadness and understanding. I could tell they were confused and amazed as tears streamed down my face. When I finished it was silent.

"We love you, Cookie!" exclaimed Shep as he fought back tears. He stood and gave me a hug.

George was sitting next to me. I could see the wheels actively turning in his mind. I could almost hear his thoughts:

That's what was going on with Cookie on our way back from Quebec back in 2003.

I was even more relieved than when I'd told Mrs. Burke. These were my friends; I needed them not to be disappointed in me or angry with me. Once they knew, once I knew they were with me and loved me, I knew I could be free from the darkness.

Then, just weeks later, I turned a major page in my life: Pastor Jim Marstaller from Cornerstone Gospel Church in Naples, Maine, approached me.

"Could you share your testimony in church two weeks from now, Marcus?"

"Of course. I would be more than happy to," I said, surprising only myself.

I had shared my testimony with the pastor privately, and he knew that this would be the first time I would be sharing my life with a group or with strangers.

The tiny church sat on the intersection of Route 302 and Route 114 overlooking beautiful Long Lake. During my years in Maine I had driven past the church more than a hundred times. I had always struggled to maintain a close relationship with God; when I was in Maine, especially, I often drifted from God's presence. That summer I began attending Cornerstone Gospel Church on Sunday evenings with a friend from camp, Anna Marie. Pastor Jim and his family lived a few feet from the church and always invited us for a meal afterward. During all those drives, all those church services, I never thought I would stand in front of a church filled with Naples residents to tell them that God is good—and how he showed his goodness in my painful life.

I began to fall apart in the days after I agreed to speak. My initial excitement faded in favor of selfishness and fear. I knew God wanted me to speak; I knew I was ready. Still I had my doubts. Telling George and the Sheperds built my confidence. I could no longer keep to myself what God had done in my life. The hand of God had been on my life well before I even realized it, but now I needed to join with him in his work in my life. Life-changing decisions that depend solely on the Lord doing his part are frightening because God demands total control. The days of me being in control were over—a harsh reality. I had run from my responsibility and from God for long enough.

Still, I wondered, what was the point of my story? How would God use this? Or was this just an exercise in humility to prove that I trusted him? Was God trying to get me to become a pastor? I loved being a teacher, and I was good at it. Was he trying to derail my whole life? I pleaded my case before the Lord in my mind, and at times out loud. I worried that my accent would find its way to the surface, and people might not understand me. I felt ashamed of my past. I felt ashamed of who I was now. I lied to my friends. I still struggled in my walk with Christ. At times I grew, and plenty of times I stagnated. From the belly of the fish, I called to God for help, for answers.

As the day got closer and closer, I became very quiet around camp. I ate my meals by myself in a bustling dining hall of about 250 people. I felt alone. I distanced myself from everyone, including Anna Marie, my closest friend. She began to worry about me. I was wasting away in the fish's belly. I was afraid to say it, but at times I wanted out so I could go in the opposite direction. Though it hadn't worked before, I wanted to run from God one more time.

I couldn't sleep. I rose before the sun on most days, so I drove through the beautiful back roads of Naples both trying to find God and to escape from him. My confidence in God had only the faintest pulse. After those early drives, I would stop at the church to pray. Everything seemed to get better when I prayed. I was not afraid anymore.

In my less fearful moments, I tried to prepare myself well. I studied Scripture and tried to recall every detail about my life, everything God had done, and how I came to know Jesus Christ. I had barely discussed most of these memories in eighteen years.

I was afraid that I would not be able to control my thoughts and emotions as I stood in front of a crowd. I was afraid of being vulnerable, afraid of being ridiculed and ostracized. I was afraid of needing help. But I clung to the truth about God's word—"For God has not given us a spirit of fear, but of power and love and of a sound mind" (2 Timothy 1:7 NKJV), and the call I was certain he'd placed on my life—"I heard the voice of the LORD, saying: 'Whom shall I send, and who will go for us?' Then I said, 'Here am I! Send me'" (Isaiah 6:8 NKJV).

Day after day, I fought back excuses as to why I should not share my testimony, and yet, the day arrived: August 3, 2008. I exited the fish, not so gracefully, and committed to following God. In an effort to remain calm, I whispered over and over a simple prayer.

"Lord, let your will be done in my life and in this situation today."

As usual, I was sweating profusely, my palms were moist and my undershirt was already soaking wet. I greeted members of the congregation as they filed into the church. Even with friends and coworkers standing close to me in the small hallway, I felt very little comfort. I had invited as many people to church as I could. Now it seemed like a mistake: they were all about to find out about my life, the shameful and sad parts of it, all that I had been through in my relatively short life, perhaps more than they ever wanted to know. *Is it too late to back out of this? How will my friends from camp handle this? Am I going to embarrass myself in front of all of these people? Can this really be a new beginning for me?*

Pastor Jim and Elder Winkler came over to me.

"Let's step aside and have a word of prayer." We went to the library and prayed. When the pastor said "Amen" it felt too soon. *He needs to keep on praying*, I thought, but I felt a little better as we walked through the doors.

In the sanctuary, I sat next to Anna Marie and the rest of my friends, about four rows from the front. I nervously looked at the program, which had my name in it. The service began, and I don't remember a thing until I walked up to the podium. I silently asked God for strength to tell my story so that he could use it, somehow.

As I took my seat on the stool, I realized that I could do it. I could speak to these people. I could pour out my heart with God-given utterance. I was like Jonah on the shore: a bit worse for wear but ready to follow God's call. I might cry. My friends' views of me might change. But I knew God was with me. I still didn't know why God wanted me to share my story or how he would use it, but I opened my mouth, took a deep breath, and began to speak.

"I was born in Liberia, West Africa."

✶ ✶ ✶

This is my story.

CHAPTER 1

Land of Liberty

My earliest memory is from sometime in 1982 or '83. I was less than five years old, and I was helping my brothers set up rudimentary traps to catch birds in our yard. I've since learned that these yellow and black birds are typically called village weavers, a species common to sub-Saharan Africa and frequent visitors to the property where I lived with my family. When the sun was setting in our neighborhood they would fill the limbs and branches of the trees around our home. Their unique voices provided a constant late afternoon soundtrack to my childhood. We called them ricebirds, because if there was one thing we knew about them, it was that they loved to eat rice.

The traps we made to catch them consisted of a huge tub turned upside down, a strong twig, and some fishing twine. When the trap was set, the tub was delicately balanced on top of the twig and the twine was tied onto the twig's other end. We would put rice under the tub and Molley, my oldest brother, would hold one end of the twine. When the birds gathered under the tub to eat the rice, he'd pull on the string and the tub would fall to the ground, trapping a bird or two underneath.

Filled with excitement and a bit of trepidation, I would watch as one of my brothers, almost always Molley, would reach under and deftly grab the trapped birds. He would tie a small string to the leg of each bird and bring them all inside, at which time we would let them fly around our house, to the dismay of my ma. These birds were bright yellow with just a few black feathers—very pretty. I loved watching them up close in the house, as well as the chaos that ensued when we let them fly around.

They would perch along the wooden curtain rods that held up our thin living room curtain or sometimes fly into our bedroom. Getting them out was almost as fun as catching them. After what always seemed an eternity to my ma, I'm sure, we would loosen the string and open up the door to let the birds go free.

This is how I got to see ricebirds up close. It was not very pleasant for the birds, but it's an experience I've never forgotten.

* * *

I was born in Liberia, West Africa, on May 29, 1979, to Roosevelt Doe Sr. and Lue Wisner Doe. Liberia, "this glorious land of liberty" as the national anthem boldly exclaims, lies about two hundred miles north of the equator along the West African coast. Bounded to the west by Sierra Leone, to the east by Cote D'Ivoire, and the north by Guinea, it is a small and beautiful country. The African continent as a whole is a beautiful place; some say the most beautiful place on earth. I consider myself lucky to be a son of Africa.

The history and geography of Liberia are unique. Known as the Pepper Coast, the land was settled by ex-slaves from the southern United States in the early nineteenth century. The land was classified as a United States protectorate until 1847 when it became an independent nation. Liberia is about 41,000 square miles in area, about the size of Tennessee. We are home to about forty percent of West Africa's rain forest, with swamplands along the coast, beautiful beaches, and wooded hills in the interior.

Like most Africans, Liberians adore their land and customs. We are very religious people. Around forty percent are Christian, forty percent are Muslim, and twenty percent follow traditional African beliefs. Religion plays a very important role in the lives of the people and the way they raise their children. In my family, for example, we went to church and had knowledge of God and Christianity, but we also followed traditional African practices, visited traditional places of worship, and met with men who claimed to be traditional believers and possessed some supernatural powers that are foreign to Western belief systems.

The people of this tiny African nation are currently categorized into sixteen ethnic groups, only some of whom share the same native language. Most people speak English, at least some version of it, and the diversity of languages and peoples is not as chaotic as it may sound. Over the years, Liberians developed a unique dialect of English, filled with humor and rich with local social idioms, words, and illustrations that most English speakers from other parts of the world have trouble understanding. The language we speak evolves more frequently than American English. There is no dictionary for its idioms and no thesaurus for its widely imaginative comparative statements. To understand Liberian English one has to spend time in Liberia or around Liberians. We as a people are generally oblivious to this. In my youth I thought I spoke very clear, articulate, standard English—I learned that wasn't the case when I left Liberia at age eleven.

*　*　*

Established on democratic political principles, Liberia became independent in a time when no other countries in Africa could boast such a thing. In the nineteenth century the "dark continent" was being carved up by European nations, eager to capitalize on colonization and exploit the native people. My homeland soon became a beacon of hope for many of these colonies and territories. The country's history of smooth political transitions was also a major draw for outsiders. Under our American style government, we enjoyed peace and prosperity.

My parents grew up in this calm political environment. My father, Roosevelt T. Doe Sr., left rural eastern Liberia for the capital, Monrovia, in the early 1960s. In Monrovia, he worked in the security detail of President William V. S. Tubman, the nineteenth president of Liberia.

Like many young boys, I admired my father. His responsibilities included planning security details for the president and, on occasion, traveling with him on official excursions. Everything my father did seemed remarkable. I loved hearing his stories when I was a child, stories of his amazing travels with the president to many countries throughout Africa and the wider world. My father had seen a world I couldn't yet fathom. I developed an amazing imagination and a thirst to travel around the world just like my father had done.

✳ ✳ ✳

President Tubman died in 1971, eight years before I was born. He was highly respected, and the nation mourned this man who had been president since 1944—twenty-seven years. According to the Liberian Constitution, the Vice President, William R. Tolbert, was next in the line of succession. Subsequently my father became President Tolbert's Assistant Director of Administration for the Special Security Service (SSS). At the time, the SSS was a highly trained force designated to protect the life of the president and other high profile government officials, similar to the Secret Service in the United States.

With the inauguration of President Tolbert some changes and new ideas came to Liberia. Throughout the 1970s the country faced many economic and social challenges, both as a result of Tolbert's rule and as a result of changes happening around the world. With gas prices constantly rising and the relationship between the United States and the USSR getting increasingly tenuous, Liberians sometimes felt as though we were caught in the middle. Perhaps we overstated our strategic importance to these two world superpowers, but Liberians felt as though our country was a major player not only in African politics, but on the world stage.

By the late 1970s Liberians had become wary of the changes that Tolbert was trying to implement. Some Liberians felt the pressure of what they deemed the "heavy hand" of the Americo-Liberians in government, and many did not understand the president and his goals. There seemed to be an ever-present glass ceiling over economic and educational opportunities for natives in Liberia, limiting their social advancement. The prospect of economic self-improvement for "country people"—as the natives are disparagingly called—was almost nonexistent. Most natives placed the blame for Liberia's lack of advancement and hope for change squarely on the Tolbert Administration.

* * *

On April 14, 1979, about six weeks before I was born, Liberia began to experience growing civil unrest. A law was proposed to increase the price of imported rice, the country's staple food. The law was meant to encourage the purchase and consumption of Liberian-grown rice. It would seem like a brilliant economic idea to help support local farmers, but many citizens couldn't see the benefit. Few citizens shared Tolbert's economic vision for Liberia. The resulting demonstrations in Monrovia were called the Rice Riots.

In the wake of the scandal, President Tolbert was accused of nepotism. He was an Americo-Liberian, a descendant of freed slaves from the United States. Most of his government officials were as well. Americo-Liberians make up a small part of the population of Liberia and were often regarded as the economic and social upper class.

The uprising gradually became tribal. Native Liberians, who generally felt like they were second-class citizens, led the charge against the new law, accusing Tolbert of favoring the small portion of the population who could afford to purchase expensive rice. They saw the increase on the price of rice as another way the upper class was endeavoring to keep a lid on the economic progress of native Liberians, thereby solidifying their lower status in Liberian society.

The April 1979 uprising passed, but the country remained tense. The uprising signaled radical change for Liberia and my family. My father was in a tight spot. He was a native but he worked in the Liberian presidential residence, the Executive Mansion, in a high-profile position. He began staying more alert, constantly working to protect himself, his job, and his family. Rumors of coming violence filtered through intelligence briefings. The nation was an open container of gasoline waiting for a match.

The match was lit in the early morning hours of April 12, 1980, when President Tolbert was killed in a military coup. To this day, the details of who was involved and who killed whom are still debated. Twenty-eight-year-old Master Sergeant Samuel K. Doe, a native Liberian, came to power. Native Liberians rejoiced in the streets of the capital city and elsewhere around the country.

Carnage continued in the following days. All members of the Executive Mansion staff were ordered to report to their places of work, where many were killed upon arrival. Many of Tolbert's officials were hastily put on trial. The charges against these men had an air of mystery about them, trumped up and bogus, most Liberians would add. A climate of fear took hold as the coup's plotters and the soldiers of the People's Redemption Council (as the new regime styled itself) forced the country to cooperate. The men of Tolbert's government were executed in public view on the beaches of downtown Monrovia.

In this climate my father was summoned to the Executive Mansion. His name was announced on the national radio. He was among those people who were to be questioned. He later told me that he was spared because he was a native and had the same last name as the leader of the military coup, although we were not related to him: Samuel Doe was of the Krahn tribe and my father was of the Kru tribe. My father was not murdered that year—I can't imagine his relief or my mother's.

The coup ushered in a period of military rule in Liberia, the Liberia of my childhood. Samuel Doe ruled as a dictator who silenced his opposition by killing his opponents, imprisoning them, or forcing them into exile. Doe and his small band of soldiers, who were for the most part uneducated and poorly informed about economic matters, announced sweeping economic changes. They decided to increase the pay of soldiers and other civil servants, without any regard for the economic repercussions that their decisions would trigger.

Growing up, my brothers and I were largely shielded from the fact that these things were going on. After all, our father worked closely with Master Sergeant Doe. The injustices that Doe committed were never mentioned in our home until years later.

Marcus is my name, but I preferred to go by "Jungle Boy." I can't tell you when the nickname started, but it described me perfectly. The only thing I loved more than my family was being outside—alone or with friends. I'm the youngest of my brothers and to the best of my recollection my first years were filled with fun.

Nicknames are common in my family. My brother Gahien is five years older than I am, closest to me in age. Mocco is thirteen years older. Roosevelt, named after my father, is eighteen years older. He later became my legal guardian. He is the one whose personality and resemblance I share most closely. We called him Boye. My oldest brother, whom we called Molley, is a full twenty-two years older than I. I also have a half-sister named Caroline, who is five years older than I am; she came to live with us when I was about seven years old. I love my brothers and Caroline, and I always felt safe around them.

Being the youngest in a huge family was both blessing and struggle. My opinion rarely mattered. Mocco, Boye, and Molley were in high school or finished by the time I was born. When I was small it seemed they were mostly busy with things I could not begin to understand. They occasionally found time to play with me, but since Gahien and I were closer in age, he was my daily playmate and companion.

When I was born, we lived in a house that was just too small for our family. It was on the Old Road, on the eastern side of Monrovia, the Liberian capital. In 1980, we moved to a three-bedroom house in a suburb called Barnersville on the western side of Monrovia. This was largely because we needed a bigger house for the growing family but also because of trouble with an old lady who lived across from our property on the Old Road.

My family believed that our neighbor was involved in traditional witchcraft and ancestor worship. Witches in our area were said to attack families and kill young children in order to use the child's life as a sacrifice to gain power and prominence in the occultist underworld of West African spirituality. My father had warned my brothers never to accept any gifts from her or even go near her. They were forbidden to stare at her or go past the mango tree that separated the two properties. They were never to make eye contact with this woman.

Later, my father told me that our neighbor had an intense spiritual battle with my family when Gahien was young, before I was born. My family lost electricity every night and strong winds blew through the house in the early morning hours. At times, my father said he could hear people walk around the house in the dark. Gahien became sick and uncomfortable during that time. When I was born, my father was afraid that I would become the next target. It was time to leave the Old Road. As a child, I didn't know what to think of this story, but I now know our move across town was a bold way for my father to protect us from dark spiritual forces.

The new house afforded our family more room, and my early memories are set against the backdrop of the hustle and bustle of a house full of people. Distant relatives, cousins, and people from both sides of my family tree would frequently come to visit and stay with us. We had someone dropping in almost daily. To this day, I love big families.

My mother, Lue, was a very light-skinned woman, known for being quiet, caring, and very soft-spoken. She was what most educated Liberians would call a 'lappa woman,' meaning she rarely wore western clothing. I do not recall ever seeing her wear jeans or pants. She always wore her lappa, a loose garment about four feet by six feet, wrapped tightly around her waist and held up securely by a single knot on one of her hips.

During the week, she worked at the University of Liberia cleaning student dorms on the main campus in downtown Monrovia, directly across the boulevard from the Executive

Mansion. On the weekends she was at home and demon-
strated her skills as a great cook. Everyone who knew her
talked about her kindness and gentle nature.

My father, on the other hand, was somewhat stern, and he
was tough on my brothers. He had a habit of gritting his teeth
when he was annoyed or immersed in deep thought, which
gave him a strongly defined jaw line. Not very tall, he was a
dark-skinned man who had grown up in the farming culture
accustomed to hard manual labor and liked to exercise. He
was always up early on the weekends to run and do chores
around the house, which I deeply admired.

Though he was stern with my brothers, Pa was gentle with
me. He often told me long-winded, adventurous stories from
his travels and his childhood. I relished my daily routine of
removing his shoes after he returned home from work, then
lying on the porch floor using both fists to prop up my chin
while my father ate his dinner and discussed what had happened at work that day. I was convinced he knew all that there
was to know about everything.

* * *

In October 1985 Liberia bowed to economic and political pressure, largely from the United States, and undertook
democratic elections to return to civilian rule. The election
was largely fraudulent, as Doe had no intention of giving up
power. He won easily. His victory at the polls simply meant a
title change from Master Sergeant Samuel Doe to President
Samuel Doe. He was sworn into office on January 6, 1986,
under a new constitution.

I distinctly remember a day between the election and the
inauguration when something, everything, began to unravel,
and I began to understand that not all things were as I thought
they were. It was November 12, 1985. I spent the night before

sleeping in my parents' room, as usual. My father was awakened by a call on his high-powered two-way radio very early that morning. Something was wrong.

It was still pitch black outside. My mother was sitting up in the bed, teary-eyed. My father was getting dressed. I watched as he nervously put on his shirt over his bulletproof vest, a purple shirt that I had never seen on him before. The voice on the radio called his code name, Planet 52. He was told to report to the Executive Mansion immediately. In my childish optimism, I thought my father was heading for a training routine.

My father took out his Swiss-made SG 551 rifle and his magnum pistol and loaded both his weapons right in front of me and my mother. Instead of making me afraid, this only made me more excited: I loved guns.

My father prepared himself, said a quick prayer, and left. I had no idea there was a military coup taking place, and my father's life was in danger.

Throughout the morning, my mother sat on the edge of their bed with tears coming down her face. She paced the room a bit and tried to lie down. She was deeply troubled. She put on her head tie, a piece of African decorated cloth two feet by two feet that Liberian women use to wrap their hair. Then she put on her lappa and sat anxiously within earshot of the radio.

As the sun rose, my brothers woke up and huddled around the radio. Ma urged us not to leave the yard that morning, and I obliged. I stayed close, constantly shuttling between my mother in the bedroom holding back tears and my brothers on the porch listening to the radio. Each had his own way of showing concern and trying to avoid eye contact.

I don't remember anyone saying too much that early morning. The radio was a small set. I doubt we had it plugged in; more than likely we were operating the handheld one using our huge, red *Eveready* batteries adorned with a black cat. Most Liberian homes had a small radio and batteries to operate it simply because electricity was an extremely unreliable commodity. The national anthem of Liberia blared periodically. The anthem usually went with a soccer game or other jovial occasions, but the looks on my brothers' faces said this was not a celebration and this, finally, made me anxious.

The deep baritone voice of a man replaced the music. The voice announced that there was a new government in Liberia and that President Doe had been overthrown—I didn't even know what that meant. The voice said the president was in hiding and declared himself the new leader of the country. My brother Gahien explained that President Doe might have been killed during the night. We sat and listened to the radio until about mid-morning. Eventually, I became bored and walked out the door, thinking I would go to my friend's house. No one was out but me. The streets were empty. I promptly returned home. The mood at our house was very somber. No one else left to go anywhere that day.

There was a roar from various points in our town. This was the normal roar that occurs in most African countries when some common interest was validated and celebrated collectively. We heard a collective roar when our national soccer team scored a goal or the final whistle blew to end a match that Liberia had won. This familiar roar also rose when electricity was restored after a long period of darkness. In the latter case, the roar was a mix of both sarcasm and gratefulness. Although the roar on this day was a bit muted, we heard it. The noise made me wonder, "Why would people rejoice if the president was killed?" This question was pushed aside when

the voice of President Doe was heard on the radio once again
in the afternoon. He said that the coup was aborted, and he
was still in charge. He also issued a curfew in the entire country from 6 p.m. to 6 a.m. Only military personnel and other
authorized people were allowed in the streets. I didn't know
what to think or how to feel. We kept listening to the radio,
but I was secretly anticipating the sound of my pa's voice, the
sound of the engine, or the sound of the tires of our car making its way to our backyard in the driveway.

Pa returned home that evening. Ma seemed happy. He
was quite serious.

Having put away his submachine gun and taken off his
sidearm, Pa sat down in the living room and stretched his legs
toward the floor as if trying to stretch them further than he
ever had. He looked exhausted. His hair was packed down as
if he had been wearing a hat all day. He had unbuttoned his
purple vest. We were all anticipating his every word, and he
launched into talking about his dangerous day.

He began rather emphatically: there were people trying
to overthrow the government. They had entered the country
from Sierra Leone, Liberia's neighbor to the west. My brothers
and I sat around as he told the story of how he climbed the
mansion wall and took some fire while making his way into
the building. He told us that the fighting was brief but intense
and that everything was under control.

I could not believe that my father was involved in a battle.
I was in awe. The neighborhood kids and I always played war,
and I felt proud that my father had seen real glimpses of combat.

When I remember that time, I think of my father, not the
political chaos. He looked like what I wanted to look like when
I grew up, his assault rifle slung around his shoulder and across

his chest. His bulletproof vest made him look more muscular. It made me want to be a soldier. In my eyes, my father was a great hero.

* * *

The leader of the coup, Gen. Thomas Quiwonkpa, was killed. His body was shown on television a few days later. My fascination with war, my pride in my father, and my age made it difficult for me to process the images. I pretended to be brave as we watched: there were soldiers surrounding him and treating his body with disgust and mockery. I still remember a soldier kicking the head of his lifeless body repeatedly while the interview was going on. Seeing Quiwonkpa's corpse left me nauseated. It left me scared. Why would soldiers treat a man like this? Some claimed that President Doe showed Quiwonkpa's dead body to send a message to those who might think about staging another coup attempt.

Other consequences of the fighting were easy for me to see and understand. The curfew was enforced and it meant early bath times and early bed times. Our family car was searched every morning going into the city for school and work. Soldiers were out patrolling the area where we lived. A few stopped in and said hello because they knew my father.

The thought of school was not on anyone's mind. The nation came to a halt. I am not sure how much time elapsed before we went back to school, but when we did, my friends all wanted to know what had happened. They knew my father worked in the mansion. I'll never forget that one of my classmates, Jefferson Sharpe, who sympathized with Gen. Quiwonkpa, said, "Wait until 1990." I did not take him seriously, but his words proved to be prophetic.

CHAPTER 2

Family Life

Let's back up. Although the political turmoil in Liberia had been brewing since before I was born, my early life was a happy one. The *first* major turning point of my childhood came in March 1983. Liberian summer is from December to March, so summer was ending, and it was time for me to begin going to school.

Until that day I'd been attached to my feeding bottle. All my earliest memories are accompanied by visions of me drinking from a bottle, even at close to four years old. That night before my first day of school, my father sat me down: Since I was becoming a big boy now, and starting school, I could no longer drink baby formula and feed myself out of a baby's bottle, he said. I had to lose the habit or risk being teased as a mama's boy at school. That night we made a bonfire in the backyard under the almond tree, and in response to my father's warnings, I decided to toss my bottles and nipples into the fire. It was my first bold life decision!

The next day the beginning of my academic career came upon me. I was very anxious about that first day at J. L. Gibson Elementary School. Its rigorous academics gave it a strong reputation around Monrovia. My school uniform for J. L. Gibson was distinct: the top was a dark green shirt similar to a sailor's uniform, with a collar so big that it hung well below my shoulder blades on my back, two pencil-thin white stripes tracing its edge. It reminded me of Superman's cape, but about one third of the size (as elementary school boys, we never had Superman far from our minds). Wearing the huge overlapping collar brought me a strong sense of intellectual and cultural sophistication—at least, in my elementary student eyes. This shirt was coupled with a pair of green shorts to match.

It was how the day started that I will never forget: I woke to find that Ma, proud of her youngest boy, had ironed my uniform for school and put out my new shoes, freshly purchased the week before. I *was* a mama's boy, for the record!

The first day of school was something I looked forward to, but the day did not at all end up the way I had hoped simply because I had not given much thought to the fact that Ma would not be there. Up to this point, for as long as I could remember, I had spent most of my time with either Ma or Pa in my presence. Despite warnings that I perhaps willfully ignored, we reached the school, and both my parents walked me up the stairs to the classroom and let me walk in. As Ma and Pa turned to walk away, I ran after them, and the tears began to flow. Tears were accompanied by loud screaming and at one point during this episode and many days thereafter I ended up on the floor pleading with Ma not to leave, grabbing hold of Ma's lappa or Pa's leg. The teachers had to use what felt like all of their strength to pull me away from my parents.

* * *

Our family owned two cars back then: a Mitsubishi Lancer and a 1978 Ford Bronco. The Lancer was sort of a light brown, and the Bronco green. We used the Lancer during the week, getting everyone to and from school and work—in fact it may have been a car issued to my father by the government, though it was ours. The Bronco was for weekends.

On Saturdays, my father would take me on rides to a plot of land on the edge of Barnersville where we had a little farm growing cassava. No one else among my brothers seemed to enjoy the planting, pruning, or harvesting like I did. My brothers will tell you the work was hard and unpleasant. I remember it differently. Of course, I was too young to do much, and I've already mentioned that my father tended to be gentler with me. Sometimes I would run off into the woods, or my father and I would just talk. On these days, instead of Jungle Boy he called me "Gingle." I have no idea why, but I loved it. Sometimes Gahien would come with us, and we three would be gone all day. As I look back on it now, those days of peace are the way I like to remember my childhood.

During our weekend drives, my father would tell us stories about Liberian history or about his favorite topic: Cape Palmas, the city in eastern Liberia where he spent most of his childhood and where he met Ma. He would tell us about mischief that he and my uncles would get into when they were growing up. Pa had three brothers that I knew of: my uncles George Sleweon, Ben Elliot, and Tom Blay. I love my uncles, two of whom are still alive today. They both remind me of my father so much that it is sometimes hard to be around them.

I never asked my father why they all had different last names. The thought never occurred to me, and I only realized later in life that someone other than their parents had raised my father and uncles. The boys just banded together with their foster parents and became a family.

✱ ✱ ✱

My mother was mostly responsible for the upkeep of the house, which included the cooking. She loved to cook, and especially took Sunday breakfast and lunch very seriously, when she always made bread to accompany our meals.

The time to visit the Doe family was Sundays. Saturday nights I would sit around and watch as rice was pounded into fine flour for rice bread and bananas were pounded by mortar and pestle. This happened every weekend. Sunday breakfast is still special to me.

For as long as I can remember we had a babysitter every day except Sunday to help my ma watch us. All of my brothers and I had an older woman who helped raise us at different times when each of us was small. We referred to these women affectionately as each brother's Ma: Mocco's Ma, Gahien's Ma, or Jungle Boy's Ma. My 'Ma's' name was Sister Kebeh. Through the years a few different babysitters came and went as we got older or a new child was born. In addition to watching us, these women helped with cleaning the house, washing clothes, and preparing for the Sunday meals.

I loved my ma, my biological ma, that is. She was very well-meaning and polite with others, and she was my dearest and best friend. When I returned home from school in the afternoon, we would always spend a few minutes talking about the day before I jetted out to play with friends.

As I got older, I realized something that broke my heart: it became clear that to me that my mother could not read or write. The world must have been strange for Ma, not being able to read, yet having children who could. I began helping her learn the ABCs. Before long, I was not always darting out to play. Instead, I stayed to help her learn the alphabet, sounding out letters and words, passing along the things I learned in school. She had a little pink copybook and a pencil, and we would practice her writing together as well. Those days are very precious to me. Ma and I developed a special bond that we never had before. She was well into her forties when she finally began to educate herself. Ma had always placed her own needs below her children's. Her amazing humility continues to inspire me.

✷ ✷ ✷

Each of my brothers brought their own personal style of thinking, working, and living to our household.

Molley was always very interested in working with his hands. He loved the police and became a high-level special security officer in the SSS with Pa. When Molley moved out of the family home, he inherited the house on the Old Road.

Boye, the one I was closest to both in looks and personality, got a job in Yekepa in the north, and then another in Buchanan, a port city east of Monrovia. He was and still is the quietest person I know. He is very smart, always studying something. He graduated from college with a degree in mining engineering in 1986. He seemed to know everything about everything and had a deft way of explaining complicated subjects. I recognized that he had wisdom before I even knew what wisdom was. Out of all my brothers, Boye and I look the most alike, and I always wanted to be like him when I was a boy.

Boye seemed to take particular interest in me as well. My mother often left me in his care, and though we are many years apart he seemed to enjoy my company. Boye always had just one girlfriend. Her name was Mildred, but we all called her Sister Lady, and she was very close with my family. Like Boye, she treated me with respect. While everyone outside of school called me Jungle Boy, Sister Lady was the only one who called me by my school name, Marcus. She always got my attention, because the name Marcus was rarely heard around the house.

My brother Mocco is very different from the rest. He was athletic, a great basketball player. Mocco seemed to be much taller than the rest of us, and was always very concerned about his appearance. He occasionally took me to basketball games, which I remember as really fun. He was also very smart, always cracking jokes, which earned him some popularity that escaped the rest of us, but it also brought him into conflict with Pa. Pa was always having tough conversations with Mocco, because he pushed Pa's patience and regularly came home later at night than the other guys. He had a very brash style that made him the cool one in the family. Even so, when Mocco explained something to me he always gave me a chance to understand instead of mocking me for not knowing already, something I didn't take for granted as the youngest of five brothers—though I should add that I always had a million questions when I was around my brothers, and they rarely dismissed me.

Gahien was, and still is, a "hustler"—which is what Liberians call a hard worker, someone willing to do what it takes to survive. He loved to take things apart and put them back together and always had some project that he was working on. When he took things apart, putting them back together was not always successful (I lost a few toys that way), but Gahien always learned something new. He had travelled to America when he was young, before I was born, and he yearned to go back. That was his big dream.

Like the others, Gahien was smart and motivated. The two of us were close in age and spent a lot of time together. Family friction meant that we fought a lot, but we always managed to make up. We often wrestled. Being older, Gahien enjoyed the privilege of frequently beating the snot out of me.

My sister Caroline, who is close to Gahien's age, came to the family all of a sudden sometime in the mid 1980s. I had no idea we had a sister until one day my father brought her home. Gahien and I were playing and fighting one afternoon after school, like any typical day, when my father drove the Lancer to the backyard. A short, dark-skinned girl in a flowery dress got out of the passenger's seat. Who was she? Why was she here?

She walked onto the porch and leaned on one of the supporting pillars next to the steps. Gahien and I stopped playing with our rubber ball and walked up. I hardly noticed that she had come with a bag of belongings.

"Her name is Caroline. She's your sister," Pa said. With that I did what I thought was appropriate. I invited her to play catch with us. She did. Gahien, Caroline, and I formed a triangle and began throwing the rubber ball back and forth to each other. We started to talk to her.

It was new and strange, one of the strangest days of my early childhood. I had more questions than answers, and it was different having a girl around. We boys couldn't run around naked as often anymore. Gahien and I had to give up the big bed that we shared and move to a bunk bed. Our morning routine relegated Gahien and I to bathing out of a bucket outside on the slab of cement next to the back porch, out in the open.

Caroline did not have a house name, so we called her just plain Caroline. Over time, we grew to love her very much, and it was clear that Caroline was definitely a Doe. She had the gap-toothed smile with the sharp canines. She was one of us.

* * *

Between my father, my mother, five growing boys, and a host of nieces and nephews who were always staying with us, the morning routine in the Doe household was crazy. Living with so many people was fun, but frenzied, and chaos around the house was inevitable. For me, losing socks was a constant issue. Finding my uniform was another. I came home every afternoon and took it off as fast and as carelessly as I could. I threw my socks, shoes, and uniform on the closest chair or bed or, most often, the floor, and I ran out to eat and play.

How we all got ready to go to school and work every day is completely beyond my understanding, and largely a credit,

I believe, to my mother's calming influence. When Caroline joined us—one more person to get ready every morning—our routine got even slower. Our route to school now included dropping her off at her school.

We had one modern bathroom with a shower, sink, and toilet. Gahien and I were forbidden to take showers in that bathroom in the mornings. I hated combing my hair and taking showers, but we used a bucket and took our baths, which I did not mind. Even better, during rainy season it sometimes rained so much that I took soap outside to take a warm, refreshing shower under the corner of the roof. To many people, rainy season might sound like a dismal time, but I remember it as the best of the two seasons we have in West Africa. Taking showers in the rain was frowned upon by my dad. He used to say that only people who didn't have running water took baths that way, but to me, nothing could beat the feeling of the warm rain rushing down from the sky, across our roof, and down onto my body. The second the water cascaded down my face I was grinning.

Breakfast was always the same: bread with a little butter and a cup of tea for each person. After we were washed, fed, and dressed, we piled in the Mitsubishi Lancer and set out from home. It was a packed car. I sat on Ma's lap in the front and my four brothers in the back. As the years went by, the occupants of the car changed. Molley moved out, Caroline came, and then Molley's daughter Princess came, and Boye left. Mocco got a car and sometimes rode to school with friends, but I was always up front with Ma. That was my spot. I sat on Ma's lap, with my skinny knees finding a resting place on hers. My left knee was always in the way as Pa shifted gears in our old Lancer.

Pa was the driver, and it was story time until we got to the city. Sometimes I would get so lost in the great stories Pa was telling that he would have to tap me more than once to move my knee out of the way so he could shift gears. This was tough, because we were always stuck in traffic.

Sometimes he would tell embarrassing stories about each person's childhood, and these were especially funny. I remember my brothers as teenagers who did not take too kindly to the idea of being embarrassed in the car. Other times Pa would launch into great tall tales about his own childhood.

The line between reality and Liberian mythology was blurred in the Lancer. My brothers had already heard these stories a hundred times when I was finally old enough to go to school, and I can imagine they were probably sick of them, but I couldn't get enough.

* * *

Around the time I was nine, things began to pick up for us financially. My father bought a blue pickup truck and started a business helping rural farmers transport their goods to markets in the city. He let go of the Lancer, kept the Bronco, and got another family-style car that made our morning rides a little easier on everyone. We used the family car for day-to-day transportation. My pa hired a driver for the pickup truck, and it was rarely around during the week. Growing up in eastern Liberia, Pa had seen far too many freshly farmed goods go rotten because of the lack of transportation. At the end of each week the driver would report back to my dad with the money he had charged the farmers, and my dad would pay him.

My father was always interested in business. In fact, we owned a store that was attached to the front of our house, a sort of convenience store where we sold things like toilet paper, canned corn beef, and necessities.

Sometimes I worked in the shop on Saturday mornings with Gahien, though "worked" is maybe a bit strong. Usually we just read the sports paper and played around. We rarely had customers.

Gahien and I were always close, and during these days we got even closer, enjoying our time together, often arguing about academic things, wrestling, or talking about football (soccer). This was perhaps the height of Liberian football. George Weah, a Liberian professional footballer, was emerging as one of the best players in the world. Sometimes our father would spend the day in the store with us and we would talk history, or he would test us on geography. He bought me my first book, an atlas, and I memorized the capital cities of the countries of the world. To this day I enjoy maps, and I still know most capital cities.

Little by little I began to learn more about the world. I'd always heard that my family had relatives in the United States. We had a granduncle whom we called Old Man Davis whose ten children we admired immensely. One of them, Charles Davis, was close to us, and he came to visit our family sometime in the late 1980s, staying with us for a month.

Charles was funny. I was so excited when he came that I could not wait to finish school and come home and listen to his American accent. America was distant and enchanted in my mind. We would watch the TV show *Different Strokes* or *The Cosby Show*, and life there seemed so perfect. But Charles told us what America was like, and to be honest, America didn't sound as good as I thought it would. He told us that crime was high and that the weather was cold. He brought pictures of snow covered cars, of everything covered in ice, and I couldn't get my head around it. The only place where I ever saw ice was in the ice box.

When Charles was visiting, all our house rules were relaxed. We went to bed later, and we ate later, because my pa said, "In America people eat in the evenings." So when Charles was there, we didn't eat immediately after we came home from school; we waited until Pa came home, and we ate as a group as darkness descended outside. That was strange for me, but I liked it because I felt American.

Charles also flexed other rules around our house; my father did not condone smoking, but Charles would sit on the porch and watch us play football while he smoked his cigarettes in the afternoons. With Charles, I tasted non-Liberian beer for the first time. We did not have alcohol in our house, but we sold alcohol in the family store. One afternoon Charles cracked open a can of Budweiser and left it on the table on the back porch. He went inside for something, and I sat watching. After a while the temptation got the best of me, and I took a gulp. If my father knew that I drank a Bud, he would have killed me, a prohibition that set high expectations for the taste of American beer. My Budweiser did not disappoint: it was nasty. Gahien and I fled the scene, laughing.

This was also the first time in my life that I saw shaving cream, and Charles let me put some on my face once. Charles was *cool*. When he left to return home, he assured us he would be back the next year.

* * *

My awareness of the spiritual world also matured as I grew, little by little. When I was small, we often listened to J. Vernon McGee, a radio evangelist from America, in the car. The familiar tune that opened his program has always stuck in my mind: "Jesus paid it all, all to Him I owe, sin has left a crimson stain, and He washed it white as snow." At the time, I didn't understand what the words meant. I just knew they signaled the beginning of the radio program, and the show meant that I was in the car with my family.

CHAPTER 3

Through a Child's Eyes

True to the name Jungle Boy, the only thing I loved more than my family was being outside. The area around our house was savannah grassland, home to all sorts of wildlife, including various species of poisonous snakes. It didn't matter. I lived to run. I spent my days exploring the area around our home, climbing trees that grew up from the tall grass. The blades and whiskers of the grass pricked my hands and brushed against my skin. Under a breeze, with the grasses swaying, I felt as if I was in the middle of nowhere.

We had four coconut trees and two mango trees on our property. The canopy of leaves made a cool haven from the notoriously unforgiving African sun. I could spend a whole day in and around the mango trees, swinging from branches or climbing as high as I could to see neighborhoods in the distance.

Stretching my wiry limbs and reaching from one branch to the next, I could make it up as far as twenty to thirty feet off the ground. I spent hours in the trees devouring ripe juicy mangoes, or plums, as Liberians call them. During plum season, I hated to see fruit fall to the ground and rot. There was nothing quite like plucking a plum fresh off the wiry stem and eating it right in the tree without ever giving a thought to rinsing it, the sticky sap from the tree dripping down my palms and onto my forearms, sometimes stuck to my shirt (another shirt forever ruined!). And if the plum was juicy enough, the juices ran down my arms too, creating a sugary, sappy mess all over. This didn't bother me much: any effort and any cost was worth the taste of a fresh plum.

When I was small, I would hang in the mango trees and watch for Pa heading home in the old car. It was from this vantage point that I began to learn patience, waiting for things that I wanted. Chief among these: I had always wanted a bicycle. Pa always told me to wait.

There were not many days when I saw our car pulling up to the house that I didn't run home hoping that he had bought the bicycle. Some days I quickly climbed down the tree, and some days I ran with purpose to get home, every day fully expecting that today would be the day. Maybe today I would get the bicycle. I would run and open the trunk of the old car, but all that was ever in it was Pa's brown briefcase, the spare tire, a lug wrench, and a jack. My hopes were dashed every day when the bicycle didn't come, but the next day as Pa drove the winding road home, with dust trailing him in the dry season, my hopes were renewed.

One day, though, Pa surprised me. He came home with a puppy. He stepped out of the car and quickly opened the back door. He plunged in and emerged with a delicate package. He turned toward me as I came around the car, just as I was carrying on my daily duty of grabbing his briefcase out of the trunk and taking it in. I saw the big surprise. The dog was brown all over with some black on his back, a tiny little guy, and very inquisitive at first. My hands were full with the briefcase. I scampered up the back porch steps and quickly dropped the briefcase in my parents' bedroom. By the time I got back outside, Gahien was already carrying the puppy. I was hit by a wave of jealousy.

Now Gahien will claim him as his dog, I thought. *Wait, wait, I am the one who has been waiting an eternity for a surprise gift,* I reasoned quietly. Gahien let me hold the dog, briefly, not before letting me know that it was his! I knew I would fight this. This would be my dog. The puppy wanted to get down, so we put him on the ground. He trotted briskly through the house, heading into each room and sniffing everything. We named him River. I forgot about getting a bike for a while.

Gahien and I took care of River together. Though he peed in our living room the first night we had him, he was very friendly, and I grew to love him quickly. Now I had a friend that would go everywhere with me, even at times when Gahien was too busy. Now, when I encountered a snake in the grass, River was there to warn me. He went fishing with me. We waded through the savannah brush and bushes together. Like me, River loved to run, and we ran everywhere together.

✳ ✳ ✳

At times it seemed as though we lived a lot closer to the Sahara than we actually did. Our house was in a relatively remote area as far as development was concerned, but we were only a few miles from downtown Monrovia. The Liberian government had built the Barnersville Estates, a series of single family homes in a planned community, to the east of city where my family lived, .

The new population brought more human and automobile traffic to the neighborhood. Though the government built homes, the roads in the area were still barely paved, and as cars drove by the dust was sometimes unbearable, especially during the dry season.

Our nearest neighbors were less than one hundred yards away until, in 1984 or 1985, new neighbors arrived. I watched anxiously from the porch as they unloaded their belongings, hoping they had children I could play with. I was not disappointed.

They had three children, all boys, two of whom were twins (a younger sister joined them later). Brimming with joy I ran over and introduced myself. The oldest son, Gbanjah, was well beyond my age, but the twins, Pretty and Deshield, were only a year older than I was, and we became instant friends. As we got to know each other, it seemed we had everything in common, the most important of which was football. We played every day.

Football became a huge part of my life. We always played barefoot. That is just the way it is in Africa for young boys. We rarely had a ball, so we improvised and used a sock stuffed with paper or sometimes foil, old shirts, socks, or anything we could find. I was frequently taking my socks—or my brother's socks!—and stuffing them with old shirts, tying them up and taking them out onto the field. Remember that "missing" socks always disrupted my morning routine.

On the field, we played two-on-two "Freetown Ball," a style of play in which the goals are reduced from the regulation eight feet high and twenty-two feet wide to a space of just a few feet. Most times our slippers served as markers for the goals. We would put one foot in front of the other for accurate measurement on the ground, place the slippers down, and begin playing. Other times we used huge gray cinder blocks as our goalposts. In either case, with nothing to use as a crossbar to determine how high the goal was, our games included frequent arguments as to whether some shots were too high.

We played all sorts of variations and drills, like the game we called "dribble and score." In this scenario, one player stands with the ball facing the goal, and the rest of the group is arrayed against him as defenders. The object of the game was for the attacking player is to evade the defenders, dribble into an opening, and shoot to score. We would make the goal a little bigger to accommodate a goalie (though still without a crossbar). Everyone got a chance to play goalkeeper, and everyone got a chance to attack. One by one we would each take a shot, while all the others formed a defensive line and tried to hold off a score.

This game, which required clever footwork to outwit the defenders, made me a great handler of the soccer ball. Juggling became second nature. With bare feet I could juggle a ball made of shirts or underwear stuffed in a sock, or even a tennis ball. The experience still helps me on the soccer field.

We sometimes had enough kids to play a real game. We would bring white t-shirts and write our names and numbers on the back. I put numbers on the back of most of my shirts regardless of what the shirt was intended for by others (my ma, for instance). Our games continued for days. If a game ended in a tie—one team or the other was always in the midst of a comeback when one of us would be called home—we promised to finish the next day. And we did finish, before starting again. The way I remember it, we played every day, in every weather. We played in dirt and in sand. We played in the punishing sun. When it rained, we played through that too.

River used to sit and watch these matches. With him on the sidelines I had my own steadfast fan, and I was always encouraged to see him watching the game, even though he wasn't roaring like the English or German crowds that I watched on Saturdays. A game for our group didn't look anything like the pros, but in my mind it was just as serious, just as real. I celebrated goals as if I had scored in London, Paris, or Munich.

All week, I looked forward to watching football on Saturday afternoons when the Liberian television station would broadcast games from the German and English leagues. The broadcast started with a local Liberian televangelist pastor named Darlingston Johnson who talked about Jesus and the gospel, urging viewers to get saved by receiving Christ into our hearts. I wanted him off the television so that my real heroes could step onto the screen.

The games they showed were sometimes weeks, maybe months, old; sometimes they re-aired games that I had already seen and knew the outcome of. I still watched, riveted by every touch of the ball, by the noise of the European crowds. They sang songs I couldn't understand, but I drank in their enthusiasm. I had dreams of playing in Europe against the top players of the world.

My dreams were fueled by the stories I read about the legends of football. While we played barefoot with cinder block goalposts, I pretended to be the famous German Littbarski or Karl-Heinz Rummenigge. These players and so many more became my heroes. In the Liberian newspapers I read about the Argentinian soccer god Diego Maradona and Englishman Gary Lineker, and Dutchmen Ruud Gullit and Marco van Basten.

For an African to dream of being a soccer player was just that: a dream. Making it to another African country was a decent hope, but making it to Europe was just a dream. I had never put my dirty feet into a pair of soccer boots. I had never played on grass, never put on a real jersey. To that point I had never even seen shin pads. Even so, I always thought that maybe one day I would possess the skill that would send the crowds in Europe wild. I would go from playing with balls made of socks in bare feet on sand in front of River and Pretty and Deshield's little sister to the grand stage: on glowing, groomed grass, striking a real ball with real cleats into a goal with a net behind it, celebrated by thousands.

* * *

Most Saturdays, after watching European games, I would take my inspiration out of the house. The twins and I would go walking around Barnersville looking for a game of football with other kids. We rarely played with kids on our side of the street. They were always working for their parents and rarely had time to play football. I rarely had to do housework. My biggest chore was emptying the garbage into the dump, a task that took all of two minutes, and I didn't do it often because when I didn't do it, someone else did. For the most part, I was free to roam the neighborhood.

On the rare occasion when other kids were allowed to play with us, the games were fierce. Most of the others that lived nearby were older than us, and they would kick our butts. They beat us regularly.

But I remember the evening when I played my best. There we were, all barefoot, chasing a ball made of our own clothes, in the dark sand with dust everywhere, having the time of our lives. Just as it was getting too dark to continue I scored the tying goal to give us an epic 7–7 tie. We headed back home that night with our pride intact. We had proved something to ourselves. We could hang with those guys.

But when I reached my house, my father was already at home and that meant trouble. My jobs around the house included bringing his briefcase into the house, taking off my father's shoes, and fetching his slippers when he got home. When I was not there he would ask me where I was and remind me how important it was to be home before he arrived. It was one thing if I was at Pretty and Deshield's house. He could see me from there. But when I wandered off he worried. It was that night that my father sternly warned me about being home before he got home.

He told me a long-held Liberian story still firmly believed by the older generation, those who were alive during the mid-twentieth century. When older Liberians share stories like this, they tell them in such a way that I am never quite sure if they are mythical or real. Our written histories tell a version of these stories, and a now-dying generation of Liberians tells them with idiosyncratic details and adds more African mystery that blends so closely with what we read in recorded history that it is hard to tell where truth finds a home.

These are the stories of Heartmen. Heartmen, as I have heard the story told, were men who kidnapped and killed children and used their bodies for tribal sacrifices, particularly during election seasons. In the incredibly shrouded culture of African animism, human sacrifice is believed to enhance and almost guarantee public, political, and even athletic success.

As a child I sat that night, and Pa told me this story. I had heard of them in passing before, but never directly. He had only told me not to stray too far lest I became the target of Heartmen. Most children in Liberia knew of and were afraid of Heartmen. Pa told me about how some children were taken away from Cape Palmas when he was growing up and were never seen again.

I sat listening to my father as he explained the way that Heartmen used the body parts of children. I was frightened. My awareness increased, yet my understanding of animism and spiritual practices became even murkier. I became more confused. Why would people steal children? It bothered me that the lives of children didn't seem to mean much. What if I was taken by Heartmen one day and never seen again?

My pa's words led to a discussion the next day with Pretty and Deshield. They didn't share my sense of worry about Heartmen, or for the children that were possibly still being taken and used for sacrifices that we never heard about, but we moved on to football before long because, worried or not, talking about Heartmen scared all of us.

Most nights after that, I made sure to be home before the sky turned orange.

✷ ✷ ✷

When no one else could join us for a game of football, Pretty, Deshield, and I would find some other way to keep busy.

Sometimes, to feed our lust for football, we would find the older guys in the neighborhood and watch their games. These older kids in Barnersville played on big fields. They had posts and cross bars, and when there was a big tournament, there were nets on the goals, and teams wore jerseys, and players wore boots with real cleats. It stoked my dreams of one day playing on a field with a real net, wearing cleats with studs underneath. There was a neighborhood team for Barnersville, but Pretty, Deshield, and I were too young to play.

Some days during the rainy season, when the swamp across the street filled, we would all go fishing. Liberian children do not have the luxury of manufactured toys and tools, like fishing rods, so we had to be creative. I spent sixty-five cents of my brother's money on a fishing hook and some twine. I spent hours looking for a good palm tree and selected the best and strongest and most flexible branch of that tree to make my fishing rod.

I found worms for bait in cool, moist areas in the soil, behind outdoor bathhouses or under rocks. I would also buy a stick of sugar cane, chew it up and use a bit of the dried, chewed leftover to make a float that we called the "watch man." I tied twenty or thirty feet of my newly bought twine to my carefully stripped palm twig and attached my watch man about midway between my rod and hook so the line wouldn't sink too far, and I could see the watch man bob when I caught something.

With my bait on the hook I would wade waist-deep in the pond. I prided myself on my patience and my sense for the right moment to pull my rod back. I almost always came back with a little prize, a fish, usually no more than six inches long.

This was just for fun. We would never eat the fish we caught, but I loved the experience even when it didn't result in a catch.

After just a few minutes in the water leeches would latch onto my skin. We all got leeches all over our bodies. We thought this was incredibly funny. I was warned about leeches by Mocco as if they were dangerous, but I rarely listened. Sometimes I went fishing by myself, got leeches all over, and came home to have my sister Caroline help me peel them off my body.

I never thought much of it. After all, my name was Jungle Boy. I belonged in the jungle. These were the kind of things young boys named Jungle Boy did. They didn't fear leeches. They went fishing. They climbed trees and ate plums without washing them.

* * *

In about 1987 another house was built between Pretty and Deshield's house and ours. We had new neighbors: the Breeze family, who had two boys, Charles and Dakar, and two girls, Mardi and Hawa. Mr. Breeze was deputy minister for education in Liberia or something big. He worked for the government, just like my father, so they became friends. The Breeze family also had cousins and other family members living with them. They had air conditioning, so I started spending a lot of time at the Breezes' house. I had my first kiss there with Hawa, my first "girlfriend." My mother became friends with Mrs. Breeze as well, and our families grew close.

Charles and Dakar added an interesting mix to the friendship that I already had with Pretty and Deshield. They did not really like football, and they weren't used to playing as often as we did. Even more, Dakar was handicapped by some accident growing up. One of his legs was shorter and skinnier than the other, so he could not walk very well, but he loved to play goalie, so we had a permanent goalkeeper. Our team grew.

✷ ✷ ✷

As I got older, small cracks began to grow in my idyllic life. I saw myself as a smart kid who loved the outdoors and football, with a growing circle of friends. Sometimes Dakar and I or the twins and I would fight but it was never serious. But everyone has a bully in life. Mine was Morris.

Morris was two years older than I was, and he was bigger, and definitely stronger. He would catch me walking around his area and whip the snot out of me for no discernible reason. This happened so often that I avoided going to his part of town. I went the long way if I had to get to a neighborhood close to his.

He was a kid that I barely knew. I didn't even know if he went to school or who his parents were. He rarely wore a shirt, and when he did, it was a shirt with no buttons, filled with holes. Whenever I saw Morris coming from a distance I would make an excuse and run home. Sometimes I would be at a neighborhood football game, and he would show up wanting to fight. Once he pinned me to the ground and stuffed sand into my mouth. I forget *why* he did it, but I haven't forgotten swallowing sand and the accompanying humiliation.

School was another crack in my blissful childhood. As early as I can remember, I didn't enjoy school—not because of classes or really even because of school itself, but because I had to be separated from my ma and pa. To add to that, my friends from the neighborhood all went to different schools, so I was separated from everyone I knew and loved.

That first day of school set the tone for how things went on a daily basis. I cried violently when I was dropped off at school every day and regularly took to rolling on the floor of my kindergarten classroom, a giant second-floor auditorium. The different classrooms were separated by movable partitions made of wood, and the chalkboards were mobile as well. It was sort of a one-room schoolhouse, which meant that you could hear what was going on in every classroom. I can imagine my teachers must have been rather unhappy with my regular crying routine. In fact, if they are still around, I would like to say I am sorry for what I put them through.

Eventually, I began to make close friends in school, particularly with a boy named Wilmot Davies who would be with me all the way through elementary school.

That first year, Wilmot and I had a very mean teacher. She seemed young and she punished us very severely, making liberal use of her whipping cane. I was terrified of her.

One day she overstepped her bounds more than usual. The class had a test and we were to bring our own pencil to school. I dropped or forgot my pencil somewhere along the way, maybe on the road somewhere or in my parent's car, so I came empty-handed.

Our teacher turned on me. She swung the cane down on me as I stood facing the board. I turned, and the cane hit me in the face. The blow left me with a diagonal line of bleeding and swelling down my cheek, and a bruise running from my opposite eyebrow up to my forehead. It hurt to squint my eyes, and the salt from my tears stung in the wound.

I went down to the office to see the principal, Mrs. Lardner, who at that time was the other scariest woman in the school. On this day, however, she was gentle. She called my father to come and get me. When he arrived, he was furious. He met with my teacher and the principal while I sat outside her office on a couch. I went home that day and got some real tender loving care from my ma, and my brothers were even extra nice to me.

* * *

My father always told me that I was a wild child. When I think back to my childhood, one thing I remember is being covered in scars from all sorts of injuries. Many of these were just accidents. For instance, I have two very prominent scars on my forehead. When I was learning how to walk, I collided with the side of a very sharp table and badly cut the left side of my forehead. The scar that most people notice is the one on the right side of my forehead. When I was three or four, I fell off the porch and hit a rock. I bled so much that my father told me later that he did not think I would survive. My parents worried about a permanent brain injury. My father joked that he and my mother thought about having another child to replace me.

Another example comes from one Saturday when I was in the fifth grade. I jumped over the banister of our back porch (again the porch!), but it caught my foot. It was about a six-foot fall right over the wall. I hit the ground hard and busted my bottom lip. Seven or so stitches later, I was back home but of course still in pain. While I recovered, my diet consisted of cream of wheat and V8 juice, and I went to school with swollen lips for weeks.

I also have scars that carry spiritual significance. My father dabbled in African ancestral beliefs alongside our occasional attendance at the Methodist church. In the villages deep in the forests of Cape Palmas where he grew up, he received traditional markings over parts of his body done by cutting the skin. My father had these markings on his upper arm, above his biceps on his shoulders, and a series of short marks made by a small sharp knife or a blade on his upper back across his shoulder blades.

My father had a traditional belief master called a "medicine man" mark all of my brothers and me. This was long before I could remember. A medicine man came to our house or we went to him. He cut our skin and took our blood for protection. We were cut with a blade on our wrists and some of us on our backs. Both of my wrists were cut in short small spaces, four times on each hand. I was also cut once on my forearms when I was a little older.

I was too young when this occurred to realize what was happening or what it meant. Unbeknownst to us, we were entering a covenant with the devil and his demons. I realize today that these blood covenants affect people, and I regret so much that I went through this ceremony. My father was trying to keep us safe and cover his bases by taking part in two religions, but these scars and the spiritual realm they represent are a tangible way that he put us at risk. My life was still apart from the healing power of the true God.

* * *

One of my wildest accidents gave me another scar that has spiritual significance for me.

It happened when I was nine years old, very shortly after River died. In 1988, he was hit and killed by a car. We took his lifeless body and buried him under the palm tree in the southwestern corner of the family compound. I lost my friend and companion, my constant fan. It took weeks for me to come to grips with his death.

I started hanging out in a neighborhood about a mile from my house. One Saturday night a friend of mine who lived there got a new football, and he promised to let me use it the next day because he was going to church. I was very excited. I told Pretty and Deshield that I was going to have a real ball for us to play with the next day. Kids from different neighborhoods did not loan out footballs for many reasons: sometimes balls got stuck in trees, dogs chewed them, cars ran them over, and broken bottles popped them. This was a rare occasion.

As Sunday dawned, I was up early. My father left earlier that morning; I was not sure where he went. My mother told me that we were going to church that morning.

I was disappointed. We rarely went to church as a family. I could not believe she picked that Sunday out of all the others. I had an appointment to pick up a football, a real football.

Doesn't she understand this is a big game? I thought. Feeling desperate, I took off running, because a brand new football was more important to me than God or church. No one saw me leave.

I ran down the unpaved road adjacent to our house. I ran all the way to my friend's house. I arrived, only to find out that he had already left to go to church. His mom was still home. Evidently he went to church by himself (that alone surprised me). I quickly decided that my trip would not be in vain.

I built up the courage to ask his mom for the ball.

"No."

Moms hate football, I thought. His sisters knew that if he was there, he would have no problem lending me the ball, but instead I left disappointed. Not only did I not get the ball after all that running, I also risked getting yelled at by my mom when I returned. I imagined that by then my father was back home and he was definitely going to be very angry. My brothers were going to be upset, because they would have been waiting on me. Pretty and Deshield were probably up all night, like me, waiting to play with a real ball (it had been so long). I was also disappointing all my friends in my neighborhood. I was sure that word had spread that was going to bring a ball for us, this rare occasion.

Disappointed, I began to walk away. I felt I had to get the ball, but how? I was lost in thought. Behind me, I heard a dog bark. I turned and saw two dogs that I did not recognize, approaching me, one brown, one black. The brown dog was moving calmly but the black one was charging toward me. My friend's mom, watching the scene unfold, tried to control the dogs, but she had little success. I wanted be brave, so I stood still.

As the black dog reached me he lunged forward at me and I reacted with a swift kick. I missed. To my astonishment, the dog bit my left knee. A small chunk of skin tore away from my leg. My bad day suddenly turned to a nightmare. Despite the pain, I ran.

I was in a world of trouble. I headed home, still upset that I had no ball to show for my efforts. Despite the blood running down my leg my first thought was not to tell anyone about my injury. I was anticipating the worst when I got home. As I neared my house, I saw that my father was home. Whatever blood was not running down my leg rushed to my brain. I felt weak. I had a pit in my stomach. I had messed up before, but not like this. I could not even imagine what my punishment would be. I sneaked into the yard by climbing through the barbed wire fence. I got into the house without anyone noticing, found Gahien, and told him what happened.

"Go tell Ma right now. You could have rabies," he said. I found my ma, who had not even noticed that I left the house. I told her what happened, and to my surprise, she said in a low voice, "Go to the nurse with your brother and do not tell your father." (We had a nurse that lived in our neighborhood.) I ran with my brother to the nurse and she cleaned up my wound.

She also gave me news I did not want to hear. I would need to get rabies shots. By the time I got home, everyone knew what had happened. It seemed I had dodged a tongue-lashing. My father was not mad at me, but I spent the day at home; no football, no church. The next day, I missed school and went to the hospital for seven injections.

I began to fear dogs because of that incident, and still feel slightly uneasy around them today. I thought God had punished me for not wanting to go to church. I promised that whenever I could, I would go to church, and I would go with my family. The scar on my leg reminds me of this promise.

All in all, I have had more stitches than I can count, and though I was a long way from realizing it at the time, God had his hand on my life protecting me. All of these accidents only made me a kid who could deal with pain. Nothing, however, would prepare me for what was about to happen.

CHAPTER 4

Death Enters

Our family spent Christmas day on the beach in 1988. We had a great time. I did not know how to swim, but my father was a good swimmer. I remember him doing all kinds of tricks in the water.

There was a damper on our celebrations, though: Mother, my best friend, was not feeling well. Little did I know that my world was going to change.

When we got home from the beach, she remained in bed. And in the weeks that followed she stopped working and stayed at home. She lay in bed all the time. We were on vacation from school, so I spent time with her whenever I could.

My mother lost so much weight. She could barely walk. She would cry constantly; sometimes I would sit and cry with her. I would often cry alone too. She got sick so quickly, and her condition deteriorated so rapidly that it was sad to look at her.

Pa took her to St. Joseph's Catholic Hospital. At first I thought everything was going to be just fine, but a week at the hospital turned into two weeks and then a month. She eventually stopped sleeping in our house. She was almost never home. We visited her after school and on the weekend. Meals without her were awful. Family traditions ceased and my days dragged.

February of 1989 was the hardest for my family. When it became apparent that she was not getting better at the hospital, my father's worry grew. He started to look for alternatives to western medicines—to the traditional beliefs and witch doctors. He took Ma out of the hospital and to different

Alladurah churches—churches that were similar to the place where the witch doctors had cut me as a child.

A couple of months before my mother became sick she had taken a trip back to her hometown, Cape Palmas. Based on a ritual performed by a witch doctor, my father believed that someone had poisoned her during that trip. So as my mother got sicker, our family distanced ourselves from my mother's side of the family. My father did not want any of us to be poisoned as well.

Pa took us to visit her at a little traditional "church" close to downtown on Center Street. Center Street ran parallel to Gurley Street, where I went to school. I was glad she was so close, but I was hurt that she was in such a place. That part of the city had a reputation for being a nighttime hang out for rough characters, people we called "societal deviants." The building itself was close to a part of Monrovia where open sewage flowed. Pa told us not to go see her without him.

The "church" was very dark and dingy. When he took us to see her, Pa led us down a long dim hallway with rooms on either side. There were other people lying in their rooms on the floor.

There was no way my mother is here, I thought. But sure enough, about halfway down the hall, we entered a room, smelling of incense, where my mother lay on the floor on a thin foam mattress.

She could barely sit up. When she saw me, she managed a smile. I smiled at her, trying to hold back my sadness and questions. She looked helpless, drained, and tired.

Her appearance that day was the most dramatic change that I had seen. For the first time I noticed how extreme her weight loss was. Her arms were beginning to get thinner, and her cheekbones and eyes were more prominent now. She managed to sit up and talk to Pa, Gahien, and me. It was a

Saturday, so we stayed a while. The sense of her suffering filled my whole body with discouragement.

On the car ride home, Pa assured Gahien and me that she would be better soon. He had a way of reassuring me that life would be just fine. I'd always found my strength in him and his ability to make things right. I tried to believe it again: my father, my hero, would make things right; he would make the decisions necessary to bring my mother back home. He was infallible.

∗ ∗ ∗

I knew Pa was trying every avenue to make sure my ma got better; ordinarily we would never have gone to Center Street. We left the "church" that day, and my anticipation of seeing my beloved mother come home turned into a strange sort of dread and mystery. I willed myself to trust my father, but I was very scared for my mother. She was sick and getting sicker, and no one could explain to me what was causing her sickness, how long would it last, or when she was going to be feeling better. I kept asking my father when she would get better. He always said "soon." Confusion and frustration crept into my fear and sadness, and as much as I wanted to keep going to visit her, I became afraid of what my eyes would see once I saw her again. I wished this would all just go away. I wanted my mother back.

I began to sense the spiritual weight of what was happening, though I couldn't understand or articulate it. This sickness was not a temporary thing, I realized. We were in a long battle for my mother, and it seemed that no one had the power to help her—not the hospital, not the traditional church, and not my father.

I really did not know where else to find comfort and assurance other than my father. As my confidence faltered, there were so many questions I wanted to ask him, ask someone.

Why did we only go to Alladurah churches for healing? Why didn't we go to the Methodist Church on Ashmund Street—the Methodist church with the huge picture of a man named Wesley on the wall? I didn't know who he was, but if his picture was up was on the wall of a big church, he certainly could help us. I believed anyone whose picture was displayed in places of authority was powerful. And I knew the church had spiritual power, just like the government made laws to make sure Liberia was safe. That was why President Samuel Doe's picture hung everywhere in the Executive Mansion, including my father's office. He had authority. What about former President Tubman? His picture hung in our living room. Though he was dead, maybe he had power of some kind. Maybe he could help. Maybe that Wesley guy could help make my mother well. In all the halls of St. Joseph's Hospital, and in the dingy rooms of the Alladurah churches, there were images of Jesus. They were all slightly different, but he was always staring at something faraway, with a great hopeful look. The glow of the sun was always behind him. What about him? He seemed to have some power. I knew he was mentioned in the Bible, and people talked about him at school and in my conversations with friends. He seemed to be everywhere, able to do everything, yet nowhere and hard to understand. These men whose faces I saw could certainly help me now. I just needed one of them to act. If they couldn't, why were their pictures hung up?

The weight of it all began to crush me. I drifted off during school. My energy was not the same. I became withdrawn. I stopped playing football and stopped doing the other things I enjoyed. I tried to ask questions about what was happening, but no one told me anything.

Then disaster finally struck.

✳ ✳ ✳

On April 24, 1989, mother died. I still cry when I think about that day. I still regret not spending more time with her in those last few months. I was nine years old.

She'd been back at home for a few weeks, rarely coming out of her bedroom. When I got home from school, she asked, "What happened in school today?" My usual response was "nothing." That was the last thing I ever said to my mother.

As I was changing to go play, my mother crawled to the bathroom. She was struggling for life. I left to play football.

Later, my brother Gahien came to get me, and as we were walking home I saw my brother Mocco running to get the neighborhood nurse. I knew something was deathly wrong. They piled into the car and raced to the hospital at about 6 p.m.

My brother Gahien and I sat behind the Toyota pickup and started to cry as they drove off. That was the last time I saw my mother alive. About an hour later, the car came back and my father got out screaming and crying. My brothers were crying, and I knew that she had died, though I never heard them say it. I'd never seen my father that way. I was stunned. The finality of it all only made my questions scream louder.

Why couldn't anyone save her?

She was gone. *Who would I run home to and show my report cards to?* I questioned. *Whose voice would I listen to at home every day? Who would I yearn to embrace?* My mother, my friend, was the person I loved to please. She had been my reason for living, the person I looked to for approval. I really did not care what people thought of me, as long as my ma smiled and hugged me every day.

That night, I remember my brother Boye looking for me. I have always considered him my caretaker. I hugged his hips and I cried on him. I do not remember where I slept that night, or if I slept at all.

The entire neighborhood was in our yard. Everyone knew and loved my gentle mother. I walked on the path to the neighbor's house in my sister Caroline's arms, sobbing as all of my friends looked on. They lined the path to pay their respects and show their sympathy. I stayed at the neighbors' for a couple of days. I did not go to school.

When I woke up I cried myself back to sleep. I hoped that I was just dreaming. I prayed—called out to any spirit that could hear me—that it was just a nightmare, and that she would be there when I woke up. I prayed my hardest that I would be studying with her again. I relived my memories again and again.

I barely remember her face now, but I remember everything about those days.

I knew it was official when I saw my mother in her casket about a week later. I walked into our house with my father. There were so many people in the house, and my mother's absence seemed palpable. My arms shook, and tears flowed as I walked toward her casket. I could not touch her. She was covered by a plate of glass. I would have gotten into the casket with her if I could. Her eyes were shut.

She could no longer speak to me. I could no longer joke with her. She could no longer call my name. I stood over the casket, and tears flowed. I cried and cried. I did not attempt to wipe away the tears; I just let them flow down my face. My tears rolled down my cheeks and onto the glass that separated us.

It seemed I stood over the casket for hours, yet it also seemed so short. My life was changing right there, and I just could not comprehend what was happening. I remember my father taking me into the back room for a Coca-Cola. It seemed he had accepted that his wife was gone. I could not.

* * *

We had the funeral on May 9, 1989, at the United Methodist Church on Ashmund Street, Monrovia, the church our family attended at times that we considered our home church. My brother Mocco sang the hymn "Pass Me Not, O Gentle Savior." I wept myself into dehydration.

I saw my mom for the last time at the front of the church. I sat next to my father in the front pew. I could feel the looks of many people that I knew as we made our way down the aisle. I was barely strong enough to stand. I mustered up as much strength as I could in order not to fall over and weep on the carpet.

This was the same church where, sitting in the pews a couple of years earlier, I had heard a sermon about how Jesus had raised his friend Lazarus from the dead. I prayed that God would work a miracle like the one he did for Lazarus and raise my mother. I prayed that she would wake up, that Jesus would show up right then and raise her. I would walk over and take her hand. Everyone would go home, and we would move on with life. Such is the mind of a child, a world filled with make-believe, a magical world in which everything ends happily. I prayed that I would see her somewhere. It never happened, so I prayed I would dream about her. I prayed I would hear her voice. I began imagining her. I still wish and pray sometimes when I visit strange places or walk through crowded airports or train stations that I will see someone that looks like her.

As we drove to the cemetery, I again sat next to my father. He was crying. I was crying. At the graveside I stood in silence while the gravediggers put sand over my mother, burying her body. Long after everyone was gone, my father and I stood there. Memories ran through my mind. Fond memories of my mother, the time we spent learning the ABCs, her smile, and her voice. I realized I would leave her there, in a strange cemetery far from our home.

My world had been destroyed. I drifted into that past world often as I imagine all children do. Things rarely happened the way they did in the books I read. The death of my mother had shot me rudely into reality.

I visited my mother with my father once a week from that point, usually on Saturdays, and I would have conversations with her at the grave. I brought her flowers and notes. Every Saturday I came with renewed hope that she would miraculously come back to life. My child mind could not let go of the hope that God would perform a miracle.

✳ ✳ ✳

After a couple of weeks out of school, I returned to class. My classmates gathered a few dollars and gave it to me to show their sympathy. Most did not talk to me about my grief, they just tried to get my mind off the situation. From those days on, I never discussed my mother's death with anyone. I never responded to questions about her unless they were from my father or brothers. Sometimes I would sit and talk to my brother Gahien, and we would cry and comfort each other. I began to put my emotions away. I tried to get over my grief quickly. That sounds crazy, but I wanted to be strong and accept that she was gone.

A month after my mother died, my tenth birthday rolled around. My father did his best to have a party for me to lift my spirits. My friends from school and the neighborhood kids showed up, and I tried to have a good time. I tried to laugh, dance, and eat. It was not the same.

All I saw and heard were things that made me miss my best friend. I knew that my friends made an effort not to bring her up, and I appreciated their presence, but I knew that they would be gone in a few hours, and I would have to deal with my grief alone. At ten years old, it is tough to find your way through.

The days after my mother's death were difficult and strange. Sadness had taken over my life and I did not know how to respond. I did not know where to turn. Those days were like a nightmare. I was constantly pinching myself in the hope that I would wake up, and it would all fade away. It seemed impossible that my mother would die, and it remained unbelievable for a long time. How could that happen to me?

CHAPTER 5

A Family Falling Apart

After I lost my mother, my world started to change. Desperately trying to control my life, I hung on to familiar things. My father and I got closer. Pa tried to understand what I was going through and tried his best to compensate for the absence of my mother.

I started asking more questions about my family history. I asked where my grandparents were, or if they were still alive. My father was surprised that I had waited until I was ten years old to wonder. To me, my family seemed to be very disjointed, so separated that the thought had never come to mind. He laughed, revealing his gapped teeth, our family claim to dental fame.

"Well, Jungle," he finally whispered, "they are all dead, on both sides." We let it stand at that.

Pain and fear began to take hold of other parts of my family too. My oldest brother Molley and his family were living in the house on Old Road where my family lived when I was born. He had four children at the time. I don't remember how old his youngest boy was when Molley started to notice the same rattling in the ceiling at odd hours of the night that had plagued my father when Gahien was a baby. I always thought my father was exaggerating, and I always believed there was a genuine and understandable explanation for abnormal things. I really didn't want to believe that witchcraft was real: It was mysterious and I not could understand or control it.

Molley talked about how the old woman across the yard looked at him. Whenever I went to visit my brother, I was fearful of the old woman. He became more and more desperate to protect his family. Molley had recently started to work alongside my father in the Special Security Service, so he had access to firearms, and he was used to getting his way. He even threatened to kill the woman. Molley's bravado did not pay off. His son died mysteriously.

After my young nephew's death, I began believe that maybe there was a dark side in the world, and I started to rethink my father's stories about what had happened when Gahien was little. Molley and his family continued to live the house on the Old Road next to the swamp and within striking distance of the mysterious old lady. I visited on the weekends, and I loved hanging out with my nieces and nephews, who were very close to me in age.

* * *

My family never quite cut ties with the occult; therefore, it followed us in spirit. Obsessed with protecting me from my mother's side of the family, my father told me not to accept food from any one of them. He was afraid that I would get poisoned as well. He said he had been warned that they were out to destroy our family.

As the baby of the family I had slept in my parents' bed for years. During the days immediately after my mother's funeral and burial, I went back to sleeping in my parents' room with my father. In dealing with his grief, he refused to sleep in the bed that he and my mother shared. Instead, we slept on the floor beside the bed. That was fine with me.

I felt safe with my father next to me. My mother and father were together for twenty-seven years. Those times must have been hard on him too. My father turned fifty years old that year, about a month before my mother passed away. Before we went to bed each night, we read a psalm and prayed. Psalm 91 was one of my father's favorites.

Despite these precautions, I also began to hear noises, a continuous rattling during the night, as if something was running back and forth on our roof. A witch doctor told my father a threat had been made on my life.

I began to imagine myself in my mother's shoes. The way she cried in pain in the last months of her life. Barely able to walk, crawling most of the time. Was I destined to suffer a similar fate? One Saturday morning, my father took Caroline, Gahien, and me to a medicine man. I had no idea what was going to happen. The medicine man talked to my father and then began to cut my brother and sister. I barely remembered the first time I was cut when I was younger, but I remember this day. The medicine man cut me on both forearms with a blade and placed a green substance in the cuts. These are some of the scars I still carry.

I thought I was tough because I did not cry, but then again, neither did my sister. At the time, I looked at the scar as a badge of honor. I had been to a medicine man—I was protected. Today I understand the power of the blood Jesus Christ shed for my sins to save me, but then I didn't know what to believe. I did not understand the spiritual consequence of what we had done: my father put me into a spiritual contract with the devil. The devil tries to imitate the blood contract that God meant for good.

After our visit to the medicine man, the environment in our house became very weird, and my worry increased continually for my life and my family. I can remember one Saturday or Sunday morning we woke up to find a huge puddle of blood on the back porch steps. It looked as if it had been poured out and left there on purpose. The entire Doe family stood on the porch and stared in disbelief. No one said anything. The back porch was about five feet from the window of the master bedroom where my father and I slept.

My father ordered my brothers to search the house for signs of forced entry. My father walked the perimeter of the property looking for more evidence. Our compound had been burglarized before. The tires of our vehicles had been stolen multiple times. Those sorts of things were easy to understand. Honestly, I would rather be dealing with petty theft than what we faced that morning. The violation of privacy frightened me, but the nature of the incident scared me even more. My father insisted that none of us walk over the blood—he poured salt on it and washed it off the steps.

I clung to my father more because he always seemed to know what to do. My father was very suspicious of everything. He tried everything to keep us safe. Down came the barbed wire fence. Up went the new concrete fence and huge red metal gates and doors. We interpreted anything out of the ordinary that happened around the house as a sign that our lives, and in particular my life, were in danger.

A few days after the blood on the porch, my father had us all outside on a very nice evening, and we actually killed a goat and sacrificed it. I'm not sure what god or spirit's favor we were trying to earn. That night, we all sat around and watched the animal burn. I do not know what my brothers thought. I can imagine they were just as surprised and confused as I was.

Paranoia crept into my daily life and I began looking at people with suspicion. I started to believe that I was going to get sick like my mother, and I was going to die. Part of me wanted to die so that I could be with her again.

Very early one morning, my father was awakened by a bird outside in one of the trees in the yard. It was an owl at the top of our almost thirty-foot mango tree. I had never seen an owl before. Owls, like snakes and black cats, are considered very bad luck in the world of the occult.

My father got up and grabbed his magnum pistol, loaded it, and walked out to shoot the bird. I stood beside him. He raised the gun and aimed. After holding the barrel leveled at the bird for what seemed like forever, he lowered it and put it away. He said he didn't shoot for fear of waking the neighbors. The bird did not fly away for a long time. It just sat there watching.

Because of the mounting danger and all the strange events happening, my father decided that I could no longer live in our house. I started spending time with family members elsewhere. My first stop was my Uncle George and Aunt Julia's house. My Aunty Julia loved to cook, and she reminded me of my mother. She was very gentle. I have never heard her raise her voice. I would get into so much mischief with my cousin Chu Chu, a year older than me. I liked living on the road at first, but I missed my home.

My father was not satisfied that I was safe, even away from our house, so he took me to live with a medicine man. I lived on the beach in a small hut close to the ocean with several men. There, I bathed in cold ocean water every night and fasted through the morning until noon every day. Every evening, I sat completely covered underneath a blanket, while strong incense burned. I stayed under the blanket for what seemed like hours.

The witch doctor made me memorize chants. They were like repeated prayers in a different language. I repeated after him, and sang along. I slept in a white gown like that of a West African Muslim and wore a necklace of strange beads. The gown came to my ankles, the sleeves came down to about my forearms, and on the neckline there was an opening like a shirt collar that could be fastened by two silver snaps. I rarely left the hut. I obeyed my father and wore the gown, though I wasn't used to anything like it. I lived with the medicine man so that I would be protected from those who were trying to kill me, but I hated life. I did not know what to do or believe.

Sometimes I walked along the beach and wondered why all this was happening to me. I would sit and watch the waves crash onto the Liberian soil, stare at the sun setting into the ocean, and wonder what lay on the other side. Boye, Molley, and Mocco likely didn't even know where I was. I did not see them for weeks at a time, and I missed them. I respected my father, and I thought he was smart, so I obeyed everything he said and did, but I did not understand what was happening. I was becoming even more unhappy and confused.

Eventually, I was brought back home, but I still had to sleep in my white gown, and had to bring it with me everywhere I went. I felt like an outcast, and even though I was back with family—sometimes at home, sometimes with my brother Boye—my sense of isolation deepened.

* * *

My father was desperate to cure his loneliness, so he began to see another woman six or eight months after my mother died. I realized that we needed a motherly figure in the house, but even I knew it was too soon. My mother hadn't been gone very long at all.

My father took me along to visit her once or twice a week after I returned from my stay with the witch doctors. I thought she was a nice woman, but I was not ready for a new mother, and I felt powerless to stop what was going on.

She was very cordial and she tried to comfort me in my loss. I appreciated her for that. She had two sons who were

around my age—I don't remember their names. The boys
were athletic, so we played football together. I do not know
where their father was, and at the time I did not care. It was
awkward hanging out with them and realizing that they could
become my family. They sometimes mentioned it, and that
made me uncomfortable. They seemed to accept the fact that
their mom was involved with my father, but I was still recov-
ering from my mother's death and having spent time with
the medicine man. My mind was totally in a fog, and I was
hurting too deeply to accept this as my future.

I was afraid to ask my father what was going to happen to
us. My mind was spinning with questions. Was this woman
going to move into our house? Was I going to have to listen
to her? Was she taking my mother's place? Would this mean
we would have to forget my best friend and mother whom I
loved so dearly? Was this going to signal the end of my visiting my mother's grave every week? What would I do with all
those memories I had of my mother?

I was upset, and Gahien seemed just as confused as I was.
Boye and Molley were out of the house doing their own things
those days. I had no one to talk to, no one to help me. I felt no
one cared what was happening to me.

I insisted on going to my mother's grave once a week to tell
her how things were going at school and what I had learned.
Those were the hardest days. I'd say hello and sit there alone
while my father cleaned around the grave or walked around
the graveyard. I pretended she was sitting next to me and
listening like she used to do. I told her stories as if we were
in the living room again. Sometimes I caught myself gesturing with my hands at someone who was not alive. I wished I
could hear her voice, that she would respond to some of the
questions I asked. I swore to myself I would not be afraid to
touch her if I came one day and found her sitting on the grave.

I just wanted to see her again. I was against the harsh reality that time cannot be rewound.

* * *

As the darkness of 1989 came to a close, our family welcomed my brother's wedding. There was finally something to celebrate. Boye and his longtime girlfriend Mildred, Sister Lady, got married on January 6, 1990. I came back from living with the medicine man just before Christmas to be part of the wedding preparations.

At the wedding, I wore a suit and tie for the first time. I was nervous about getting ready. Before she died, my ma always helped me with all the details of my clothing. Since she'd been gone, getting ready for school had become a challenge. She always had my uniform washed and ironed, and if I could not find socks or underwear, she would help. Now I was on my own, even in a house of so many people.

I started to wash my own clothes that year. We washed everything by hand in giant tubs. This required getting water out of the well numerous times. I actually enjoyed this part of daily life. Now that I was working on my own, my clothes were not as clean as mom would have wanted, but I was doing things for myself and this brought a certain feeling of independence. But getting a suit and tie ready was a new challenge for me.

The day of the wedding arrived and we all went to celebrate. It was the first wedding I had ever been to. I sat close to the front alongside my brother Gahien, both of us in suits, excited that Boye was getting married. I was proud of how well I'd taken care of my outfit. Gahien seemed to know all of my older brothers' friends. Boye was very nicely dressed in a tuxedo matching his groomsmen. My father, who was very proud of Boye, chose to wear an African outfit with a hat. I liked that about him: while everyone was wearing western clothes, he was wearing African attire. It made him stand out.

The wedding ceremony took place at a church called Philadelphia Church on the outskirts of the city next to a famous ice cream shop where my father would occasionally take us for special treats. The church was a huge, oddly shaped building where Sister Lady attended services. The reception was held across town at the OAU conference center and hotel, the finest resort in Liberia at the time, built in an elegant design sometime in the 1970s for the Organization of African Unity leaders meeting. I had visited there once before with my father for lunch on a Saturday after my mom had passed away.

The wedding celebration refreshed us as a family. I enjoyed dancing and taking pictures and shaking hands with so many people, and I could not help but wonder what my own wedding would be like. My brother paid tribute to my mother and I imagined that I would do the same on my own wedding day. I looked up to all of my brothers, but I especially looked up to Roosevelt T. Doe Jr. He'd been there for me up to that time, and I sensed that we would be close for many years to come.

* * *

The wedding ended that evening and we made our way back home. The next day I left to go back to the medicine man. During those few days I was at home, I had begun to hear about a political uprising that was taking place in northern Liberia, a movement led by a man named Charles Taylor to topple the government of President Samuel Doe. This was the first time I heard Taylor's name. I did not take it too seriously at the time, because it seemed like every year there was an attempted coup in Liberia. My father worked for the SSS, so we heard of small uprisings within the government that never reached the ears of ordinary people. He always knew about these political rumblings around the country, but this time the dark clouds of uncertainty grew stormy.

I think my father knew that our family was about to change even more. He got us all together to take a picture. We rarely took pictures as a family. All of my brothers and our father stood on the front steps of our house. It's one of my favorite memories. It was great to see all of my brothers who no longer lived with us. At the same time, there was a sense of finality about that moment.

On the back of the photograph my father wrote our ages at the time of the photo. He did it with great pride and great attention. His handwriting was impeccable. His boys were all grown up. Molley was thirty-two, Boye was twenty-nine, Mocco was twenty-four, Gahien was sixteen and I, Jungle Boy, was a mere ten, with a birthday around the corner. My father, Roosevelt T. Doe Sr., age fifty, stared at the photo in admiration for a long while and smiled. I wish I had a copy of that picture today.

I watched as the smile faded. He sat cross-legged, dangling a leg back and forth over the edge of the porch. I didn't know then what he was thinking, but I realize now that he saw further into the uncertainty of the future than I did.

CHAPTER 6

A Country Falling Apart

Even in the midst of the family turmoil I was excited to start sixth grade. My school was an elementary school, and sixth grade was the final year. Sixth graders were the senior students, and all the lower grades looked up to them, so I had always been excited to make it there.

When the school year started, I lived just down the road from my family's house with a classmate and his parents, the Johnsons. They took good care of me, but spending time everywhere but my own house continued to take a heavy toll on me. I rode with them to school past my family's house. I could see my family getting ready to leave for the day. I longed for the chaos of my family's home. At the end of the school day I rode home with my family, but they dropped me off at the Johnsons.' I was not allowed to come home.

In sixth grade, students were beginning to distinguish themselves academically, and my ability to memorize facts and dates set me apart from others. Geography, civics, and history came naturally to me. In an era when the heads of state of almost all the African nations changed often, I kept up with African political leadership. The atlas was my companion. The capital cities of the smallest nations of the world became my fascination. I even knew the names of the members of the Liberian cabinet at the time. My academic ability made me a classroom leader.

There were about thirty students in my class. I sat in the back impressing my classmates (especially the girls) with how much I knew about my two favorite topics: world politics and football. Students always wanted to sit next to me on test days: I was always willing to help. If someone needed an answer I would provide it. They helped me at lunch with extra food. There was a girl named Sandra whom I thought was the most beautiful human being God ever made. I helped her for free.

Every morning before school my friends and I would walk down Gurley Street to the corner of UN Drive and buy huge pieces of corn bread. The lady sold them for thirty cents apiece at the lotto booth corner.

We couldn't leave the school grounds during the day and by the afternoon the corn bread lady was gone, so the morning was our only chance. Some mornings we would get to the lotto booth before she got there. When she finally arrived the corn bread was hot. Whenever she was late, we made the choice to suffer the consequences at school. Old Mr. Woodrow, our former first grade teacher and master disciplinarian, would be waiting to whip us in front of the entire school. The corn bread was well worth the whipping we got, and we enjoyed those few precious minutes together before school started. We ate all the corn bread on the quarter mile walk back to school. Sometimes I would save a piece for Sandra, but she always refused it.

"Who wants old corn bread from the pockets of a sixth grade boy?"

✳ ✳ ✳

As sixth graders, we had the responsibility and honor of leading the entire school in raising the Liberian flag and saying the pledge of allegiance. I loved raising the flag and leading the entire school in saying the pledge. Since I knew a lot about politics and loved raising the flag, and because my father worked for the government, my friends began to ask me about the uprising and the war that had begun in the north of Liberia. I never knew what to say and brushed their questions off.

But it became more and more apparent that I couldn't ignore what was happening. One day early that year, around March 1990, my teacher noticed that I had on pants with pleats on the front waist. This violated the very strict uniform rules: shoes had to be white, pants had to be ironed, and t-shirts with the school logo had to be clean. We had to wear belts, to look distinguished. My pleats were considered too stylish and were not appropriate under uniform rules. Three of my classmates were in the same boat. My teacher consulted with the principal about what to do with us. He initially decided to make us to do some push-ups. After we did countless push-ups, we were told we had to go home and come back with new pants.

My friends and I stood outside the gates of the school in the middle of the city and debated what to do. Someone suggested a movie at one of the downtown cinemas, another suggested a walk to the beach.

Finally, I proposed that we walk to the Executive Mansion where the president lived and my father worked. It was not that far from school, and my classmates had never been to the Mansion, so I thought it was a fantastic idea. All of my classmates liked my father; we had invited them all over to our house for my party the previous year. So Jefferson Sharpe, Wilmot Davies, Charles Wade, and I walked to the Executive Mansion. Charles and Jefferson lived in the city, so they were comfortable. Wilmot and I lived in the suburbs. To show what a brave leader I was, I took us on a short cut across the Barclay Training Center barracks. This was the main headquarters for soldiers in Monrovia. Some of these soldiers were gearing up to fight in the war that was going on up north.

We naïvely strolled down the middle of the compound. Soldiers approached us and demanded to know where we were going. A tall, dark-skinned soldier in full military uniform approached us. We stood still as he walked over. He wasn't smiling and did not treat us like young boys. His dark face made his bright pink gums and clean, straight white teeth very distinct. As the rest of the soldiers shouted at us from the closest building, he asked us, sternly, to turn around.

Being the leader of this misguided adventure, I calmly said we were walking through. The soldiers threatened to arrest us if we did not turn around and walk outside the barracks. They were tense, and the interaction was not a pleasant one. I did not realize that the war was getting serious and the soldiers were on edge, preparing to face Charles Taylor's men.

We arrived at the Executive Mansion gates around midmorning. The armed soldiers at the gate greeted us and asked us the necessary questions. My friends seemed a bit timid. They stood wide-eyed as I boldly handled the questions from the soldiers, but then I wasn't scared of soldiers with guns. After all, my father had taught me how to operate all of his weapons.

Soon we were allowed to enter the grounds of the Executive Mansion. I brashly explained the story of how my father had jumped over the wall under fire during the 1985 coup attempt. I was feeling more and more proud of myself and our bold excursion.

We arrived at the doors and we were escorted through the metal detectors. I saw some of the men who knew my father. They called me "Small Doe." My friends were surprised and I felt very powerful.

We got to the elevator and I pressed the button for the fourth floor. My friends were excited. Once we got to the fourth floor I knew to turn right and my father's office was the last one on the right, next to the communications area. My father had been alerted that we were on our way up on the elevator. I knocked on the door and entered. As I explained to him what had happened to us at school, my friends looked around his office. On the walls hung pictures of President Samuel Kanyon Doe, awards that my father had won, and his SSS dress uniform with all of his military insignia hanging off the shoulders. Behind his desk was a huge window through which we could see the capitol building that housed the Liberian legislature. My friends sat in the cushioned armchairs in front of my father's desk.

My father called the school and apologized for us not being in proper uniform. He was upset that I brought my friends to the mansion, but he took us all to lunch and then back to school. We were allowed back in, but we had to get new pants for the next day.

Looking back, I now recognize why my interactions with the soldiers were so tense, that our beloved nation was about to be shaken to its core. Even so, I can't help but remember it as a great day with my father.

* * *

My childhood playfulness stood in contrast, though I didn't realize it quite yet, to the political situation in Liberia. The climate was beginning to get tense. A coup attempt was possible at any time. The neighborhood around us began to thin out. People were gradually leaving. Students at school were not showing up for classes regularly, and there was a sense of inevitable doom. It was as if everyone knew something we didn't know, or were afraid to admit. My classmates, for once, had more information about political climate of Liberia than I did. They were not sheltered by a father who worked in the SSS. The newspapers reported rebel advances into central Liberia.

Slowly, I began to get nervous, catching glimpses of newspapers here and there: there were rumors that the rebels were killing members of the Krahn and Mandingo ethnic groups in retribution for the killing of the Gio and Mano ethnic groups after the 1985 coup. President Doe was a Krahn; my former neighbors and good friends, the Breeze family, were Krahns. I knew and liked many Krahns, and it seemed that the government was losing the war. The rebels were gaining territory fast. Generals from the government claimed that they were winning, but kids at school and the international news were reporting otherwise. At home we did not listen to international media since my father worked for the government. We were not Krahns, but that was difficult to prove because none of my brothers or I spoke our native Kru language. We had tried to learn Kru, but we never took it seriously. Now it seemed our lives could depend on it.

Gahien became a bit frantic—that scared me the most. He was usually calm and supportive, but he wanted desperately leave Liberia for the United States. He applied for his passport; he saw something that perhaps we all did not see.

"If the rebels are killing people for simply being of the same tribe as the president, what are they going to do those who have the same name as the president?" he said. I went to sleep that night very scared. The thought that I could be killed because of my name was unsettling. I thought about other innocent people named Doe. Were they going to be killed? I immediately thought about my new sister-in-law. She was in danger of being killed because she had married my brother.

Uneasiness occupied me more and more. The military seemed to be facing a shortage in soldiers. Sometime in early 1990, President Doe somehow passed an executive order or law of some sort making all Mandingoes citizens of Liberia. Mandingoes are predominantly Muslim people who immigrated to Liberia from neighboring countries. Most Liberians had some strong prejudices against them. Doe was making a politically desperate move, some people said. He needed men to help fight the oncoming rebels.

Monrovia was a pressure cooker. It was difficult for me to concentrate on anything. Key officials began to desert the government, and I suspect many soldiers did as well. Amidst all this pressure, we still went to school. I started living with my family again, to my relief. It seemed to be because no one wanted to be around someone named Doe, so no one wanted to look after me. My father also wanted to keep us all close. I felt safe in our compound because my father received a security detail of three heavily armed soldiers who guarded our compound at night.

The impending war hit home in other ways too. Robert, a young man whom our family loved who came around our house periodically to cut the grass, do chores, or just hang out and play, joined the military. He was in his early twenties. We had known Robert for years. My father had also begun to build another house for our shrinking family about three or four miles from where we currently lived. Robert watched over that property for us.

Our family also loved our driver, Mr. Matthews, who was of the Gio tribe, the tribe that supported Charles Taylor's uprising. Despite the rising tensions Mr. Matthews was still very nice to all of us, but he and other family friends were becoming very concerned that something might happen to us. After all, our name was Doe, and my father worked for the government.

I was beginning to wonder what would happen to us. Were we going to be slaughtered in our house? Would we have to escape to another country? Death seemed a real possibility.

Pa did not seem too concerned. He felt sure if there was a regime change, he was still going to maintain his position under the new leader. It had happened before. For some reason, his nonchalant attitude did not do much to inspire confidence in me.

* * *

On a day in the middle of May that year, there was a rumor that rebels had reached the Coca-Cola plant on the outskirts of Monrovia. The news ignited panic in the city. We were in school as the situation unfolded. Parents began picking their children up and taking them home. Mr. Matthews, who usually picked us up from school, was nowhere to be found. Wilmot Davies, my niece Princess, and I were the only ones left at the school.

The principal decided to close down the school. I could not go to the mansion this time, and I could not find my brothers, so we started to walk the eight to ten miles home. This was perhaps the dumbest idea I ever came up with.

We decided we were going to try to take a bus home after we made it over the main bridge that ran out of the city. There were so many panic-stricken people running across the bridge that afternoon that I nearly lost my niece, Princess. I had never been on the bridge before and it was quite scary.

Luckily, as we crossed the bridge into the Clara Town neighborhood, we saw a familiar face. An old neighbor, Mrs. Vinton, saw us, put us into a taxi, and got us home. I was tired and scared about what my father would do to me when he got home, but I knew he could not leave the Executive Mansion right away because of the crisis—that's also why Mr. Matthews could not pick us up from school.

When my father finally got home, he was tired and, yes, he was furious with me. Gahien made fun of me, as he usually did when I got in trouble. Unlike me, he had waited patiently at school for Mr. Matthews or my father to pick him up. My adventurous spirit had risked the lives of other people again, and this time my niece was almost the victim of my poor judgment.

Shortly after that incident, our school closed its doors indefinitely. It slowly became obvious that war in the city was inevitable. Whenever I thought about the possibility of encountering rebels, my heart skipped a beat. I knew for sure our world was going to change. We stayed home during the day, waiting for news that the war was ending. Our new next-door neighbors, who were Mandingoes, left their home and headed for Sierra Leone, afraid for their lives. Gradually people we knew began to desert the neighborhood and the country. The government said one thing about the war, but I heard other things from people in our neighborhood. I did not know who to believe.

One thing that everyone was sure of was the fact that the rebels were definitely killing Krahns, Mandingoes, and, no doubt, they were killing people named Doe. The rebel leader Charles Taylor had promised to kill President Doe, and it seemed he was going to achieve his goal. The Liberian military put up very little resistance. Rumors circulated about how well-trained the rebels were: incredible stories of how a single rebel solider could take over an entire village or kill numerous government soldiers. I felt like we were sitting ducks waiting to die, and I wanted to leave Liberia. Peace talks between the government and representatives of the rebels, held in neighboring countries, fizzled out. It seemed inevitable that there would be a bloodbath in Monrovia. I do not know how well my father slept during those days; I cannot imagine that he did at all. He spent more and more of his time at the mansion. Most nights I was asleep by the time he got home.

Eventually, he made a critical decision on my behalf: to send me, his youngest son, across town to stay with my newly married brother. My father sat me down, as he often had since my mother's death, and broke the news to me.

"Jungle, you are going to spend time with Boye," he said to me, with a hand on my shoulder. He told me this move was temporary, perhaps a couple of weeks until everything was back to normal. I had become familiar with saying goodbye to my brother Gahien, my sister Caroline, my niece Princess, Mocco, my Uncle Sakor, and our maid, Gladys. It had almost become routine. I had spent so much time away from home that I felt like I should not mind leaving again, but it still hurt. I loved my home and my family, but I sensed something different about this farewell.

After my mother's death, I had told myself that I would spend as much time with my father as I could. I was determined not to lose him. He perhaps felt the same way, because we spent a lot of time together during that year. My father told me that he remembered how my mother told him and my brother that she wanted Boye to take care of me if anything were to happen to her. I love my brother Boye, so I was glad to be heading to his house. This seemed like the next best thing after being with my father. This decision changed the course of my life.

* * *

On June 4, 1990, I left home early in the morning with my brother Mocco. I'd packed five pairs of shorts and some shirts and underwear. No toys, no books. Nothing else. I felt like I was deserting my family, even though there was no way I could know what would happen.

Boye and Sister Lady lived in a two bedroom townhouse in Congo Town, and they welcomed me with open arms. When I arrived, my sister-in-law was happy to see me. I remember thinking that their house was very clean.

They let me have my own room, something I had never dreamed of having before. They both worked during the day, so I spent much of my time by myself. Boye worked for a satellite station of the news service Voice of America, and Sister Lady worked for the West African Examinations Council. At first, my brother locked me in the house all day by myself. I remember staging mock World Cup tournaments on paper, very bored. The real 1990 World Cup was about to start and I couldn't wait: I was rooting for the Argentineans and Diego Maradona.

During this time, as my eleventh year began, out of the sheer boredom of being stuck in the small house all day, I began to read the Bible. I do not remember if Sister Lady gave it to me or if I just picked it up. I mostly read the Old Testament books: Samuel, Kings, and Chronicles became my favorites. I liked all the kings and wars. I had never sat and read the Bible before, but I enjoyed it. Characters like King David, Solomon, and Josiah were new to me.

I also began to listen to international media coverage of what was going on in Liberia. I remember one of the first broadcasts of BBC's *Focus on Africa*. I heard that the Liberian rebels had advanced to the Firestone rubber plantation. I knew where that was— it was pretty close to the city. For the first time I heard the voice of Charles Taylor, the leader of the uprising. It scared me. It was the voice of a man who I had heard was killing people like me.

My father came to visit me a couple of times while I was living with my brother. He stopped by during the late afternoon before it got dark, just to say hello. I always asked when the situation would be over. His answers did not do much to comfort me.

"I don't know, Jungle."

The last time Pa stopped by—the last time I saw him—was June 14, 1990. He was wearing a Liberian-made suit: light brown and short sleeved. It had four pockets sewn to the front, one on each side of the chest and two on each side by the waist. These suits were popular with men in Liberia in lieu of the traditional European shirt and tie.

He took my hand, and we walked out of my brother's house and onto the road where he had parked. I do not remember what we talked about that day: probably my mother's grave and World Cup football. If I had known I would never see him alive again, I would have held on a little longer. I would have said something important, but it's hard to imagine anything appropriate to say to someone the last time you see him or her.

I was crying as he drove away, and I didn't even know why. I never thought it possible that I would never see him again. As I watched him leave, I had that same uneasy feeling I had on the night of April 24, 1989, as my brothers drove my mother to the hospital for the last time. Bringing myself to eat that night was nearly impossible. I remember Sister Lady chided me for not eating. Food was getting scarce, and prices were skyrocketing. Everything seemed to be caving in.

We were heading for a massacre. I tried to avoid thinking about what was happening on the other side of the city, where my brothers and sister were. I had no way of finding out what was going on. News from that side of the city was rare. I had no idea what was in store for me or my family.

CHAPTER 7

The War Arrives

"Everybody get out, right now," the soldier demanded.

Boye slowly opened the door and walked out. He told me to remain inside the house. Sister Lady also went outside. All of the neighbors in the tiny compound came out of their houses.

I watched the soldier through the curtains from the living room. I grabbed a tiny piece of curtain fabric and pulled it back ever so slightly to see what was happening. He was a very tall, dark-skinned man. The uniform he wore was unkempt, and his boots were dusty. The pockets of his faded uniform hung unbuttoned, and the chin strap of his helmet was loose. His helmet dangled atop his head as he spoke. He was a soldier from the Armed Forces of Liberia. These were the government troops who were trying to keep the country from crumbling? They were fiercely battling rebel troops loyal to Charles Taylor, and from what I'd heard, they were losing ground badly. I had not left the neighborhood in a couple of days, but it seemed the situation in and around Monrovia had grown quite tense. A sense of lawlessness was spreading across the country.

We lived in a compound of eight relatively new houses on a back road. The houses in the compound were parallel to each other with a huge cement paved area in the middle. It was almost entirely fenced in besides the opening in front where cars came in. Surrounding the homes on three sides was marshland. We were very close to the ocean. My brother and his wife had lived in this area for a few months before I moved in with them.

Just before the solider arrived, my imagination had been running wild about war stories: David, Joshua, and all of the great men of Israel winning great victories in the Bible.

"Give me money," the soldier screamed, in Liberian English, "or I will do all of y'all!"

Money or die. That was the choice the soldier offered us. My brother Boye and a few other men in the compound began trying to reason with him. I could tell that he had been drinking, as he struggled to keep his balance. His words were slurred. He was erratic and forceful.

"Y'all give me my money," he repeated. He started to get more boisterous in his demands.

My whole life government soldiers had been very kind to me. My father worked with them. I saw them as very safe people. I knew the rebels the government was fighting were trying to kill me and everyone that I loved. Now these facts I'd depended on started to seem less solid. Right here in our compound was a government soldier trying to kill my brother and our entire neighborhood. As I looked on through slightly parted curtains, the soldier kept demanding money, and I became more afraid.

My thoughts turned to my brothers on the other side of the city. Were they experiencing similar things? Were they safe because my father was with them? I wished that I was with them. Maybe my father could show this soldier where he belonged. If he knew our name was Doe, he certainly would not act this way. My brother did not seem to be telling him that our name was Doe and that we were on his side.

The soldier hoisted his rifle and fired several shots in the air. It was incredibly loud, and what was an intense argument had now escalated. He was cavalier with the weapon and used his thumb to push the trigger. He demanded to search every house for rebels, a common practice during this time of early chaos. Some citizens who supported the rebels hosted re-connaissance troops. My brother refused to back down. Our neighbors also did not want to give anything. They realized that if they gave this soldier money, he would be back for more, possibly with his friends.

The soldier made demands more loudly, and shot off more rounds from his rifle. Everyone kept their distance but no one gave in. As darkness arrived, and the alcohol began to lose its hold on him, the soldier agreed to settle for some rice, though he promised to return for more.

As he slung his rifle over his right shoulder and his un-kempt uniform faded into the darkness of the warm, stale Monrovia night, I slumped into my chair inside the house. Our neighborhood's relief was tangible, but this soldier had not just taken our rice. He had taken my sense of security and he had taken my trust in the government troops. We crossed from fear into full-blown anxiety and panic that night. Now I knew that anarchy was descending on Liberia.

My brother walked back inside and quietly shut the door. The worried look on his face alarmed me. I could see the questions going through his mind: What if the soldier comes back tomorrow? Should we leave? Where would we go? What would happen to the house? What would happen to our neighbors? The war had reached Monrovia. My hopes of the war ending with a government victory faded. A new, ugly reality took over.

I ate in silence. The more I thought about our situation, the more I shook. The rebels, whom I knew were killing any-one affiliated with the government, were only weeks or maybe even days away from capturing our area. They were closing in on our neighborhood. The night watchman at our compound said he'd seen a few rebels walking along the beach close by. The government troops who were supposed to protect us were trying to extort all that we had. These thoughts sent a bitter chill down my spine. I did not sleep well that night. I could think of nothing else.

* * *

Every night we all gathered around to listen to the radio, hungry for news, any news. Batteries to power the radio had become a rare commodity. Replacements were suddenly hard to come by.

The rebels were on the outer edge of the city, the BBC news reported. It was just a matter of time before Taylor's troops overran the capital. President Doe was holed up at the Executive Mansion and he vowed to "fight to the last man." I tried to imagine that the government troops would eventually defeat the rebels. I did not know why anyone would want to kill the president. I had heard that he was not a good president, but things seemed fine to me. Worry and confusion overtook my senses. I honestly did not know how we would survive. I was terrified I'd lose my pa.

By mid-July 1990, while the rest of the world was watching tension in the Middle East, Liberians were falling into a struggle all our own. We were on the brink of our own catastrophe.

A few days after the soldier had harassed us, the electricity went out all over Monrovia. A military siege of the city had begun. There were very few means of transporting food into Monrovia: the airport was closed; the rebels controlled the major roads out of the city. There were rumors that running water would soon be gone.

Our night watchman seemed to enjoy telling us that the rebels would be in the area soon. He said that he would join the rebel ranks when they arrived. Many young men wanted a change in government, so they joined the rebel army. Over the seven months since fighting began, the rebels had grown from a few hundred to thousands by the time they reached Monrovia.

We started saving food, only eating one big meal a day. I hoped that this situation would not last long: I loved food, and my sister-in-law was a great cook. By late July, amid rumors that the rebels were going to overrun our area, we moved three or four miles closer to the city into my sister-in-law's childhood home where a number of her brothers were living.

Her family was Americo-Liberian—descendants of freed slaves who were mostly upper class and considered more civilized and educated than most native people of Liberia. They and their descendants were almost always more educated and better off socially and economically than most Liberians.

Sister Lady's mother, whom everyone called Ma, lived in a four-bedroom house in the Old Road suburb, within walking distance of our old home. The house was on a hill overlooking a little swampy ravine. She had a garage and a bigger kitchen than the one at my house. There was a huge bookshelf in the living room. The bedrooms lined a long hallway that led ultimately to Ma's room at the end. My brother and sister-in-law slept in the room across from Ma's. Everyone wanted to be close together when the inevitable happened. Sister Lady's brother, whom we called Uncle Mac, also lived in the house along with a few others whom I didn't know.

Ma was a tough disciplinarian. I had met her several times before, and I knew that she did not put up with much. She had actually taught my father while he was in school back in Cape Palmas, Eastern Liberia. My father always told me stories about her strict discipline style. She lived next door to her oldest son, St. Jerome, whom I called Uncle Nat, a well-educated man who walked and spoke with great confidence. He always seemed to be able to explain what he thought was going on, even when others were at a loss. He had spent time in the United States and had a degree from the University of Indiana. Uncle Mac, Ma's second son, had a degree in History. I admired them both. They would sit and discuss the war and the government's options and I would sit and listen, though when Uncle Nat was around, I felt invisible. The whole family seemed more educated. They were well-spoken and often corrected my poor English grammar and sloppy table manners.

I liked living at Ma's house because I had company. There were three children there who were close to my age. Uncle Nat's daughter, Nathifa, was nine. Nuku Boy, who was related to the family in some way that I never learned, was ten. Evelyn, the younger sister of Uncle Nat's wife Aunty Ethel, was twelve. I was eleven years old. The children had time to talk during the day, but we rarely played outside.

While we lived together in Ma's house we had two jobs: picking rice and filling the water barrels.

During the early hours of each day, we would separate rice. In Liberian-grown rice there were always a few grains that were dark brown while the rest were white. We poured uncooked rice onto the dining room table and went through it grain by grain getting rid of the dark brown ones. I hated this tedious task, and it took all morning. I had never done this at my parents' house. We just cooked and ate the rice we had.

The rumor that Monrovia would lose running water came true, and the water supply to the city and the surrounding suburbs was cut off. We had to rely on a well to get water. To provide the water for the family, Evelyn, Nathifa, Nuku Boy, and I would walk up the small hill across from the house, then over a little log bridge across the swamp to the neighborhood well. We would then carry the buckets back to the house and empty them into huge fifty-gallon barrels.

Ma's house had two barrels, one in the kitchen and one in the bathroom, and Uncle Nat had two barrels as well. Carrying the water on my head was tough. This process took at least two hours. Back and forth we went. I hated it. My family had a well inside our compound back in Barnersville. As I carried the buckets back and forth, I would daydream about what my brothers were doing across town.

✶ ✶ ✶

Several days after we arrived at Ma's house I was told that if rebels asked my name I should say it was Marcus Davis, for my own safety. It had been confirmed that the rebels were killing anyone with the name Doe. Uncle Nat and Uncle Mac tested me on my new name.

"What's your name?" they'd ask without warning. I would respond as confidently as possible, "Marcus Davis." My reply was never confident enough to avoid reprimand, advice, and sometimes a little laugh from Uncle Mac.

"You better remember when they ask you," he'd say. I had to repeat to myself that my name was Marcus Davis, not Marcus Doe. It was hard, but I knew my life might depend on how well I answered that simple question. I also had to say that I was America-Liberian, that I was Congo, and not of the Kru tribe.

In the evenings, we listened to the news on the BBC to learn how far the rebels had advanced that day. These days took on a sense of inevitability. In the midst of all those people, I felt alone. I felt I was waiting to be killed, while the others were waiting to be liberated. I was afraid of the rebels and what they would do to me if they ever found out that my name was Doe. Separated from most of my family, I really did not expect anyone to stick up for me if I was interrogated by the rebels. I grew accustomed to feeling lonely but was still crying myself to sleep at night.

Some people felt this was a hopeful time: The rebels were coming, and people seemed happy at the prospect of a change in power. I felt sure the situation would get worse before it got better. I knew many people would lose their lives—quite possibly even my family. I missed them constantly.

The Liberian government issued a curfew during this time. No one was allowed outside of their homes or in the streets at night except for military personnel. If a person was found outside between dusk and dawn, they were to be treated as a rebel. I knew that most of these people met their end. This was not the first time that a curfew had been declared in Liberia. I remembered that the country was under a curfew in November of 1985, the time immediately after the failed attempt on President Doe's life.

I felt safe at Ma's house, with Uncle Mac watching out the living room window for soldiers or rebels. As dusk approached each day, we would all take a bucket bath and take our places. I slept on the floor in one of the rooms, using my bag of clothes as a pillow. The house was filled to capacity. I was just happy to have a place to lay my head. We tried not to have candles burning or a lantern at night for fear that soldiers would harass us.

If I had to go to the bathroom at night, I held it until morning. I didn't want to risk anyone's life for a trip to the toilet. I tried to be as anonymous as possible: I did what they asked me to do, and I kept quiet. When darkness fell, we went to bed.

Sometimes the other kids and I stayed up telling spider stories, popular West African parables and children's stories that teach moral lessons. We would share them as we faded off to sleep. The stories took me to a different place, a fairy tale land where everyone was happy. There were no rebels in those stories, no government troops, no guns, no paralyzing fear, and most importantly, no sadness. There were only make-believe characters.

Little did we know that a few miles away, the rebels were systematically killing anyone from the Krahn and Mandingo tribes. They were killing hundreds of people. They were killing fat people (if you were fat it was assumed you worked for the government), former soldiers, and anyone affiliated with the government.

This was in direct contrast to what our neighbors were saying. The children at the well were enthusiastic about the impending arrival of Charles Taylor's troops. I feigned interest and made myself laugh along with them, but I knew that if the rebels won, I would lose at least one family member, and possibly all of them.

The children at the well told me that the rebels—who called themselves Freedom Fighters—were friendly and gave people food and treated them nicely. Very few people had spent time behind rebel lines, so no one really knew what the rebels were like. I could not wait to get my bucket and start walking back down the hill. At times as I carried the bucket on my head, water dripped down my face onto my clothes and hid my tears.

At night I prayed. I had never prayed so much in my life. I prayed for my family on the other side of the city and I prayed for my life and the lives of those around me. It was hard to tell how long the rebel siege of the city would last. Many of the adults predicted a few weeks at the most. But I wasn't sure: would they try to starve the people in the city to death in hopes that the government would give up? Would they bring the fighting into the city and forcibly remove President Doe from power? President Doe continued to vow that he would not resign the presidency.

* * *

As I began to settle into a routine at Ma's house, there was occasionally a gunshot or two, but nothing too alarming. Everything seemed fine until a night in late July. It was not quite dark yet and we were getting ready to head to bed. From the windows of the back rooms you could see up the hill into the neighborhood.

That night, we heard noise coming from the house up the hill. We had a clear view of the house owned by a man Ma knew. As she parted her curtains, Ma saw government soldiers crowded together and her neighbor on the ground in front of the house. He was on his knees. There were a few government soldiers harassing him. Things were happening quickly. We watched in silence.

The government soldiers were looking for any prominent members of the Gio or Mano tribes—the tribes that made up most of the rebel forces. The government soldiers were killing all Gios and Manos in their controlled areas, while the rebels were killing all Krahns and Mandingoes in their territory. No one was safe.

Ma's neighbor must have been Gio or Mano. He was being harassed by the troops. Uncle Mac told the children to sit in the living room. A few minutes later, we heard the shots. The innocent man was killed. This sent chills over my body. We heard the man's son run to his father's lifeless body, screaming, "My pa! My pa!" More shots rang out. Then silence.

The adults turned from the window. The looks on their faces said it all, yet left it all unsaid. It was a look that one gets when things don't make sense, are unbelievable, and one is desperately fearful and helpless. It is an unforgettable look. Watching them come out of the room, I felt so vulnerable and scared. I felt sure that the soldiers were going to go house to house through the neighborhood. I felt we were next.

I doubt anyone in our neighborhood slept comfortably that night. Even as a tired and scared child, I lay there just hoping there would not be a knock on our door. Tears streamed down my face. I wanted to be in any other part of the world. All the places I had memorized from my atlas felt so distant: Copenhagen, Amman, Pretoria, Sydney, and Buenos Aires. *Take me anywhere but here, anyone, please.*

I pictured my own death at the hands of ruthless rebels. I imagined myself crying and begging, hoping to avoid torture or death. The rebels would have no mercy on me. They would not care that I was eleven years old. I wanted to leave Liberia. I wanted to disappear into one of the spider stories and never come back.

There was no way out of the country then. Everyone who was left in Monrovia was in for the long haul. The next morning, the gunfire became more consistent. We did not live too far from James Spriggs Payne airport, the last possible escape route for President Doe and his officials.

A few days later, things had returned to relative normalcy, and we were back to our routine of picking rice in the morning and drawing water from the well in the afternoon. I headed up the hill slowly, dreading every trip back down with a bucket of water.

Taking a break halfway through the afternoon, sitting by the well daydreaming, I was slammed to the ground by the loudest noise I have ever heard—so loud I nearly fainted. All the children at the well started to scream and run. We scattered. I dropped my bucket and sprinted down the hill.

The government troops were firing rockets onto rebel positions close to the city from a road nearby. The government had purchased these rockets from the Romanian dictator Nicolae Ceaușescu some years back. They blazed across the late afternoon sky like the sun was racing across the sky at five hundred miles an hour. It sounded louder than if I was standing next to an airplane taking off. Three rockets were fired that evening. I reached the makeshift bridge before the third rocket, sweating from every part of my body. Extreme fear had me breathing heavily as I ran, goose bumps popped up on my skin, and I began to shake uncontrollably. A few minutes later, when the firing stopped, I ran back to get my bucket, but that was the end of drawing water that day.

The whole family sat and talked that night. It was clear the war had officially reached our area: there was regular fighting in the swamps a few miles to the north of us. The rocket fire became more regular and other artillery fired onto rebel positions nearby. The noise of fighting filled the air at unpredictable times, sometimes at night. The days were sunny, but everyone was in a gray mood and no one moved around. It was the middle of the rainy season, but it rarely rained. The stifling humidity never broke. Relief never came. The days seem to drag. Government soldiers walked through our neighborhood often. I eavesdropped on the adults' conversations to hear what they thought the rebels were doing. They were all predicting a rebel attack anytime. My life—and everyone else's—was hanging by a thread.

As early August rolled around, we listened to more news about where the rebels were. My uncles always chatted about world affairs, and while Uncle Nat always seemed the most intelligent one, Boye was knowledgeable too and I enjoyed learning from their observations. They said Iraq had invaded Kuwait and the United States was sending troops to help.

I prayed that the United States would help poor Liberia. We were slaughtering each other, but no one in the entire world seemed to care.

CHAPTER 8

Entrenched in War

Early in the morning on August 10, 1990, the fighting reached our neighborhood.

I was wide awake. The gunfire sounded too close, the walls were shaking, and the pictures on the walls were barely hanging on. I only had time to brush my teeth before everyone rushed into Uncle Nat's house. He recommended that we lie on the floor. Aunty Ethel commanded us to be completely silent. No one said a word.

The sound of bullets whizzing by the house filled the air. Sometimes there were a few minutes of silence, a lull in the constant gunfire. Periodically I could hear the voices of the fighters shouting instructions. At one point in the early afternoon, I heard combatants running through the flowers just outside, where Ma and Uncle Nat had planted trees and shrubs between the two houses. Soon enough, I could hear constant traffic of soldiers rustling through the undergrowth.

I lay on the floor in the hallway, sweat pouring down my back, my palms moist, trying to make sense of all that was happening. I was afraid to even roll over. I periodically closed my eyes and imagined myself in a different place. The sounds of big guns interrupted my escape, making the windows of the house shake. I hoped that the soldiers would not enter the house and that I would not get struck by a stray bullet. I was completely paralyzed with fear. At the same time, I was a boy who loved guns, and a part of me wanted to see the fighting as it was going on.

Uncle Nat would periodically crawl around the house to make sure that everyone was doing fine. Morning turned to afternoon. I was getting hungry, and I had to go to the bathroom. Evelyn was close to me, and I was itching to talk to her, but I was not willing to risk one word slipping out of my mouth, not even a sneeze or a cough. I started to think that if the fighting went on through the night I would probably soil myself for fear of getting killed while I was using the bathroom.

I dared not get up and go, and I didn't dream of opening my mouth and asking for food. I was sure everyone in the house had not eaten. I had been lying in the same spot, in almost the same position, all day. Aunty Ethel was in her bedroom with my young cousin Moe Dee, who was about a year and a half at that time. Amazingly, he did not cry once during that whole ordeal. The fighting raged on outside the house, and hunger and my full bladder raged inside me. As the battle wore on, the gunfire would sometimes cease for a few minutes, and the neighborhood would fall into eerie silence.

Sometime during the early afternoon Uncle Nat crawled around the house with a box of crackers. He handed me two crackers and smiled. He always seemed to be in control of any situation. As bad as that day was, he was still in a quiet world, it seemed. I grabbed the crackers and devoured them, but they only made me want more. I did not realize yet that hunger would follow me from that day on during the war.

As the afternoon wore on, the shooting got sparser. The sounds of gunfire seemed to have moved well west of where we were, and I could hear our neighbors calling out to us. Finally, as afternoon turned to early evening, the neighborhood began to clear out.

But just as relief was settling onto the house, rebel soldiers arrived and commanded everyone to leave their homes.

I could hear their voices from the roads and up the hill. The neighbors were screaming and alerting people and relaying the message to leave the area. I was dreading my first rebel encounter. I had heard so much about these "freedom fighters." I imagined them as giants. They said to grab what we could and leave the area. Everyone looked afraid.

I ran over to Ma's house and grabbed the blue book bag that I had used for school and was now using for all my belongings. I had left my parents' house two months earlier with this bag, expecting to be back in two weeks.

In that moment the bag seemed to represent how the world I knew was rapidly falling apart. I had a new last name, new friends, and new family. I lived in a different place, and now I was heading into the unknown. I waited as everyone else packed their things—feeling lucky because I already had a bag packed. On our way out, a neighbor explained that the rebels had told him that we needed to leave the neighborhood because the government troops would launch a counterattack overnight, and the neighborhood would become a kill zone.

Ma and Uncle Nat locked their doors, and we began walking up the hill toward the well. We moved faster than a normal walking pace, not quite running. With a bag on my head this pace was a bit frantic. I stayed close to Boye and Sister Lady. Everyone else in the neighborhood had already left. We avoided the main road.

★ ★ ★

I was anxious to see what the rebels—or freedom fighters, or whatever I was supposed to call them—looked like. I imagined them to be well-dressed, trained, and friendly. I also imagined them as ruthless killers.

When we hit the first unavoidable main road, I saw the rebels for the first time. There were three of them, and they were screaming, "You free now!" They didn't look at all like how I imagined. They were not in military uniform. They wore wigs. They were teenagers. As we walked toward the main road that led toward the western suburbs of Monrovia, I saw a few more rebels heading toward the fighting.

As we were passing Sophie's ice cream shop, where my father would take us to celebrate good grades, artillery from government troops began to land on all sides of us. I heard the loud screaming whistle as the explosive projectiles traveled through the air. Then I saw and heard them land. I had heard the piercing scream of artillery in war movies, and I knew soldiers were supposed to get into their foxholes and cover their heads. We had nowhere to take cover and no one to tell us what to do. We were walking on a main road.

With the shells falling all around us, we just kept going. I could not help but wonder where my father was, my brothers and sister. I became concerned about Ma. How could she walk all this way? I was close to Boye and he looked back to check on me. We carried on together.

I put my bag on top of my head and held it with one hand, alternating hands to give the tired arm a rest as we continued our frantic pace. The bag was too heavy to carry by my side.

There was a long line of people all walking toward Paynesville, moving further away from the fighting. Another rebel stood in the middle of the road. He had on a plain white t-shirt and jeans. He held his gun in his right hand slightly above his shoulder with the muzzle pointed upward and urged us to walk faster. He too was a young man, older than me but not by much.

As we walked eastward, rebels on the side of the road shouted, "We are fighting for your freedom!" They told us Charles Taylor was now our president. All this was strange to me. As we walked out of Congo Town, I noticed that many houses had been broken into. I figured the rebels must be using people's houses to sleep in while they were "fighting for our freedom." The further we ventured, the more I noticed empty houses whose doors had been busted and defaced with graffiti.

Every moment, I was learning firsthand the horrors of war. At the intersection where the Liberian football stadium is located, the rebels were gathered into crowds. They were looking at the fleeing people very closely. They were taking people from their families and walking away with them.

There were a few dead bodies lying on the road. Some were people who had just been killed. Blood flowed across the street and the air was full of its smell. Flies were all over the bodies. I remember passing close to a man's body that had been stripped completely naked. Flies crawled over him. Some of the bodies were women. Most of the bodies were in civilian clothing. The rebels were not just killing government soldiers.

I began to get scared. Were these people innocent victims hit by stray bullets? Were they suspected Krahns or Mandingoes? Did they say something that annoyed the rebels? Were they rebels killed in action? The most chilling question: Would my body soon be lying on the side of a road, being devoured by flies?

The gruesome sights did not seem to bother the rebels at all. The further we got behind rebel lines the more I realized that the rebels were not who they said they were. They were not what the children at the well had promised: freedom fighters coming to bring new order and wealth and food. No. They were killers.

Where were those kids now? Where were those children who could not wait to see the rebels, and get all the rice they could eat from them? Where were those children who could not wait to live behind rebel lines?

* * *

The hunger pangs that I felt earlier that day had vanished, and so had the urge to go to the bathroom. Things were getting uglier and uglier. As the light of the sun dimmed, and the sky turned orange, my own mood darkened from curiosity to extreme fear: a fear that I had never felt before, a real fear that I might not live to see the war end, perhaps even the end of the day.

A young rebel soldier, maybe my age or a little older, called out as we walked by.

"Ay, you, stop. You'n hear me? I say stop!"

No one dared turn around or even look toward him. I quickened my pace, and so did the others around me. I wanted to walk faster, even run, but I knew that would make me stand out. I was desperately trying to blend into the few people around me as we shuffled past the rebel.

A group of rebels began walking toward us, among them the young man who had called out. He repeated his command, this time more forcefully.

"Old man with the gray hair, stop!" The man he was referring to was walking just ahead of me. He looked well-educated and possibly more than twice the age of the young soldier. The old man ignored the young rebel.

"I say, old man with the gray hair, stop! You'n hear me calling you?" The young rebel raced past me with a few other fighters and grabbed the old man. He looked shocked that a young man would address him in such a disrespectful manner. I was surprised, too. Africans are respectful to their elders. The rebel pulled the man away from his family and started interrogating him.

"You working for Doe?" The man stayed silent. Three or four rebels dragged him away. I remember seeing that one of them had a machete. People slowed down to see what was happening. I kept on walking. I didn't want to do anything to anger the rebels, and I didn't want to watch them kill this man. Behind me, I heard the old man begin screaming.

"I beg y'all, oh!" I dared not turn around to see. They led him away. I tried not to hear his pleas. I tried to swallow, but my mouth was dry. It was clear: these were not "freedom fighters."

I could not walk straight for a few hundred feet. My legs felt like noodles. How could they call themselves freedom fighters when they were killing innocent civilians? I could not fathom children killing their elders. Where was morality in all this chaos? Where was God? Was there any respect for human life?

Most of the rebels I saw seemed to be working in small groups with little or no supervision. Who was in charge of these soldiers, if anyone? And if someone was in charge, were they approving of these random killings of innocent people? My mind and emotions raced. That dreadful afternoon was wearing on, and we were still walking. I was tired and my hunger pangs were beginning to show on my face.

We reached a checkpoint at Duport Road where many rebels had gathered. The sun was setting. The rebel-imposed six o'clock curfew would begin soon. We stood in line, waiting for who knows what. I was just glad to stop walking.

I tried to make sense of my day. I had walked miles. My heart and my body felt weak. I was scared. I tried to avoid eye contact with every rebel. My feelings had changed dramatically about the rebels. I had distrusted them before, but now I hated them. I was fearful of them, yet in a strange way I also wanted their power. I hated them, but I wanted to be one of them. I realized that in order to survive I had to interact with them. How could I deal with people who wanted to kill me?

As we turned onto Duport Road, elderly people around me were pleading for food and water. Young children were crying. The fast-paced walk that had dominated the earlier portion of our day had slowed to a crawl. We were in some sort of line. The rebels were trying to find people of the Krahn and Mandingo tribes. I hoped that no one would recognize me or my brother as we stood in the line and walked through the checkpoint.

From what I overheard the rebels saying, I gathered that the rebel forces had splintered. Now there were three warring factions all vying for power. Prince Johnson, a man I had never heard of, was now heading the second faction of rebels. He too was trying to kill President Doe. He was once a part of the original uprising but decided that he would split from Charles Taylor and reach the capital first. This turned the war into a three-sided conflict, with each side fighting on two fronts.

My new "cousin" Evelyn was just ahead of me in line. My brother was a little ahead of us. As we stood in the line, waiting to pass the rebel inspection, I began to daydream about my mother. She was buried not too far from where I stood. At least she is not alive to go through this awful situation.

My daydream was rudely interrupted by a young rebel pointing his gun in my face.

"Is this your sister?" he demanded, pointing to Evelyn. He looked me in the eye, and I was frightened. Before I could respond he said, "I am taking her as my girlfriend."

All I could muster out of my weak, scared body was a feeble shrug. At that moment I lost feeling in my entire body. It felt like my sweat glands froze. It felt like I was going to soil myself and faint all at once.

He told us he would be right back for her. He was not much older than I was, if he was older than me at all. As he walked away I realized that this was a boy I could've played football with in a different time, a time that seemed so far away at that moment. How did he become a rebel? He had so much power, power over me and over Evelyn, over everyone in that line. I breathed deeply, and Evelyn turned around and gave me a look of betrayal. Every cell in my body wished I had shouted "no!" to his demand.

In the end, he did not come back to look for her. I am eternally grateful. I could never have forgiven myself if Evelyn had been taken away, and I did nothing about it. I tried not to think about what I would say if he came back.

✳ ✳ ✳

Most of the rebels I saw were young men who belonged in a high school or university somewhere; some even looked like they should have been in my class. I wondered what kind of life they hoped to have after this. Were they even thinking about life after this war? I couldn't bring myself to imagine life *after* this.

I realized then that I could not see past that day, let alone what I would do if war ended. It had only just reached me, but I saw no end to the conflict. I was tired of looking away from rebels, of being startled by gunshots. I began to imagine that I would eventually die a painful death brought on by starvation. I pictured myself: a skinny boy with a huge stomach, suffering from malnutrition, barely strong enough to blink my eyes or brush the constant barrage of flies on my face, flies that could not wait for me to die so that they could have my remains.

I had seen this on television; now I was seeing it in real life. Would I drop dead, starved in the midst of this conflict? Or was there a bullet destined for me in one of the guns held by a rebel soldier not much older than I was? Would I cry as they led me away to kill me? Or would I be thankful to be done with hunger, with all of this? I knew that if my family was killed, I wanted to die too, so that I would not be left on earth by myself.

In my despair, I looked up and saw a man standing in front of the checkpoint. Dark-skinned and young, he was wearing a cowboy hat and motioning people toward a house. He even smiled. On a day when I had not seen any smiles, or anything to smile about, his face was deeply refreshing. He encouraged everyone to find a place to sleep for the night, as curfew was approaching. He brought water to those who asked. He made sure that everyone found a place to sleep.

It was a stroke of luck at the end of a supremely unlucky day. I did not have to go through the checkpoint and face questions from the rebels who seemed to be hungry for human blood. And the smiling cowboy, who said his name was Prince, seemed to have something to do with the house that we slept in that night. I remember thinking that he was very graceful. But he was also a rebel, and he carried an AK-47. I knew he would kill me if he found out that my name was Marcus Doe.

I grabbed my bag and followed everyone else who had left Ma's house. The place was already overcrowded, and the people inside didn't seem at all happy to see us. The woman who carried herself like the owner of the house did not want strangers in her home. There were probably fifty or sixty extra people in her house that night. The more people walked into her house, the more she sneered. Prince assured her that it was just for the night. Uncle Nat made his rounds to make sure everyone in our group was accounted for and encouraged us that things would be all right.

I dropped down on the cold marble floor. My father had warned me, rather sternly, that I had to wear the white gown from the witch doctors every night as I slept. I believed, as my father had, that the gown would protect me from evil spirits as

I slept, but Mandingoes were the only people in Liberia that wore long flowing gowns. If anyone saw mine, I would be killed. I was torn between my fear of evil spirits, my respect for my father, my desire to blend in and be anonymous, and the feeling of looking absolutely ridiculous. Honoring my father won out. I pulled on the gown for protection and used my bag as a pillow.

As I drifted off to sleep that night, I knew I would have to stay quiet to survive, to escape notice. I was hungry, but I was even more exhausted, and I fell asleep quickly.

✳ ✳ ✳

Footsteps on the marble floor woke me up that morning.

"Who this boy in a white gown?" It was a woman's voice. The question seemed to echo and repeat itself through the house. Was it the owner turning me in to Prince the rebel? I felt naked, like the way one feels after saying something in public that shouldn't have been said. She had exposed my secret. I was wearing a gown like a Muslim in rebel territory.

For a few moments I did not know where I was. I knew I was in a war, but I was disoriented. What was I doing on the floor in this strange, crowded place? I slowly pulled myself together. I could feel everyone's inquisitive looks upon me. I wanted to shrivel up and disappear.

As I became aware of my surroundings, I knew that my fears were coming true and my white gown was making me a target. Death was staring at me. Anyone in that house could have said, "He is a Mandingo boy," and that would have been the end of my life—and the life of anyone who came to my defense. No one spoke.

Without thinking, I ignored the question, got up, and changed into regular clothes. The source of the question never surfaced. I didn't put a face to the voice, and I didn't want to. I brushed my teeth in the front yard with a cup of water, and I washed my face. I saw countless rebel fighters along the street and all around me.

I stared at the roadway, eyes glazed, my mind empty and tired. A face caught my attention: my uncle George Sleweon, my father's brother, was walking along the road in front of the house about fifty yards away. I wanted to make eye contact with him, but he did not see me. I wanted to shout, but I couldn't say anything. I did not want to put his family's life in danger.

He looked tired. His wife, Aunty Julia, was next to him. I had lived with them when my mother died, and my heart ached to run to them now. I wanted to tell them what I had seen and been through. I wanted to ask them if they knew where my family was. Was Pa still alive? What about Caroline, Molley, Mocco, and Gahien? I couldn't stop the questions in my mind, but I was afraid of the answers. I was afraid to hear that my family had been killed. I cried as Uncle Sleweon and Aunt Julia walked away.

Prince walked into the compound as I hurried back inside the house. His cowboy hat sat on top of his head. His jeans and his sneakers were clean. The owner of the house wanted everyone out, and Prince began helping new arrivals to the area find a place to stay permanently. He was being a Good Samaritan, but I was scared to be around one of the rebels.

I gathered my things that morning in silence and prepared to keep walking. Prince herded us all back outside. I had no idea where we would end up. Maybe I would see my brothers. Maybe I would befriend a freedom fighter, and he would look after me. Maybe someone would recognize me, and I would be killed.

I wanted to stay in the house. It felt safe. I had survived a day of walking past hundreds of rebels and a military battle. I had not eaten since the afternoon before. I wasn't sure I could do it all a second time. Nevertheless, we prepared to set out again.

CHAPTER 9

Life behind Rebel Lines

I was exhausted the next morning as we walked further from home toward an uncertain future. We were now well behind rebel lines.

I had been transformed. My old face, a boyish gap-toothed grin, had morphed into a new face, a hungry frown. My joy had been replaced with fear, doubt, and worry about my survival. It was a bit safer here, farther from the front lines of the fighting. I studied the rebels out of the corner of my eye, fascinated, trying to make sense of what was happening to me. Thoughts of my death and the demise of my family and friends crossed my mind continually. My daydreams shifted to dark questions: *Will I be better off dead? Will death be painful? How do I want to die?* I made the solemn decision that if a rebel decided to take my life, I would not beg and suffer humiliation and torture. I would simply disobey, that way the killing would come quickly.

It was the rainy season. During this time of year strong thunderstorms come along the West African coast, bringing strong winds and heavy rains. It reminded me of those carefree days in Barnersville, the rainy days that I loved as a boy when I would play in the downpours with Pretty and Deshield and the times I took the soap outside to shower under the roof, feeling free and refreshed. Now I longed for that cleansing. My mind and body were caked with filth. Picturing the rain cascading down the roof and onto my face gave me hope.

Thinking of the rainy season also reminded me of fishing, wading waist-deep in the pond across from my house in

Barnersville with the fishing rod I made myself. I remembered Caroline helping me get leeches off my body, looking me over from head to toe and making sure there weren't any hanging on where I couldn't see. That memory of family, of being cared for, jarred me back to my present state.

* * *

We arrived at what was to be our new temporary home along Duport Road in a gated compound well off the main street. There was a long, unpaved side road leading to the house. We arrived in pouring rain.

There were about fifteen of us in our party, and there were already many people milling around—some seemed to have been living here for weeks or months. I am not quite sure how we found this house or how we knew these people, other than the fact that Aunty Ethel seemed to know the house's owner. There were a few children my age running around the front yard of the compound.

The house was big. The tree-lined driveway was made of cobblestones, shifting to concrete as it got closer to the two-car garage. It looped left, forming a semi-circle that led back out of the compound through a second gated entrance. The front porch of the house was on the left side. On the right side, close to the house, was a huge almond tree, much like the almond tree in my family's yard in Barnersville. Next to the fence on the edge of the lawn was a newly dug well.

I was relieved to finally put my bag down and rest. I was also eager to make new friends and feel human again. We climbed up the stairs in the garage and made our way through the kitchen and dining room. The living room sat a few feet lower than the surrounding rooms and had a homey feel. At the end of a long hallway with rooms on both sides and a bathroom about halfway down, we arrived at a rectangular shaped room with blue carpet: our room. It had several huge bean bag cushions. I put my bag down near the door, and Nathifa and I walked out to meet the other kids.

It took a few days to figure out the new place. I was eager to run and play, but I quickly learned that sitting and playing cards was a wiser choice—staying out of trouble and avoiding hunger was more important than fun. As scarce as food had been for the past couple of months, it was even harder to come by on Duport Road. We ate once a day around 4 p.m., our food heaped in a huge serving bowls. Nuku Boy, Evelyn, Nathifa, and I ate together out of the same huge bowl. The usual fare was rice and greens, but sometimes it was just rice and palm oil. Mealtime was what I looked forward to each day.

The four of us came up with rules for eating because we wanted everyone to be fair. Nuku Boy tended to chew faster and eat more quickly than the rest of us, so we decided that we would all take spoonfuls of rice at the same time. We chewed each spoonful slowly so that no one got a bite ahead of the others. We also compared spoonfuls as each child pulled their spoon from the bowl to make sure we all had roughly the same amount. We fiercely policed each other, and there were frequent arguments at meal times over food.

The water in the well in the compound was always brown. I used it to bathe with no shampoo or soap. I washed my clothes in it, too. In the months that I lived there, I was perpetually dirty.

Every day around noon, I rolled the empty fifty-gallon water barrel out of the compound to a nearby creek to fill it with water to drink—the only times I left the compound. Nuku Boy always disappeared when it came time to labor, and the work was too difficult for the girls, so it was up to me most of the time. The creek was about sixty yards outside the compound. When I got there, I filled the barrel with water, sealed it, and then rolled it back to the compound on its side, pushing it with my foot.

I risked running into a rebel every time I left the compound. I hated this chore, but we needed water, and even while I hated the work, leaving the compound was my only time to myself. No one else came down to the creek with me, so I could sit and think. I was free to let my imagination run away with me.

Most days, I sat by the creek and cried. I longed for my family. I wondered what had happened to them. I had no way to find out information about their whereabouts.

The children in the compound had very few things to do. As long as I took a bath every day and filled the water barrel, Sister Lady rarely gave me a hard time. She had given me a Bible of my own, and I continued to read the Old Testament stories about all the great heroes. A few weeks after we arrived at the compound, she organized a midday prayer service with the kids. We read from scripture, and we prayed. It felt pointless to me. I prayed for my family sometimes, but I was losing hope that they were still alive, and I wasn't sure prayer was much help anyway.

In the afternoons, the kids played cards and took part in our new favorite pastime: talking about what we would do after the war was over. We did this every day, making sure the adults didn't hear us. These conversations ran wild among the four of us. We went into vivid detail about how our lives would be different. Nathifa always talked about her future and so did Evelyn—going to America, getting married, jobs, and school. Nuku Boy and I talked about what we would eat if we survived the war. We made a pact between us that we would never let food go to waste in our presence. For years after I left the war, I ate everything off my plate wherever I went, sometimes even eating unfinished food off other peoples' plates as well.

I kept my desire to see my family to myself. It hurt too much to talk about. I started to accept that they had all been killed and began to dream about how all the rebels would be brought to justice for all of the senseless killing they had done. I envisioned myself living permanently with my brother and his wife.

The atmosphere of the compound got tense whenever a rebel came. Rebels showed up in our compound maybe once a week or so, sometimes to see who lived in the compound, and sometimes demanding food. Sometimes they were just milling around looking for Krahn and Mandingo people.

I had to hide because of my name. The gate made a distinct sound and as soon as I heard it I ducked into a bush or ran into the house. Nathifa and Evelyn always warned me when they heard the gate.

* * *

One afternoon I did not hear the gate open, and before I knew it there were two heavily armed rebels in the compound with two men they had captured, all perhaps in their twenties. The two prisoners were completely naked. Each one was tied by the arms so his elbows touched each other behind his back. The men's genitals were also tied up and the rope was tied around their necks, so their backs were slightly hunched over. It looked awful. The pain and fear on the faces of these men is hard to forget. This punishment was called *taibay*. Sometimes when the rebels taibayed a person, they would touch the tightly stretched skin of the prisoner with the sharp blades of their knives, splitting the prisoner's chest open revealing the white cartilage of breastbone, and they would laugh.

These men whom the rebels brought into the compound had tears in their eyes, perhaps from the pain of the tying, the fear of death, or the humiliation of their torture. They were crying and begging for their lives. According to the rebels, they had been caught stealing from a house that no one lived in. This was a crime in rebel territory, even though the rebels routinely commandeered other people's houses once the owners were forced to vacate the premises. Many houses had been abandoned during the war. Sometimes the rightful owners had been killed, or the house had been claimed by a rebel who was still on the front lines. One could always tell whenever a rebel had claimed a house because his name would be written on it in charcoal or paint. No one could touch the property, let alone live in the claimed house.

I stood on the front porch of the house, about twenty to thirty feet away from the men, frozen. I wanted to run into the house. Panic and fear gripped me from head to toe, and I stood motionless. The other kids had disappeared into the house. I was the only one standing on the porch, and I felt then that if I moved, I would be the rebel's next victim. Drugs made the rebels extremely unpredictable. They could have called me down and taken me along just for looking at them.

There were a few people in the garage and they stood still and silent as well. No one dared come to the defense of these two men. The men were crying and asking us to beg the rebels to forgive them. I stood on the porch looking down and I saw in their eyes a look that I was beginning to recognize: the look a person gets when death is near and certain. It's a look of desperation and vain hope and repentance. Many people never see this look. I can never efface its imprint on my heart.

The rebels taunted the men and made jokes about how stupid they were for trying to steal from an abandoned house. They asked us if we knew them. No one knew the men, or if they did, they dared not say. Getting nothing from us, the rebels eventually took their prisoners and left, hitting the men as they led them out of the yard. As they left I felt sick and light-headed. I can never forget the faces of those men who probably met their end that day.

After that encounter, I listened even more keenly for the sound of the compound gate, and we sank further into anxiety and fear for our lives. As August became September, thunderstorms owned the nights, and fear and hunger ruled the days.

* * *

My overall health was deteriorating. My gums bled all the time and I lost more than one tooth. The simplest and most basic hygiene items were nowhere to be found. Toothpaste was very scarce. We simply put a dash of baking soda on our toothbrushes and scooped a cup of water from the barrel of drinking water that sat in the kitchen. I went out under the almond tree on the left side of the yard and brushed my teeth. I had never been to a dentist in my young life, and until my gums began to bleed and my teeth began to fall out I didn't see the importance of dental hygiene. The water we used to brush our teeth was from the creek or the well—it was a miracle that no one contracted dysentery.

I was lucky to eat a meal every day, but the steady diet of rice and any green plants we could gather from the bushes was not sufficient to keep me nourished. I was losing an incredible amount of weight. I did not own a belt then, but if I had it would have been of little help holding up my khaki shorts. The elastic waist in my athletic shorts could not keep up with my shrinking waistline. By mid-September I was using my shoelaces to hold up my pants.

I didn't recognize myself when I looked in the mirror—a surreal feeling. My eyes bulged from their sockets. My veins dominated my arms and legs. My lips were chapped and bleeding. I knew the face in the mirror was me simply because it had the scars on the forehead that I had come to recognize as the marks from my childhood accidents.

Despite all of this—the fear of rebels, my poor health, the chaos, my homesickness—I managed to look forward to simple things: playing football and eating well. I had great plans for after the war consisting primarily of eating until I fainted and having a full belly so I had the energy to play football. I drummed up energy and hope by sharing my plans with the other kids, but daydreaming alone is what got me through those days. I wasted away on the outside, but my imagination became more vivid, and I fed my sense of appreciation for the things I lacked.

The nights in the compound were long and scary. It was difficult to fall asleep on an empty stomach. Then the artillery would begin, filling the night with random, constant gunfire that kept me awake or woke me if I happened to doze off. Based on the closeness of an initial blast, we could tell whether it was incoming artillery or outgoing. We preferred the outgoing. The whistle of the incoming was terrifying. Sometimes we would mistake the noise of thunder for artillery—and the other way around. Thunderstorms at night still frighten me.

One night someone thought they heard a soldier in the bushes in the yard. If a rebel was in our yard this late, we were in grave danger. The adults woke us up to sit quietly, ready, as they listened for sounds. It was raining. I was tired and scared. I needed to go to the bathroom. We sat unmoving in the pitch dark, waiting to hear something and hoping to hear nothing. Everyone—all thirty or so of us—was silent. The adults communicated in nearly inaudible voices. The spirit of fear flowed down the hallway and into the room where we slept: a fear that stripped away all clear thinking, a fear that collects sweat below your skin, holding it in until the danger is past.

As thunder rolled and lightning lit up the backyard, I strained for a brief glimpse of light. We sat that way for close to an hour waiting to go back to sleep. Waiting for the restless fear of a rebel outside to loosen its paralyzing hold. Finally, the all clear: I felt the sweat pour out of me as I lay down. Someone said it was about 4:30 a.m., and I knew it would be impossible to fall asleep again.

I remember that some nights I could sleep through anything: sensing no danger, I'd fall asleep and passively give my cares over to God. When I was afraid and sleepless as a child, my father would hear me rolling around in bed and take me out to the porch and comfort me in the open air.

I missed him that night. He was nowhere close. In my mind he was still in Barnersville, but how could I be sure? I imagined he was somewhere in the country just as worried about me as I was about him, not knowing where I was or what I was doing. I could no longer be sure that my father was still alive—a notion I tried to fight off. We had heard reports from the BBC that President Samuel Doe had been killed in early September. Anything seemed possible.

I tried to make sense of the war as I lay awake. I thought the fighting should have ended with Doe's death—he was the dictator that Charles Taylor and his rebels were after—but a loyal remnant of Doe's soldiers fought on. Prince Johnson had splintered from Charles Taylor and formed his own faction of rebels, which was also prolonging the fighting. I was even more afraid of Johnson's men than of Taylor's, because Johnson was the one who we heard had captured and killed Doe. My mind flooded, my stomach growled, and I waited for daylight.

In the morning I was eager to find out what had happened the night before. I'd eventually dozed off, but I was one of the first to wake up. I listened to the radio with the men every morning, and I felt safe with them, listening intently as they gave their thoughts, feelings, and predictions. Some of their pronouncements were full of gloom, while others were cautiously optimistic about our survival. They all gave timelines for when they thought the war would be over: most predicted the fighting would be over by Christmas of 1990.

Listening to their opinions gave me hope and left me discouraged by turns. On this morning they didn't mention much about the night before, but they were all talking about the West African peacekeeping forces, the Economic Community of West African States Monitoring Group (ECOMOG), that had been sent to Liberia from neighboring countries. These peace keepers were battling Charles Taylor's rebels on the outskirts of Monrovia. They carried food and medical supplies with them. Their presence in Liberia brought renewed hope that I would survive. I clung to every word the adults uttered. I could barely imagine what Liberia would look like when the war was over.

But even in days of more hopeful news, I began to imagine a world without me. My dreams of becoming a football star— first for the Invincible Eleven, then AS Monaco of France— seemed to slip away with every loud and visible heartbeat, with every rib that began to show and every day that wasted away. Six months ago, the idea of sitting around playing cards all day was unimaginable. Living on one meal a day was not supposed to happen to me. Those things happened to other countries, not to Liberia: not in my country, not in my home, not in my family. Would our community get to the point where we would have to decide who was worthy of staying alive, who was worthy of precious scraps of food? Would I be forced to join the rebels and kill to survive? Would it be survival of the fittest? Would I be lost?

As I began to feel fear's roots digging deeper into me, I started to attend the daily prayer service more eagerly. I'd do anything that gave me hope of survival. In retrospect, I did not really believe in God, and I had no relationship with him. At the time I was unsure of who he was, what he could do, or whether he cared about us. But I prayed often—what else could I do? I thought of God as a distant figure, inconsistent and slow to intervene. Questions nagged me: Why would God allow these terrible things to happen?

There is a certain desperation one develops when death seems to be just around the corner. Cynicism crept into my behavior, demeanor, and my outlook on life. When the next meal is your priority, few things seem to matter, certainly not a passive God. And yet, when two weeks into the future becomes hard to imagine, one seems to become more reserved and thoughtful. I wondered whether God could offer me more than my cynicism.

✱ ✱ ✱

Around the end of October we began to hear the sounds of different guns at night. I had become accustomed to the sound and rhythm of the AK-47s used by Charles Taylor's men: a rhythmic two-shot sound with a distinct pause, or wild and continuous fire. But these new sounds were more measured, mostly single shots, sometimes two. They had a different cadence, not rhythmic, more deliberate.

The BBC reported that Taylor's men were being pushed back out of the city by Johnson's men and the peacekeepers. I was hoping for the arrival of the peacekeepers from Ghana and Nigeria with food, medicine, and some semblance of sanity. But I was conflicted: they had joined forces with Prince Johnson, whose troops had killed President Doe. I did not feel too safe with them. I didn't know what to expect if they arrived. Johnson didn't seem to bring safety or peace. But if there was more food, we could survive.

Taylor's men became even more volatile as they continued to lose ground. As the fighting got closer, they encouraged people to move further inland with them as they retreated further away from the city. At times they demanded that people move with them. These reports were coming fast and furious. Many of the people who lived with us in the compound bowed to the pressure and left as the fighting got closer. Many feared that Johnson's men were going to unleash another onslaught of killing comparable to what we had seen when Taylor's men took over the area. Rebels began knocking on doors throughout the neighborhood. They were angry and persistent. Most people in the compound who were loyal to Taylor left with the retreating rebels. Our population began to dwindle.

Our group of displaced people had to make a decision. Were we going to defy the Taylor rebels and risk death by staying? I stayed close to my uncles to eavesdrop about what they would decide. I was eager to know if we were going to be moving, or if we were going to sit and hope that the rebels did not come into our compound and find us waiting for their enemies. I was torn between leaving with the rebels or staying and hoping to be found by ECOMOG troops. Leaving the house could mean another death march through a gauntlet of angry rebels eager to show their prowess by killing indiscriminately. Marching with rebels who were angry at their defeat to an unknown, unspecified location—maybe five miles away, maybe a hundred—would be brutal. Would we just keep retreating with the rebels and hope they didn't kill us in their anger? What about food? I imagined that march and the many victims of hunger whom I knew would die of starvation on the way. I thought about being left at the side of the road with my cousins to die. I actually imagined my lifeless body lying along the highway, my life ending with a whimper.

ECOMOG's arrival brought another threat: ECOMOG had an air force, and they conducted bombing raids day and night. This was an advantage for them, of course, as they used bombing raids to soften Charles Taylor's positions. But we weren't sure how they went about gathering information and selecting targets, so we were afraid that they would drop a bomb on our compound. It was a big building that could have been confused for an ammunition depot or some other military building.

I went to sleep those days hoping not to wake up in a flattened house with dead people around me. When I left the compound to get water, I would go during the early evening to avoid rebel contact, and I scanned the sky for war planes.

Threats around us multiplied, and we waited, weighing our options. One day I was out by myself filling the barrel from the neighbor's well. I was rolling the barrel down the unpaved road with my feet when an ECOMOG war plane seemed to be rushing straight at me.

The plane was very loud and flying low. I could tell it had dropped a bomb because I saw the smoke rising in the distance. In a panic, I took off running toward the compound, leaving the barrel behind. My heart was racing. My feet shook. I covered my head and braced myself. The ground seemed to be shaking beneath me. The seconds ticked by. It was a short distance, but it felt like forever. The plane was far enough away that I was in no danger, but my instincts took over. I made it through the gates to find everyone in the compound outside on the pavement staring at the sky: innocent civilians hoping not to get bombed. Uncle Nat cautioned us not to point at the aircraft for fear that the pilot might confuse our upraised arms for weapons and rain bullets or bombs on the house.

From then on we had to remain inside the house. The gate to the compound was locked for fear of rebel entry. We stayed extremely quiet all day and all night. The rest of the neighborhood was quiet as well. Either they had left with the rebels or stayed in silence. We were scared to go find out if the neighbors were still around.

Rebels knocked on the gates to make sure we were all gone. When they did, it sent chills down my spine. There would have been a bloodbath in our compound if they had found us hiding in there.

Citizens of ECOMOG countries who lived in Liberia were also at risk of being killed. Taylor's men were ordered to kill all Ghanaians, Nigerians, and any other foreigners who lived in Liberia. We had four Ghanaians living with us in the compound. This was a source of contention in the group. If we were found to be hiding Ghanaians, we would be afforded little mercy. Each one of us faced death if these people were discovered in our compound. Some in the compound were not comfortable risking their lives for the lives of foreigners, but letting them go would have meant certain death for them. They would stand out: Ghanaians and Nigerians had very noticeable accents when they spoke, having been colonized by the British. Their cadence and intonations were very different from us Liberians.

Without coming to a resolution, we continued to harbor them in our compound as the rebels continued to search houses for foreigners while they retreated from the oncoming peacekeepers. Whenever there was a knock on our gate, the children in our compound would alert the adults and signal to the Ghanaians. What followed on a nearly daily basis— sometimes multiple times a day—would have been comical if our lives were not at stake: we had to get the Ghanaians into the ceiling as quickly as we could. This was a process we had planned but not practiced. One of the Ghanaian women was out of shape, and it was always hard to get her into the ceiling.

I won't ever forget the looks on their faces while we struggled to hide them.

Caring for them was not difficult for me. They were such kind people, and acting as a liberator gave me hope. Watching them climb up into the ceiling gave me courage not to let the rebels control my life. These Ghanaians were hiding for their lives, and we were there helping them, saving lives instead of being accomplices to their murder. I felt I was sticking it back to the rebels who had been the source of so many of my nightmares.

I have no doubt now that it was God who kept us there and blinded the rebels to our presence. They never chose to open the gate and come in. The wait for the arrival of the ECOMOG troops seemed to be never-ending. All the same, I could hardly shake my constant sense of dread. Prince Johnson's men were hostile toward people like me. I had gotten used to living in Taylor's territory. Now the rules were going to change, but I was not sure how. Part of me felt as if I was just waiting for someone different to kill me.

CHAPTER 10

Imperfect Liberation

"Everybody in the house, come outside!"

A soldier in Johnson's army shouted orders inside the compound. His voice was threatening, demanding. Everyone filed out quietly. We lined up against the railing just below the front porch. The now-familiar fear and anxiety gripped my eleven-year-old body. Other inhabitants of our compound filled the garage and the walkway between the porch and the lawn. The Ghanaians that we hid during the rebel retreat emerged from the house for the first time in weeks. Trembling with fear, I stood with my feet very close together. It was a clear day, but it seemed the breezes stopped blowing and the leaves stopped rustling. Everything and everyone around me stood still.

There were about ten soldiers. Prince Johnson's rebels were better dressed than Taylor's men. They wore military fatigues and carried automatic rifles. They were all adorned with belts of ammunition. They looked just like I had imagined a soldier should.

They wanted to know if we were harboring any of Taylor's men. The adults answered that we were not. They searched the house. A few minutes later more rebels emerged from the backyard and stood in front of us. My hope was slowly rising: would we be free now?

My growing admiration and hope evaporated in an instant.

"Any Krahn people here?" As well dressed as they were, they were still rebels, interested in ethnic cleansing.

One by one, they asked everyone their name. As they made their way down the line, I knew I would have to lie for my life. If I slipped and said "Marcus Doe," they would kill me and anyone who knew me. They would assume we were all Krahns. I had to do this not only to preserve my life, but the lives of those around me. I practiced in my head, *Marcus Davis, Marcus Davis, Marcus Davis.*

I felt like I was going to soil myself. I could have fainted and remained on the ground until I died from anxiety. I wanted to shrink into the cracks in the pavement and join the ants that crawled so peacefully right beside my bare feet.

My turn arrived and they passed over me. The rebels didn't even acknowledge me. They asked at random. I was among those who never had to answer.

I breathed a sigh of relief, feeling proud of myself. We survived to starve another day, to live in fear another day, to hope another day.

The rebels left the compound, joking as they walked toward the gate, laughing as if there was not a war going on. We were no longer governed by Taylor and his rebels. We now belonged to Prince Johnson's army and the West African peacekeepers. The peacekeepers had not made it to us yet, but I was already imagining what they looked like.

The Ghanaians were elated. They could finally get some fresh air. It felt good to see them happy. They had not smiled in weeks, it seemed, and now they walked around the yard with renewed confidence. They talked openly about returning to Ghana. Most importantly, they asked us to join them. They were very grateful to us. They promised us everything they had back in Ghana because of what we had done for them.

Tears filled my eyes as I watched the Ghanaians soak in the little bit of daylight left. They sat on the porch and enjoyed a simple pleasure that we had come to take for granted. They were so happy just to be outside, enjoying loud laughs and speaking their native language. I felt hope for the first time in a long time. Watching them have a conversation I could not understand, I slumped against the wall in the garage and cried, torn between my joy for the Ghanaians and my continuing fear.

As I drifted off into my solitary world, I wondered when I would truly be liberated. I yearned to be reunited with my family. This day had been was sweet for us all, but worry still loomed. I could still be caught by Johnson's men and killed.

Something deeper changed that day. I had become willing to lie to preserve my life. I began to be ashamed of my name. This habit of lying grew as I grew, and it became easier to lie about my family, my country, my people, and my continent. Unable to change my circumstances, I started to change myself, reinventing myself to fit my situation. It became my impulse to deny who I was, a habit that followed me for many years.

✳ ✳ ✳

The next few days were strange. Charles Taylor's ruthless men had not completely relinquished control of our area and Johnson's forces were not numerous enough to provide protection for their newly captured area. There were rumors circulating that Taylor's rebels were infiltrating the surrounding neighborhoods and killing people. There were also rumors that Taylor's men were planning a counterattack on our area. We heard that Taylor's men would probe the area at night and break into homes to massacre or torture the residents because they chose to wait to be liberated by the ECOMOG forces. The peacekeepers and Johnson's army had not properly mopped up lingering detachments of Taylor's rebels. Our neighborhood was far from the nearest main road, so we were standing targets.

The owner of the house in which we were essentially squatting had the idea of asking a Johnson rebel to guard the

place, and when she did, the rebel agreed. The owner somehow knew this rebel from before the war, I think. I wasn't
sure of the relationship. He came to the house at night. The
sense of danger was heightened when he was around. The
child in me came out: was he putting us at greater risk of
Taylor's retaliation?

At night, the children gathered around the soldier to hear
him talk. News from the city was scarce, and we were all curi-
ous. I held back at first, but my hunger for news soon overtook
my timidity. Like every other anxious, wide-eyed child in the
compound, I was eager to hear from a real soldier. I wanted
to understand what it was like to fight in real combat. Like the
other boys, I was wired to see combat as the valiant work of
heroes. Quickly forgetting that this man could have ended my
life, I gave in to my fascination with his role in the fighting.

He claimed to have been there when President Doe was
killed. He described in detail what happened that fateful day,
including the battle to capture President Doe inside of the
compound close to the city center. He explained how Doe
was tortured and brutally murdered. His description jolted
me back to what was real: fear. *This man is not a liberator. He
may have killed my father!* Desperately trying not show my
disgust, I tried to smile and put on a face of approval. But no
one warned me to stay away from him, and I wanted to know
what was happening. So I kept listening.

One night, the rebel arrived as usual at nightfall. Someone
at the house had begun saving him some food. That night as
he ate his meal, he began to tell stories of another battle. I
listened to his story, sitting relatively close.

As the evening was winding down, he asked for someone
to hand him his AK-47. My childhood love of soldiers and
guns arose. Without thinking, I jumped up before all the other
children, grabbed the weapon, and handed it to him. At that

moment, Uncle Nat walked into the room and saw me. He said hello to everyone in the room, then acknowledged me with one word: "Marcus."

He left the room. A few minutes later, Nathifa, Uncle Nat's daughter, came and asked me to follow her. I knew I was in trouble. My sister-in-law and my brother were going to be furious with me. As I walked across the hall I began to tear up, realizing the gravity of my mistake: *How stupid am I? This rebel will kill me if he finds out who I am. Why was I helping him get his rifle? Why did I want to impress him? How could I have been so thoughtless?*

Whatever I got, I knew I deserved it. Fear built up in me like never before—fear of the rebel, fear of my family. My cousin barely looked at me. All the adults in our group were in the room: Uncle Nat, Aunty Ethel, my brother, and Sister Lady. The room was very dimly lit, but I recognized faces.

The moment I closed the door, Boye said, "Were you just playing with a gun?"

"Yes," I responded, realizing that trying to deny the allegations would only add to my punishment. Everyone in the room began scolding me at once. I tried to explain the situation, but it was a vain attempt. I could tell Sister Lady was not just angry, but very disappointed. I stood right behind the closed door, trying to plead my case, trying to beg for mercy.

I was filled with shame. I knew I was ungrateful to have put them in danger after they had kept me out of harm's way for all these days. I was scared that they would send me to find my other brothers, that they would no longer allow me to follow them. Now that we were liberated and we might have a chance to leave the country, I feared that they would leave me with the first family member they could find.

Defenseless, all I could do was listen. Every time I tried to speak someone said, "Close your mouth." My chapped lips quivered, my legs shook, and I began to sweat. I hoped the berating would end, and this whole thing would be over— but it was far from finished. Frankly, I would rather have taken a beating. Instead, they continued the tongue-lashing, each person trying to make me realize how stupid my actions were.

Finally they told me to begin "pumping tire."

This was one of the worst punishments for a Liberian child. Essentially, "pumping tire" is doing squats with your hands on the sides of your head, your thumb and forefinger holding on to your earlobe. The up and down motion resembles an air pump for tires and soccer balls, hence the name of the punishment.

My body sank to the ground and rose rhythmically. Up and down I went. My knees began to ache. My hamstrings and quadriceps began to fatigue. My mind shuffled between remorse for my actions, anger at being punished, and a calm distant blankness that sheltered me from it all. When I began to slow, I was commanded to keep going. My legs weakened and began to tremble. Sweat poured from every pore on my body. The hunger that I usually felt intensified. I knew that I deserved to be punished, and I tried to take my share like a man, but I couldn't hold back the ugly flood of tears down my face. I had never been punished like this before, not even by my own mother.

I felt like a disappointment to my brother, whom I adored and loved to please. That was one of my regrets as I continued to "pump tire."

Finally he said, "Take your stupid self to bed." I stopped and walked slowly toward the door. My fatigue and anger mixed with my genuine shame and remorse.

"Sorry," I whimpered as I opened the door. I hung my head and walked down the hallway. I didn't know what else say.

I wiped the sweat from my forehead as I stepped into our room. The barrel with drinking water was outside in the garage, and I dared not go there. My thirst lasted until morning. I laid my head on the bean bag that I shared with my cousins, curled my trembling legs toward my body and cried myself to sleep. I knew I'd made a mistake, but I wished my parents had been there to save me.

* * *

The next few days I could barely walk. My energy was scarce, but I was still required to fill the water barrel. Gathering all my strength, I rolled the barrel down to the well, filled it up, and pushed it back with my legs much more slowly than usual. After getting water for everyone else I had very little energy left to go to the well to get a bucket of water for a bath, so I did not. Not bathing for a couple of days was fine with me.

Leaving the compound was what I focused on. Word spread about what I had done. The other kids in the compound made fun of me, mimicking how I walked. Even my cousins chimed in. Pretending to laugh along, I hid my internal pain, a feat at which I was becoming very adept. Soon my legs felt better, but the pain of being mocked lingered. My internal scars would last a long time, long after I could walk without discomfort.

Soon after, our group decided to move closer to the main road. The dangers of living under the constant threat of attack from Taylor's men became too much to bear. Aunty Ethel and Uncle Nat led our entire group to a house just off Duport Road. Boye had a friend who lived a few hundred yards further from the main road. His home was in a more densely populated area. Sister Lady, Boye, and I settled there.

During the war, many families were split up and houses were filled with people from all walks of life, including people grieving the loss of family members. Some were lucky enough to have all members of their immediate family alive, well, and within hugging distance. Others were left alone, all family members unaccounted for.

We settled into this new house. The owner, Sam Glover, had known Boye in high school and college. He was very matter-of-fact, very practical. Intellectual sophistication oozed from his speech. I hung on his every word until I found a quiet corner to lay my head that night and faded off to sleep.

That night was one of the noisiest nights of the conflict. ECOMOG forces launched an artillery barrage on rebel lines. Cannons blazed, and rockets flew high into the night, sometimes lighting the sky for more than ten seconds. The peace-keepers also launched flares as if they were conducting a major offensive. Clutching my bag of clothes, the only things that I owned on earth, I hoped that every hand-fed mortar, rocket, and artillery shell would find its intended military target.

The night seemed endless. Boye and his friend Sam sat and traded war stories while keeping a keen ear on the situation outside. At times it was difficult to tell who was launching the artillery: were Taylor's forces laying the groundwork for a counteroffensive? If so, we were in mortal danger—their soldiers were not well trained, meaning the threat of misguided bombs loomed larger.

For my peace of mind, I led myself to believe that the opposite was true: ECOMOG was launching these rockets in order to soften rebel positions in the surrounding areas in preparation for a more thorough ground offensive that would push Taylor's forces out of the suburbs of Monrovia. I fought off sleep just in case we were hit by misguided munitions.

I found out later that our move from the compound that day was preceded by a dream or premonition Aunty Ethel had. She had a bad feeling about staying close to rebel lines and thought it wise for our group to relocate closer to the main road, leaving others in the house. That decision was the work of God. While I rested my head on my bag and listened to artillery that night, back at the compound, Taylor's men had barged in, woken everyone up, tied up a few people, and accused them of siding with the Johnson. They had been watching all along as the hired soldier came into the compound, day in and day out. We had escaped just in time. Had we not left that day, I am convinced that we would have been the victims of a massacre.

I believe God intervened on our behalf. Even though my knowledge of God was faint and I didn't think much about him at the time, he was looking out for me. He was keeping us safe.

The night dragged on, the sheer madness of it still beyond what I knew. I began to fade to sleep. Thoughts of freedom competed with dreams of my family as I slowly gave in to my exhaustion. I would have traded freedom for time with my family. The deeper my fear got, the more readily it triggered prayer: "Lord, please let me survive this time. Please save me. Please protect my family."

My head ached to know whether my brothers and sister were safe. I pulled my knees closer to my body, escaping to my world of ideas, where the war was distant: a place where my dreams still had a chance of coming true, where I had hope, peace, and most importantly, my family. It had been five months since I last saw them. I tried not to wonder what their lives were like now—if they were even alive.

CHAPTER 11

The Decision to Get Out

When I looked outside I could see dead bodies lying in the streets. Most of them were probably civilians whom the rebels had accused, tried, convicted, and executed within minutes. It was early November 1990.

We prepared to head to downtown Monrovia to get closer to the peacekeepers and look for family members who might have survived. I gathered my few belongings, and we began walking with the rest of the group heading toward the city. I was not sure exactly where we were going, but for my safety's sake I shut my mouth and fell into formation like a good soldier would. The trip to Monrovia was about six miles.

Shell casings lined the streets as we walked toward the city. The stench of dead bodies filled the air. Flies hovered in clouds over the dead. Some of the bodies were barely clothed. Some were completely naked. No one seemed too concerned for the dead—people almost didn't notice the corpses. For the first time I realized that these bodies we live in are so temporary: we take the time to dress, clean, and sometimes idolize and adorn them with fancy clothes and jewels, but our breath can be snatched away in an instant. I am sure these people whose bodies I walked past thought highly enough of themselves to wear nice clothes and probably ate well in order to prolong their lives. But now their bodies were feasted on by flies. Birds and dogs picked apart their swollen skin.

I glanced at the bodies, hoping I wouldn't recognize any of them but unable to fully suppress my curiosity. These people were gone. Some had been there a week or two, some for just a few hours. Tongues hung out of their mouths, arms and legs had stiffened with rigor mortis under the stifling African sun. Their blood had long since dried up. All the dead had the same look of horror permanently stuck on their faces, pride and dignity gone and families nowhere to be found. They wouldn't get a proper burial—their bodies simply left to the elements. I remember them as a sign of futures dashed, hopes faded, dreams unfulfilled, accomplishments forgotten. These were the casualties of the war, victims in a conflict that did not make sense to me. Was God there when these people cried out?

I found myself more and more drawn to the dead, peeking back after I had walked past, praying that it would not be a family member. I looked at their faces, into their lifeless eyes, taking careful notice of hands, fingernails, hair, the color of their shoes. There were so many. Maybe I knew them. Maybe I would run into a family member asking about them. Would I be the bearer of bad news?

Those faces haunted me for years—even now. How could I forget them? Even in remembering them I feel a sense of guilt for beholding and remembering their humiliation, their bodies eaten by dogs. Yet somehow I also feel I can honor them by bearing witness to their suffering, by recounting the end of their stories: the face with sharp cheekbones, the head with short hair, the body with the white unbuttoned shirt.

Inevitably I began to think about my fate and the future of the people around me. The dogs would not find much meat on my bones. Maybe I would be a meal for birds and flies. Would anyone care enough to look into my face and tell my family? Would anyone care enough to give me a decent final resting place? Most people were concerned about their own survival, shuffling past and squeezing their noses to avoid the horrible smell. I felt sorry for the dead, though I did not know them. I couldn't stop a few tears as I balanced my belongings on my head.

✳ ✳ ✳

A pickup truck with a few ECOMOG soldiers offered us a ride as we arrived at the Red Light Junction, an open market in Paynesville, Monrovia. It's aptly named. The intersection had the only traffic light for miles. Red Light Junction used to be a booming marketplace; now the war made it almost unrecognizable. Rusted sheets of zinc, once used as a roof for makeshift market kiosks, were strewn through the unpaved area. A few potholes filled with muddy water left over from the rain scarred the ground of this deserted area. Johnson's men lined the side of the road, just milling about, smoking cigarettes and chatting among themselves, standing among dead bodies.

The pickup truck sped off toward Barnersville, slowing down intermittently to weave its way through sandbag checkpoints manned by ECOMOG soldiers. We used to take this route home from school when Mr. Matthews had to see his family. We also had driven this way home when we had to pick up soft drinks from the Coca-Cola bottling plant for the family store. We stopped by the bottling plant about twice a month. A smile slipped onto my tired face as I thought about fighting with Gahien in the back of the car to open a bottle of Coke. As we got older, we disobeyed our father a little by drinking a bottle of Fanta or Coke before we brought it home to the shop. Usually we just hid the empty bottle back in the crate. We knew Pa would be disappointed when he found out, but it seemed we always got away with drinking a bottle or two in the car.

As we drove by in the soldier's truck, that all seemed like years ago, another time. Up until that moment I had not thought of Mr. Matthews and his family. He was from the Gio tribe, who accounted for most of Taylor's loyal soldiers, the men doing most of the killing behind enemy lines. I hoped Mr. Matthews was still alive.

We had developed a special bond over the years. He drove us home every day after school. He always parked along Gurley Street on the same side as our school. When I would burst out of the gates shortly after the school bell rang, I looked for his friendly face and jumped into the car. Mr. Matthews was patient when I carried on talking with my friends. He was a quiet man. He simply brought us home from school, ate his meal, and returned to the Executive Mansion to give the car back to my father.

Now, I couldn't help thinking over every detail about him. He had dark skin and salt-and-pepper hair. He wore his uniform with pride: a sky blue top adorned with military regalia and navy blue pants. His shoes were always well polished. He carried a .38 caliber pistol. His shirt was always tucked into his pants and his sidearm neatly fastened along his hip—hardly the dress of a chauffeur. I was also struck by how little I knew about his life. I didn't know what his duty was, aside from picking us up every day. We never saw him on weekends. I knew he had children, but I never saw them. I knew his wife worked here at the Red Light Junction. That was all.

The pickup continued down Somalia Drive, getting closer and closer to the intersection that led to my family's house. As we drove past the crossroad, I wanted to leap out and walk the rest of the way home. Fear forbade me: fear of seeing them all dead, seeing the house destroyed, or worse, not seeing anyone at all. The Barnersville Junction was as close as I would come to seeing my family.

The truck snaked its way through checkpoint after checkpoint, winding westward. Now I began to see familiar buildings that had been destroyed. Everything looked abandoned. There were very few people moving around. We crossed the bridge right before Jamaica Road. We were getting close to the Monrovia harbor, known as Freeport. Everywhere in the city the stale air reeked of human flesh and raw sewage. It was difficult to see Monrovia, a city that once brimmed with pride and bustled with trade, left in ruins—streets covered in shell casings, roads badly damaged by artillery shells, bloodstained sidewalks, buildings torn apart by bullets.

✳ ✳ ✳

We reached Freeport and climbed out of the truck into a crowd. Around me I saw what seemed like hundreds of people who looked worse than I did, including children with bellies so swollen they seemed to have trouble breathing. They were barely dressed and had hunger in their eyes. I felt a bit better about my appearance, felt a little less self-pity. Both adults and children seemed to be moving in slow motion. I saw many people with yellow eyes: jaundice and chronic malaria were exacerbated by the standing water and no medical treatment. There was no running water, no food, and sewage backed up in the street. Most of the doctors were dead, in hiding, or had left the country.

We sat outside the port resting. I waited for instructions from the adults and began picking up shell casings. There were more than I could hold: big ones, small ones, oddly shaped ones. Bullet holes riddled the outside fence, the border between the ECOMOG headquarters inside the port and the hungry and desperate people outside.

A few Ghanaian and Nigerian soldiers, recognizable by the flags of their countries sewn onto the shoulder of their neatly pressed military fatigues, walked past me on patrol. They carried British-made rifles that I hadn't seen before. A couple of soldiers carried American-made M16 rifles. All the soldiers had strange accents. My friends and I used to make fun of the accents of other West Africans at lunch time. Now these men, who spoke their British accented English with a slight West African variation, were patrolling our soil.

I instinctively felt safer, but I didn't quite know why. They had come to Liberia to save us from ourselves, and I suppose I was grateful. The looks on their faces revealed their thoughts: pity, prejudice, and disdain. Perhaps they thought I was a child soldier, one that they had faced in combat.

I tried to meet their gaze with confidence, but the feeling in my stomach, the current state of my capital city, and the appearance of my fellow Liberians telling a different story shook my foundations. The destruction was too much to hide. In that moment, I was ashamed to be Liberian.

Mentally, I surveyed my life, my appearance. My oversized head dominated my pencil-thin neck, which seemed barely connected to my shoulders. My hair had not been combed or cut in five months. Dirt stuck to my hair and skin, and I assumed I smelled terrible. My ribs stuck out so far I could count them easily, though my constantly growling stomach was still not swollen and held my organs in—a blessing because a bulging stomach is among the signs of malnourishment. My shoelaces dug into my hipbones, holding up my pants. My knees seemed a whole lot bigger than they were before. The black high-top sneakers I had been so proud to own the previous year were in ruins, the tongues flopping everywhere as I struggled to walk. My finger- and toenails were pale white, and I imagined my eyes were also yellow.

All of this was obvious, but the psychological weight on my shoulders was invisible to those soldiers. My visible collarbone could barely carry the bag that I lugged around, but my shoulders carried so much more than just the weight of my earthly possessions: hardships, loss, hunger, nightmares, extreme fear, disorientation, unbelief in myself, my people, and

God, a loss of innocence, ruined dreams, uncertainty about my family, hidden tears. My pain might have been invisible to those soldiers, but I could not hide the scars of war. I hid in the shade recounting my priorities to myself: cling to life, hang on to my belongings, and never, never lose sight of the family I had left.

Eventually everyone in my party gathered their belongings and headed to Mamba Point, the southwestern part of downtown Monrovia and the place where I had lived with the witch doctor. It rose into a hill overlooking the entire city on the east and the Atlantic Ocean on the west. The American embassy was located there. I had always thought about travelling on the high seas, and going back to Mamba Point made me wonder whether one day I would see the United States or Brazil. Mostly, I wanted to just sit by the ocean and dream—dream of a belly filled with food and peace in my homeland.

We walked through Clara Town toward the two main bridges that led into downtown Monrovia. The area was deserted. Shops that used to carry the latest fashions and goods had long been shut down. Most had been looted. The metal doors that once stood between thieves and their targets hung open. There were a few people walking along as we made our way down Bush Rod Island toward the city center. As we got closer to the bridges, we veered right in an effort to cross the river along the older of the two bridges. My body tensed up. The bridge was old and there had been heavy fighting in the area. Was the bridge still safe? I fought the crowd to get closer to my brother. If I was going to die crossing the bridge at least I would die close to my hero.

We reached the bridge over the Montserrado River. It led into what used to be the busiest, most popular open-air market in Monrovia: Waterside Market. The river was brown and dead bodies floated by in the water. Before the war, the river changed color when rain washed the dust and mud from the Slipway neighborhood just a few hundred yards away, but it hadn't rained that day. This was not mud.

Chills ran down my spine as we began to cross over. It seemed the bridge swayed back and forth slightly in the late afternoon breeze. My short, tired legs wobbled as we crossed. Trying not to look down, I stayed close to Boye. The bridge was long—at least it felt that way. The sidewalk section of the bridge was not enclosed. There were big holes at key points along the bridge. I could see clearly down to the water. To keep from looking down, I looked toward the tall buildings of the once proud capital of Liberia. Now deserted, all the buildings appeared to have suffered damage during the fighting. When my gaze fell to the river, I saw the trash that had always flowed down the Montserrado now clinging to the shoreline. The blood-tainted water flowed toward the Atlantic Ocean. As the sun began to fade over the Atlantic horizon, so did my strength.

Walking up to the Mamba Point neighborhood was difficult. We walked through the Waterside Market area, avoiding the trash that lay everywhere. Dirty standing water made parts of the area impassable.

Waterside was a busy center of commerce before the war. We'd seen it from time to time on television, when it had seemed to be an irreplaceable image of the third world. Then, hordes of people would crowd onto streets that were too small, carrying over-sized loads on the top of their heads. Yellow taxis squeezed their way through the foot and vehicle traffic. The streets had no distinct lanes for traffic and no discernible patterns, and it always seemed like complete chaos. The partially paved roads gave way to pools of mud and puddles that bred mosquitoes. Those scenes used to be an everyday affair at Waterside Market.

Not today though. Today there was very little car traffic. Soldiers—I couldn't tell whose—were patrolling the neighborhood, and a few people were milling about, but there were no crowds. The stores that lined the streets had long been closed, then looted, then abandoned.

As we began the trek up the steep hill, my imagination got the best of me. A fond childhood memory played in my mind's eye. I was about five years old. My mother and I were walking hand in hand down Waterside. We were looking for a pair of shoes for me. Back to school shopping was not usually a big deal, but for me, getting a pair of shoes really mattered. I had anticipated that day for weeks. My mother and I walked along from store to store to find a pair of shoes that would last the entire school year—that would endure through a year of constant walking and hundreds of soccer matches. Ma and I held hands and talked about what school would be like this year. It had rained prior to our shopping trip, so the sidewalks and streets were muddy and slippery. Makeshift kiosks were everywhere, and shoppers and merchants mixed together. We went into five or six places. Ma couldn't find a pair she liked. Finally we saw a man with several shoe boxes in his hands. Ma got his attention. He had something that fit me and seemed quite durable—brown leather with a very thick rubber sole. I put on the left shoe and walked a bit. Ma liked it and so did I. She paid for them and we were on our way back to the car.

At home, I showed the shoes to my brother Mocco. He opened the box and scowled. Mocco seemed to always have something smart or cynical to say—I love and despise him for that—but this time he was not being a cynic. To Ma's horror and embarrassment, we had bought two left shoes from the street vendor. There was virtually no way we would find that guy again. She laughed and Mocco joined in. I didn't see the humor in me having to wear two left shoes to school. *Oh great*, I thought. Ma told me she was sorry, but we didn't have enough money to get another pair. She still had four other boys to worry about. I could wear Gahien's old shoes or my two new left shoes. In the end I chose Gahien's, even though he'd spent the previous year playing football in them. I had told everyone I was getting new shoes, so when each of my brothers got home, they would ask, "Jungle Boy, where are the new shoes?" and I would show them. Molley asked, as did Boye, and finally when Pa came home he asked too. It was more of an embarrassment for Ma than for me. After a few days, I put the shoes away into the compartment over the closet in the room that Gahien and I shared.

My mind tumbled back into the present. Our long walk continued. Our final destination remained a mystery to me. That was nothing new. Deep in daydreams, I rarely paid close attention to the adults' itinerary—besides, plans were always changing.

The streets of Waterside were strewn with lotto booths. Each little kiosk was about seven feet tall and three or four feet wide and was painted with the flag of Liberia. They were usually manned by two people in that cramped space. When business was booming, there were frequently lines in front of the lotto booths, people trying to strike it rich, wide-eyed optimists putting their hope in little tickets. Now as I walked past, I saw that, like our economy and government, they had toppled over. A few had been partially burned. Bullet holes pocked the wooden walls. The zinc roofs had ripped off and long since disappeared. Another symbol of national pride and collective optimism destroyed.

My legs had reached exhaustion when we arrived at a house and met a few relatives of Aunty Ethel's. We would be staying with them that night. Curfew was getting closer. Now that we stopped and the mystery of my future resurfaced in my mind, I listened to the plan: we were going to get back to the port in time to board the refugee ship. We were heading away from Liberia. I was shocked. Was it really possible to leave the war and the constant threat of death behind?

I thought of my brothers. I didn't even know where they were. Should I leave the country without them?

But I knew I couldn't be completely safe in Liberia. Too many people wanted me dead. Johnson's men would be glad to end my life. Taylor's forces would as well. These two factions controlled nearly the entire nation. Leaving Liberia was the right thing to do, I resolved. I would not let my shame at deserting my family consume me. I knew I had to leave if I could. I would move ahead, cling to hope that they were alive. Maybe I would run into them on the ship. Maybe they would be there!

✳ ✳ ✳

Our entire group was up with the rising sun the next day. I quickly prepared my things, changed my clothes, and began the walk with everyone else in our party. Thick, dark smoke billowed in the distance. There seemed to be a constant dark cloud over the city. It felt like an overcast day even though the sun was shining. The smoke seemed to be pouring up from the ground. *Even the earth has had enough of the conflict,* I thought.

We made our way across the bridge, through Clara Town, and to the port. The chances of getting onto the ship were slim. We were not the only people who had dreams of leaving the country.

We stayed in a huge warehouse inside the port that day. There were rumors about when the ship would depart and what the destination would be—likely Ghana, but who knew, and what city? Most people weren't concerned about where the final destination would be, and neither was I. We were all thinking the same thing: anywhere but here.

Finding food at the port was tough. No one wanted to leave the area for fear of missing the departure of the ship. To distract myself from hunger, I walked around the port admiring the uniforms of the foreign soldiers who roamed the area. They must have felt like heroes: the coalition that had come to save Liberia. They looked healthy, strong. I had not seen healthy men in a long time. They looked almost superhuman.

I had always romanticized the life of soldiers. There was always something manly and admirable about them. As a boy I often fantasized about being a soldier. We fought neighborhood wars all the time, but among our various games, the Christmas Day war was an especially beloved annual tradition.

Every Christmas morning, without fail, my parents gave me a new toy gun. In 1987 it was a toy submachine gun similar to ones that the German army used in World War II. Later that afternoon my friends and I, all of whom had received a toy gun for Christmas, fought against the children from the opposing neighborhood. In fact, kids from all over would come to take part. There were a few children whose parents could not afford to buy them anything for Christmas, so they cut down branches from nearby trees and shaped them into weapons. Four-inch nails hammered into short pieces of two-by-four also made great automatic rifles and side arms.

We fired on each other from far away and close by. Those with homemade weapons used their voices to simulate the powerful sounds that a real gun would make.

Pow! Pow! Pow!

Brrrrr! Brrrr!

Chew! Chew! Chew!!!

We screamed while pointing rifles at each other.

Boys ran through the neighborhood with gusto, chasing each other and shooting, hiding high in trees, staying low in tall grass, resting behind buildings, and running through our neighbors' properties and gardens. When a participant was "killed" and he could be made to agree, he sat out the rest of the war. Being dead was always a subject of contentious debate. No one wanted to stop fighting. Older brothers became judges to decide whether someone was shot fatally or not. Sometimes the battle lasted for hours.

The war—the real, nation-shaking war—shattered those childish fantasies. All the boys from my neighborhood had surely learned the reality that not all heroes survive every battle. Even more shocking, most of the soldiers I encountered were not heroes at all. They were cowards. They killed unarmed civilians.

Most were not even old enough to understand the atrocities they committed. Guns in the hands of untrained youth produce chaos and tyranny. Now I knew the truth: war is ugly. Human beings become desperate to survive. People are dying, and there is no solution in sight. Heroes cannot simply come to save the day and make everything all right.

The only heroics I saw were the feats done by men who risked their lives to find food for their families. Uncle Nat, my brother, and my uncle MacDonald Davis were heroes. They didn't need a weapon to earn my genuine respect. They didn't need to intimidate to gain influence. They shielded me from the realities of war as best they could. They managed to keep their sanity when our whole world lost its way.

CHAPTER 12

The Refugee Boat

November 5, 1990, was the slowest day of the war.

That morning our entire group—my brother and his wife, my aunts and uncles and cousins—had walked from Mechlin Street across the bridge to the port. Once inside the harbor, we seemed to be waiting for an event that would never come. We were holed up in a warehouse previously used for storage. Now, in place of the goods, there were hundreds of people crammed into the building, and there was filth everywhere. The sight and smell of human feces surrounded us. We awaited orders from the peacekeepers as to when the ship was leaving.

We were waiting to desert our country, a country that had long since deserted us, it seemed.

The cargo ship we were waiting for had brought equipment for ECOMOG forces, and it was now transporting refugees out of Liberia. There were no criteria for who was eligible to leave and who was not. Apart from those who looked physically ill or wounded and who could come up with a monetary bribe, there seemed to be no rhyme or reason to who was eligible to leave, as far as I could put together. This was not going to be a legal process, filled with paperwork, visas, and travel documents.

Fearing a free-for-all, I stuck close to the adults in our group. I imagined a scene of people pushing each other into the harbor waters trying to make their way onto the ship. It was our last hope to escape the desperate, starved, death-dealing city.

Some people in the warehouse were wounded and needed medical care. There were pregnant women and nursing infants. I was eleven years old, and I was starving. I could only imagine what a nursing child was going through. Only the grace of God kept us all alive.

Rumors ran rampant. We kept hearing that the ship was not going to leave until the next day. As time wore on, it became apparent that we would be sleeping in the port that night. This was a terrifying proposition. I shuddered at the thought of sleeping in an open area with hundreds of other hungry, sick, and tired people. People were coughing, sneezing, and even defecating close by. I could feel their desperation in the air.

The soldiers brought some rice, and the masses fought over the food. I held back from the clamor, afraid to get in the way should desperation turn to panic and violence. The food was not enough for everyone. It ran out quickly. The sun was beginning to set, and it appeared that I was going to be going to bed hungry once again. It was my first day without food since August. As I prepared myself to sleep that evening, I thought about what life would be in another country. Since I was uncertain where the ship was going to end up, I could not plan accordingly.

More food finally arrived later that evening. Again, rice, but this time, it was rotten. The rice had a reddish color to it, as if it had been cooked with tomatoes and nothing else. The stench hit my nose before the taste battered my mouth, but I could not refuse it. I ate, placing spoonful after slimy spoonful in my mouth. It was yet another symbol of what life had become for us.

It was beginning to get dark as we sat in this huge hangar in Freeport. Years earlier, what now seemed a generation ago, I trapped birds using rice. The traps I set for the birds were simple—just a bucket, a stick, and some twine. Now I was caught, but this trap was much more complicated than anything I could have dreamed of as a boy. I had trapped the birds just to look at them. It was the work of a moment to set them free again. I was trapped in war, wrapped in the reality of death by starvation or dysentery. I longed to be a ricebird, feeling my way anxiously in the darkness, awaiting my freedom. I was caught under the dark canopy of war, my lungs filled with the stench of feces, and my hope of freedom anchored in the harbor so close by yet so far.

Everyone ate slowly, in contrast to how we usually ate during the war. I gathered that everyone else was thinking what I was, but no one dared say anything: we were all caught between disgust at the horrendous food and gratitude at having something to eat. I came to the dismal conclusion that eating something that might kill me was better than starving to death. I ate a few more spoonfuls and I felt sated. The horrible taste and the smell lingered long after the meal was finished. The ugly aftertaste of the rotten rice hung on my taste buds as if for its life.

As the day wound down, the soldiers ordered people to start lining up, beginning with the sick and wounded. Everyone looked sick. They also gave preferential treatment of foreign nationals—Ghanaians and Nigerians who had survived the carnage of Taylor's manhunt. It seems we—the simply starved, not sick, Liberian-born males—had no business getting on the ship. We would have to beg or maybe even bribe the peacekeepers to reach safety.

At the front of the line, the soldiers selected who would get to go on the ship, packed them by loads in shipping containers, and hoisted each container onto the deck of the ship with a huge crane. They did their best to avoid pushing and shoving. Container after container was lifted up.

Ma got a place and was lifted aboard. Sister Lady got one as well. One by one, family member after family member quietly recited a goodbye tinged with hollow sadness. I was standing next to my brother and my Uncle Mac as darkness fell. The rest of our group was now on the ship. We'd already been through the line once and been rejected. I began to get the feeling I would be staying in Liberia, the feeling that I was not going to be selected for freedom. I felt sick to my stomach. Maybe it was the rice. I started to cry.

Uncle Mac was upset with the soldiers' inconsistent and unfair approach to the selection process. In a moment of frustration and impatience he walked off. Boye and I stood patiently and waited our turn, going through the line again. We were frustrated and scared, but we didn't know what else to do. I stayed within arm's length of Boye; he was the only family member whom I knew was alive.

"That is the last container," the soldiers announced. We watched as the crane hoisted the giant metal box onto the deck of the ship.

My heart sank deep into my stomach. My knees got that familiar weak feeling. My eyes began begging me to roll back into my head and mucus flowed from my nose. I felt an immense magnification of the eerie feeling that I was at school, and everyone in class had finished a test. The teacher was collecting them, and I knew I had failed.

My brother patted my bushy hair and held my hand. He guided me over to the soldiers and told them that his wife was onboard the ship and whispered to the soldier that she was pregnant (something I did not learn until later). The soldiers had sympathy on him and were going to let him aboard, but I overheard them saying something about not letting me get on the ship. They would let Boye on— but not me?

The soldier who was in charge said, "He could be one of those small soldiers."

I stood paralyzed, tears streaming down my face.

What would I do now?

The peacekeepers beckoned for a few other men to enter. They shuffled past me and into the container.

My brother whispered something to a peacekeeper with a clipboard, gesturing in my direction. The soldier paused, considering his response. I barely felt the time pass.

I felt already alone, already dead.

Breaking the spell, the soldier lifted his arm and motioned for me to get into the container. My blood pumped again, alive. My tears of sorrow turned to tears of joy.

Wiping my eyes, I jumped onto the container with my bag of belongings in tow, afraid that if I dawdled, the soldier would rescind his offer. As the container was lifted, I forgot to breathe. I felt light-headed, so I leaned onto one of the men in the container. It was smelly, but if that smell was the price I would pay for freedom, I was happy to smell it.

As the crane lifted us and the container swayed in the breeze, I glimpsed my homeland one last time. I said goodbye to Liberian soil. The crane seemed to be taking more time to arrive on the deck of the ship than it had for the previous loads. It was as if the operator knew this was the final lift, the last people allowed on the ship.

Relief swept over me. I looked over at my brother, and he smiled right back at me. He was my biggest advocate, the one who always believed in me more than I believed in myself. My mother entrusted him with my well-being in her final days on earth. His decision to talk with the soldiers that night saved me again.

What would his decision have been if the soldiers had refused to let me onto the ship? Would he have chosen his defenseless, almost-dead little brother or his pregnant wife? I knew he would pick her over me, and I could not have faulted him, but by grace it didn't come to that.

It didn't come to me alone on the streets of Monrovia, waiting for death by starvation or bullets.

With a loud bang the container landed on the deck of the ship, breaking my introspection. It was close to 10 p.m. I stepped off the container and onto the deck amid hundreds of other Liberians glad to be leaving our home. I was relieved, excited, and tired.

It was amazing how quickly we found the rest of our group, though the excitement of finally being free was quickly curtailed when I remembered we were missing a key member: Uncle Mac had walked away from freedom.

✶ ✶ ✶

Families and friends laid down their blankets and sheets and formed makeshift beds, establishing territory to retrieve a bit of pride. Being the last people to board the ship had an unexpected privilege: we got to keep the container for shelter to protect us from the elements.

In minutes I was up to my old ways. I jumped around the container until I decided to explore the ship. Sometimes I forgot where I was during the war and reverted to being a boy again.

"Nathifa, you want come with me?" I inquired. She refused. She was not in the mood to get yelled at.

I was. I had been on a ship only once before, and I was excited to see what it was all about. Jungle Boy was out of the jungle, but it didn't mean my desire to explore had been quenched. I climbed down from the upper deck of the ship and landed along the railing a little ways from the bow.

Leaning over the rail I could see the water about forty feet below. The water in the harbor was calm. I headed toward the back of the ship, walking along the railing on the lower deck. I could see the peacekeeping soldiers in the harbor. I was just the right height to look over the edge of the ship without being seen from land.

The soldiers were beginning their night maneuvers, switching shifts. More and more soldiers were milling about. I could tell from the flags on the shoulders of their uniforms that they were Gambians. From the height of the deck I could see downtown Monrovia, almost completely dark. The usual gunfire echoed in the distance, and occasionally a flare lit up the sky.

Suddenly a realization broke through my exploration: not only had we left Uncle Mac, but I was leaving my father, brothers, and sister. Everything I had lost up to this point, possessions, home, country, paled in comparison to this cavernous loss.

I was heading to a strange country. Perhaps I would never see my homeland again. Standing there looking over the city, my young mind was overcome with emotions: joy and sadness filled equal portions of my being.

Just then it began to rain, and it poured! Some civilians hurried past me as I stood there looking over the harbor. The raindrops got heavier, pelting the rust that had gathered along the floor of the lower deck of the ship.

My old excitement at rain resurfaced—refreshment was here, cleansing, but that clashed with my confused emotions. I felt hope and despair at once. Finally the rain stirred me to action. I ran back to the main deck and my family in the shipping container and watched as other refugees sat getting drenched by the rain. Many were nearly motionless, as if they didn't feel the rain. Were they just happy to be free, or were they too weak to move? It occurred to me that these people were lost in their thoughts as I was.

"Maybe it is washing us clean," Uncle Nat said.

Back with Boye and the others, I stepped out from the protective covering of the container to enjoy the rain. I hadn't bathed in days.

After about fifteen minutes, the skies cleared up, the moon came out, and wispy white clouds rolled overhead, standing out against the dark blue sky. The breeze felt cold against my skin, and I trembled a bit from my wet clothes. Looking at the sky, I could not help but think of my new freedom.

That night the ship stayed in the harbor. I settled into my spot in the container for the night and slept, forgetting where I was, lost in a dream.

The loud ship horn startled me awake. My mind grappled with the unfamiliarity of my surroundings. My sleepy eyes saw the ten to fifteen other people who'd slept in the container that night. Most of them had also been surprised by the horn and were slowly rising.

Sister Lady gave me a pea-sized amount of toothpaste with a tiny cup of water to brush my teeth. I hurried down to the lower deck, brushed my teeth over the railing, and spat into the harbor. I counted—one, two, three, four—the seconds until my spit hit the water. Boyish, I smiled every time I saw my spit splash and make ripples. I performed a very cursory wash of my face, and then I headed back up to the main deck to return the cup.

The ship's anchor pulled up, and the ropes that moored the ship in the harbor were untied and released. The tiny boat that led the ship out of the harbor revved its engine and began to pull us out to sea.

I was conflicted: reluctant to leave family, home; but ready, more than ready, to put the war behind me. Slowly, the ship exited the harbor, and the only home I had ever known faded behind us. I watched until Liberian soil was no longer visible on the horizon.

CHAPTER 13

Freedom's Sky

I could smell freedom. It smelled like fresh sea water.

The ship rocked back and forth gently, gliding forward with a barely perceptible thrust. I was standing near the railing close to the bow of the ship, which I called the USS Freedom, looking into the blue Atlantic Ocean. The water was so clear that I could see huge fish swimming in the wake of the ship. There was nothing around us but open sea in every direction, as far as my eyes could see. It was a two-day journey to Ghana.

I was free. Free from the tyranny of Liberian rebels. Free from the constant threat of death. Yet uncertainty lay ahead for me: a new life. Would my future include the squalor of life in a refugee camp? Would I ever be reunited with the rest of my family? With every splashing wave, I inched closer to freedom, though that freedom was a mystery. I had never left Liberia, so I was terribly excited to be heading to a different country.

After I had been standing along the railing for hours, the crew served lunch. I climbed onto the main deck, lifting myself by my weak arms, to where food was being served. The queue was long, full of men, women, and children holding cups and big bowls. I ran to the shipping container where we slept and grabbed a cup. Nathifa and I stood in line for the food. The line moved fairly quickly. Once we got close, I could see that the soldiers were serving *gari*, the ground root of the yucca plant, a cheap food and a West African favorite. Gari was not even considered a meal in Liberia. It was merely a snack. The soldiers prepared it in the most basic way: with water and sugar. The man handing out the food had a huge ladle and an equally big bucket. He dipped the ladle in the bucket for some gari and dumped it into the outstretched bowl or cup.

"Next person," he yelled with his thick Ghanaian accent. All of the people in line avoided eye contact with each other, humbled by the fact that they were standing in line desperate for such cheap food.

One after the other, proud Liberians walked by me with their chins close to their chests, humbly carrying their share of gari back to their families. Everyone was hungry. As my turn approached, I got excited despite the meager fare. The solider poured half a cup for me.

"Thank you," I murmured, and walked away. Without hesitation I put the cup to my mouth. To my surprise there was barely any sugar in the gari, leaving it bland. Disappointed, I slurped the food down anyway and headed back to the container.

Across the main deck, along the side of the ship, I saw one of the most heartwrenching sights of the war. A middle-aged Liberian man, who looked sicker than most, crouched in a quiet corner alongside the railing holding rice. Rice! I am not sure where he got it from, but he had spilled a portion of it onto the rusted deck of the ship. As I squeezed by him, he barely looked up, intent in his hunger. He ate directly from the deck. There were particles of rust all over each grain and he did nothing to brush them away. He picked up the grains of rice one at a time and ate them, risking his life and health to satisfy his hunger. *Is this what once-proud Liberians have become?*

* * *

I dropped off the cup with Sister Lady and hurried back to the side of the ship to watch the clear, blue, endless ocean. I loved watching the fish jump up and out of the water along-side the ship. Very few people were moving about on the deck. Many were content to enjoy the freedom from conflict, the sense of escape. Others were seasick and weak from lack of proper nutrition.

Leaning against the railing, I slumped to the deck and pulled my knees close to my body. I looked up at the cloudless sky. I thought about screaming my name out loud. *Marcus Doe is my name!* I repeated it in my head. No one would kill me because of my name now.

I wished my brothers were on the ship with me. More than that, I missed the person I very well knew would not be anywhere, my ma. I was leaving her there, buried in Paynes-ville. As so often happens when thoughts of her fill my mind, tears filled my eyes, and in no time they were bubbling down my cheeks. What if I was an orphan now? What if the only family member I had was my brother? Had I become one of those kids I used to read about from other wars? I realized that in most ways I already was one of those kids: malnour-ished, dirty, a refugee. Other children around the world were probably reading about me now.

Terrifying thoughts of what could have occurred at my former home in Barnersville, what could've happened to my family when rebels stormed it, were hard to ignore. I was al-most paralyzed with questions as to the whereabouts of Mocco, Gahien, Caroline, Molley, and Pa. I did not want to accept the fact that they could all be dead. Deep down inside me, I imag-ined the day that I would hug them and hold them close again, though clinging onto that hope seemed futile. Maybe that hope would ease the pain when I found out the inevitable. I was wait-ing on a moment that might never come. Why hadn't I said something more significant when I left Barnersville six months earlier? I regret not hugging them. I'd just walked calmly to the car that day, and Mocco had driven me across town to Boye's. I had gone without so much as a whimper. During the ride, Mocco and I had talked about Argentina's chances in the 1990 World Cup, hardly the stuff of last goodbyes.

Dusk fell on the ocean before I knew it, and I had to get back to the main deck for the night. Rather than sleeping in the container, I wanted to quietly fade to sleep looking up at the stars on the deck. There was a gentle breeze.

* * *

The next morning as we approached land, I felt alive. It was as if my heart was beating fresh blood, and my lungs were breathing more deeply than they ever had. I had never seen a piece of land so welcoming. It wasn't so much how the land looked, but the fact that I knew there was no war there, that there was no smoke from explosions rising from the landscape.

We had another meal of gari just as the ship docked in Tema, a port city east of Accra, the capital of Ghana. We made our way off the ship and were immediately vaccinated. For the time being, we had to stay in the port area, waiting until we could be properly processed. I remember that the port did not have proper bathroom facilities for the refugees so we had to make do with what we had. There were outdoor latrines and other places to relieve oneself, but they offered very little privacy or dignity.

The Ghanaians whom we'd hidden in the ceiling wanted to pay us back for saving them. Since they were Ghanaian citizens, they were allowed to leave the port. They promised that they would return and take us for a meal.

The time in Tema seemed to move slowly. I was anxious to leave the port. Thoughts of the land I had abandoned faded with my desire to explore a new place, though being on foreign soil was still strange. In truth, I felt Liberia had abandoned me—taken my childhood and my innocence, and thrown me out. The land was contaminated with the blood of hundreds of thousands of innocent people.

Ghana was my fresh start, I decided. For the first time in my life I wanted to go to school. Having been out for six months, which felt like a lifetime, I was desperate for something to read. I had not read a book in a long time, not since the Bible that Sister Lady gave me in Congo Town. Ghanaian culture, I imagined, would be very different. I anticipated new languages, friends, and teachers. I imagined fitting in right away, and I looked forward to a semi-normal life. I missed the social environment of a school. I missed learning. It was strange to realize that I had taken school for granted.

After several days, when we were finally able to leave the port, many Liberians opted to be transported to the refugee camp outside of Accra. For some reason our group did not follow. We chose a hotel close to the port and close to where our Ghanaian friends lived.

The first night out of the port, our Ghanaian friends prepared a feast for us, and it proved to be yet another embarrassing moment in my young life.

There was food everywhere—all the Ghanaian staples and favorites: fufu (an African dish made from yucca that's been pounded using a mortar and pestle), peanut stew, rice, and kenkey (made from ground corn and usually eaten with hot pepper and fried fish). I could not believe all the food they had prepared. I can only imagine the look on my face when I saw all that food.

It was all I had daydreamed about for the better part of a year while I was only eating one meal a day. I had not seen that much food in almost a year. When we started to eat, it was a pitiful scene. We ate heartily, desperately, along with the Ghanaians. I'd become accustomed to eating quickly, and I was done within a few minutes. I asked for a second round, and to no one's surprise, I was back for a third in no time at all.

My dream had come true. I had survived to eat my heart out, and I was determined not to let any of it go to waste. Eventually, everyone else seemed to be giving up. As the rest of my party sat digesting and reminiscing about the war and trying to process what had happened to us in the past few months, I continued to eat. After all, I had made a vow never to let good food go to waste in my presence. Soon enough, I had packed my stomach so tight I could barely walk and I had to go to the bathroom.

"Where is the bathroom?" I shouted.

"Around the corner," a man replied, his arm pointing toward the door. I shuffled out quickly. My stomach was filled to capacity. Suddenly, while I was on my way, I felt I could barely move or breathe. I struggled to walk. I started to slow down, my head ached, and I could not bring myself to inhale because it hurt. With every step I felt I was going to explode. I tried to hurry, grabbing the seat of my pants in a last ditch effort to keep from soiling myself. *A few more steps!* I told myself. I reached the door, relieved, quickly yanking on the handle.

There was already someone inside.

"Oh no," I screamed. It was Sister Lady. My heart dropped into the pit of my stomach. I felt warmth on the inside of both my legs. My body could no longer hold it back. All my pride was slipping down my pants.

Just then my cousin Nathifa and Evelyn came walking around the corner, and Sister Lady came out to find me mired in my own feces. My cousins were there to see her let loose on me for being such a greedy and undisciplined child. I had never been quite so ashamed in my life, even when I was pumping tire.

When Sister Lady was done, my cousins taunted me. "Marcus, you pupu on yourself?"

"Yeah, oh," I said, and burst out laughing to try to hide my embarrassment. They began to laugh too, and it was hard to tell whether they were laughing with me or at me.

That evening I walked back to the hotel holding my soiled clothes in my hand, wearing borrowed pants, having left my dignity at the doorway to the bathroom. I washed my clothes. I couldn't afford to throw them out. My stomach still ached from all the food I ate, but going to bed with a full stomach was the best feeling ever. Despite the embarrassment, I did not regret eating all that food. I just wished no one had been in the bathroom when I got to the door. As I lay down that night, embarrassed that I had soiled myself at eleven years old, I couldn't help but smile.

* * *

The next few days were like a whirlwind. We moved from one hotel to the next trying to find a home.

Sister Lady had worked in Liberia for the West African Examinations Council (WAEC), a non-profit organization that was responsible for providing culturally unbiased standardized tests to English-speaking West African students throughout their academic careers. Students usually faced tests in the sixth grade, ninth grade, and just before heading off to university. The organization was highly regarded in West African academic circles. Sister Lady was able to gain employment with the council again in Ghana.

Her association with the council provided us with housing at a guest house. Boye, Sister Lady, and I settled in Achimota, a suburb of Accra, Ghana. The other option was the refugee camp miles from the city, so we were extremely lucky.

From the day we arrived at the guest house, I felt immediately at home. Achimota was more upscale than the other neighborhoods I had seen. Almost all of the houses were surrounded by high, elaborately designed walls that were punctuated by massive iron gates. Most residents had people who looked after the lawns and gardens that surrounded the houses. Rumor was that the world super featherweight boxing champ at the time, Azumah "Zoom Zoom" Nelson, lived within walking distance of our house. There was a particularly huge house adjacent to ours, though we only saw the owner periodically. The neighborhood had many kids; some attended school, and some did not.

There were three other families living in the compound with us, all refugees from the war. The Flomos, another Liberian family, had a toddler we called "Bay Bay." Mr. Harrison and his son Yao were native Ghanaians who had immigrated to Liberia some years earlier.

Mr. Safo, an employee of the council, was the overseer of the property and lived there with his family. They greeted us with genuine hospitality. The Safos had three children: Justice was the oldest, and he was about six months older than me. Gloria was the only girl, and Confidence was their youngest. Their names were very peculiar to me, but I never bothered to ask the stories behind the names.

There were seven bedrooms, one huge kitchen, and five bathrooms in the guest house. I was used to crowded, shared-space living by now. I had not lived with fewer than ten people in the same house all of my life.

Justice loved football, both watching and playing. He and I became fast friends. The first few days were filled with questions from Justice about my experience in the war. He told me he could not wait to get home from school to talk with me.

We shared a tiny room full of bed frames and furniture that served as the storage room for the house. He and I shared a single bed. After sleeping on various floors for almost two years I was happy just to have a bed to lay my body on. We thought nothing of sharing the space or the twin mattress that sprouted broken springs.

Everyone cooked and ate with their respective families each evening. Justice ate his meals with his family. Sister Lady cooked for us, and Boye and Sister Lady ate together. I ate by myself; I was the only one who ate alone. I would some times sit outside on the steps happily eating my food as fast as I could.

Eating quickly gave me more time to explore. The archi-tecture of the compound was unlike anything I had seen in Liberia. The house was white with light blue trim. The front door had a metal gate and a regular wooden door. The walls around the compound were about seven feet high and there were two gates: one for cars and another for foot traffic, a light blue gate that locked from the inside. The entire left side of the compound had been paved with concrete. The right side, where the Safos lived, was not paved. There was a huge front porch where we sat or played table tennis.

Inside, the floors were made of granite-like stone, and the furniture was very comfortable. The common areas were all built in a straight line. There were two living rooms: one as you walked into the house and the second, a sunken lower level, about ten feet past the first. The table in the dining area was designed for buffet-style meals: it was huge and could seat about twelve people comfortably. Since we all ate as fami-lies, the table was rarely used. From there, the back door gave way to the half-paved backyard, surrounded by white walls. There was an outdoor faucet, so we were able to wash our feet and get quick drinks while we played outside. What lay beyond the fence fascinated and terrified me all at the same time—after all, I was still Jungle Boy!—a huge swamp that my imagination populated with all sorts of creatures.

The front of the house had a unique architectural touch: there were stairs that led up to the roof, where there was a patio with a few chairs. This was my favorite part of the house. Justice and I spent the evenings up there sometimes, talking and looking at the stars. Whenever I looked at the sky, I saw a world of possibilities. Gazing at the sky at night revived my imagination and helped me to dream and hope. Under the stars I could somehow try to be a child.

After leaving the war, the world came alive again. I was no longer waiting to die; instead, I could plan to live. The stars came to represent freedom for me.

On the roof, I got my first lessons on Ghanaian languages. Justice spoke Ewe, Twi, Ga, and English. We started with Twi, since it was what everyone in the area spoke. It came in handy when I had to go to the local market to purchase food. I learned the basics, and within a few months we moved on to the Ga language. Justice wanted to improve his English, and so we traded language lessons.

During breaks from the lessons I told him about the war and my family back in Liberia. When he noticed the tears in my eyes, he said he was optimistic that my family was indeed alive. He was intrigued by how I made it out of the country. I told him stories of Liberia over and over, and he never got tired of them. We also discussed our dreams, letting our imaginations run wild, sitting twelve feet above ground on the fold-out wooden chairs, with our feet up.

We both wanted to play football for our respective countries. He would play for Ghana, while I would be playing for Liberia. Justice had not seen me play football yet during those initial days—he was in for a surprise. We were quickly becoming like brothers—we even looked a bit like each other. I trusted him, and we went most places together.

In January 1991 my absence from school ended after seven months. I picked up where I left off in the sixth grade. African Child Elementary School in Achimota was quite different from J. L. Gibson Elementary School in Monrovia. It was housed in an abandoned, unfinished building two or three miles away from where we lived. There were no windows or doors, no cabinets, just desks for the students, a desk for our teacher, and a blackboard. When it rained the rain came in and water dripped down the walls or through holes in the weather beaten roof. Rain was a disruption rather than a reprieve, and when it was hot, we studied in the heat. The cement walls and the thin roof did little to keep us separated from the elements and the other classes.

The building had no bathrooms. The latrine was just a hole in the ground outside the school in a room six feet by six feet or so without a door, surrounded on three sides by standing sheets of zinc, which were usually used for roofing. The latrine was only good for urinating, otherwise one had to hold other bodily functions all day, or run home. It taught me great discipline in controlling my bowels—for me it was about a two to three mile run to get back to the guest house.

During the months of January and February the weather in sub-Saharan Africa shifts dramatically. The Harmattan winds sweep down from the Sahara Desert and bring very dry weather. The winds stirred up the red gravel in the school-yard and blew directly into our classroom, interrupting our lessons several times a day for several minutes at a time. We would all put our heads on our desks and hold on to our papers. Sometimes when the windstorms had passed, the entire class was covered in red dust. After a brief period of sweeping up the classroom floor we would go right back to learning, seemingly undeterred.

The sixth grade classroom was on the second floor of the school. There were about twenty students in my class, and Justice was one of them. I did not speak Twi very well, but I was able, with great effort, to understand a bit. Most students detested speaking English outside of the classroom. The Ghanaians, who had been colonized by the British, considered English the language of the oppressors or the higher class. Though they'd won freedom thirty-five years prior to my arrival, the wounds were still fresh. As a result of this history and my lack of language skills, it was difficult for me to get a word in edgewise in conversations outside of school and during lunch. I relied on Justice to translate for me, and sometimes he could not because his English was not great. I lived in the gulf between where his English ended and where my Twi began.

In the cruel world of adolescent boys, I was often the butt of my classmates' jokes in their native tongue—about me personally, my struggling country, or my refugee status. A very nasty version of nationalism was sometimes the underlying tone in those conversations. Not being able to speak the language enough to defend my country and simply not having a country to defend was painful. Eventually I could understand just enough to get the jokes, but I still lacked the Twi vocabulary to respond. When I responded in English they could not understand me, and by the time Justice interpreted my rebuttal, my wit and wisdom were lost in translation. *Why did the rebels have to ruin my country? Now it was the butt of jokes.*

After a few weeks at school under those circumstances I began to feel distant.

"Go back to your country" was one of the few the English phrases I heard from the other students, both boys and girls. I was a spectacle for students in the younger grades. Some would sneak by to catch a glimpse of "the Liberian," the *obroni*—the Twi term for a white man or foreigner. Since I was lighter skinned than most of them, the term seemed to fit. The color of my skin became an issue with the other students, and I wished I was a bit darker skinned. I needed something to get me into their good graces.

The routines of the schoolday helped me adapt. I loved lining up first thing in the school yard every morning for roll call and marching to class while singing songs. We sang the Ghanaian national anthem, and then we listened to the day's announcements from the headmaster. He was a very tall, well-spoken man with a well-groomed afro who was very polite to all of the students. He took the time to introduce himself to me and remembered my name throughout the time that I was attending African Child Elementary School. At the end of the day and at the end of marking periods, the headmaster assembled us by class and recognized students who achieved high academic marks. He also distributed letters for students who had received them. Since most students did not have physical addresses, letters were addressed to the students through the school's post office box.

I became very interested in these letters, which only a few students received. I came to understand that the students had pen pals in different countries. I began spending my lunch money on sending letters: I would starve just to gain a friend overseas.

First, I wrote to bogus addresses across the world, only to have the letters returned. Then Justice and I spent weeks rummaging through old magazines looking for addresses of people around the world who were our age, hoping to find a friend who lived in the United States or Europe. Several months later, I hit the jackpot: a girl named Ingela Mattsson wrote back. She was from Malmö, Sweden. I loved writing letters to Ingela. It took weeks to hear back from her, but it was a great feeling to receive a letter from overseas. I was the envy of my friends whenever I received a letter from Ingela. We took an interest in one another, and I started looking forward to after-school assemblies.

I spent the rest of the school day in fear of our teacher, Mr. Kesse Foster, whom we called Mr. Evans. He was, and still is, the meanest and most impatient teacher I ever had the displeasure of studying under. Justice had warned me about him. He was always impeccably dressed and had a great smile, but it was a trait he rarely displayed. It always seemed that he was angry about something. In particular, it seemed he had trouble understanding why some students could not grasp the basics of mathematics.

We began my time there by studying ratios and proportions. I was terrible at multiplication tables and division, so I suffered in his class. A year out of school had really hurt my already pathetic math skills. We began each day in Mr. Evans' class with a math warm-up problem of some kind, and I never got a single one of those problems right. As a result, I was whipped every morning to begin the day.

Nearly every day, I took six lashes on my back or behind. It became a routine for me and a few other students. I tried my hardest, but eventually I resorted to preparing my backside for the caning rather than preparing my mind for the math.

Sometimes everyone would get the problem right, and only I would get it wrong. The students began to feel sorry for me.

Other than in math, I asserted myself quickly as an elite academic student: I dominated geography, history, and all of the English components of my classes. My ability to memorize facts, dates, and political subjects helped me greatly. I accomplished enough to get the attention of a few girls, especially a quiet classmate named Janet Ofori. Like Justice, she helped me learn Twi, and I helped her with English. Sometimes I walked with her to lunch before I met the boys.

I won the boys' respect at recess with my footballing ability. I dominated the field and got the attention of one of the boys I admired: a great footballer named Desmond Ofori. Desmond pulled me aside after my first day of playing football at recess and told me in his best English that our class needed just one more player to beat the neighboring sixth grade class, and I was that player. My arrival catapulted our class to repeated victory against the other teams.

It was working: my academic ability had won me a few female admirers, and my talent on the field had gotten me the respect I wanted among the boys—I even had a pen pal in Europe. I felt that my luck was beginning to change.

But one particular school day shattered this feeling. It was right after lunch. Mr. Evans was teaching mathematics, and he asked a question. I had no idea what the answer was, which was not surprising.

"Doe," Mr. Evans demanded, "come up here and solve this."

My stomach tightened, and my palms began to sweat. I walked up to the board, paralyzed with fear. I summoned all the math I had ever known, prayed fervently as I fumbled with the chalk, and slowly wrote down an answer after meticulously calculating.

To no one's surprise, I got the question wrong. Mr. Evans was angry and told me to stretch out my hands and place my palms on the chalkboard.

"Twelve lashes," he yelled, "and if you remove your hands from the board we will start again." After about nine hard lashes across my back, I had no choice but to drop my hands to touch my aching, pinching, burning skin. As a result we began again. The beating continued, and I could not help but drop my hands time after time. And he began again, and again, and again. I had received about forty lashes when I tearfully begged him to switch and whip me on my buttocks, even though they were already sore from the previous day's beating.

I couldn't see it at the time, but my classmates cringed as blood began to soak through my shirt and shorts. It was only then that he stopped.

I defiantly walked to my seat, grabbed my things, and walked out of class crying. It was a lonely walk home. I could feel my swelling skin under my blood-soaked shirt. As I walked, I pulled off my shirt and used it to wipe my tears. Those tears brought memories of all my grief washing over me, and I sobbed all the more. My family was missing, my mother was dead, and my future was uncertain.

I washed my shirt as soon as I got home. I told no one about my horrible day. Justice and I laughed it off that night as we lay in bed. I returned to school the following day, expecting more whipping because I had left school without permission. To my surprise, Mr. Evans never mentioned it. He had done enough; he had broken me.

CHAPTER 14

Assimilating in Ghana

"Marcoss Doe."

Ghanaians had an amusing way of pronouncing my name, but I enjoyed hearing them say it.

I'd been waiting for about an hour. It felt like an eternity. The floor was spinning, and I felt close to vomiting. Huge drops of sweat poured from my bushy hair onto my forehead and down the side of my face, yet I shivered and kept my arms folded in an attempt to keep warm.

As I'd walked the mile there early that morning, the sun's rays mercilessly beat on my body, and the ache in my joints was indescribable and unbearable. My elbows felt as though they would disconnect at any moment. My back hurt. My head and shoulders were too heavy for my body to support. My knees and ankles caused me pain with every step. My eyes were bright yellow, and my temperature was, I would come to find out, well over one hundred degrees.

"*Marcoss Doe!*"—this time with more force. I'd sprawled onto the wooden bench, and it was hard to peel myself from the unforgiving stiffness of the boards. Few people sat in the small waiting room, and even fewer gave me a second look. I had labored to put my clothes on that morning and came into the office looking gangly and shabbily dressed. I pulled my knees toward my body and attempted to get up from the bench. I nearly failed. It was even harder to lift myself out of my self-pitying, miserable state. My steps slowed as I made it toward the door.

I missed school to come to the Achimota Clinic. A female doctor looked me over, and I could see the sorrow in her eyes as she asked me in Twi, "Ou wor whor Mamie?" ("Where is your mother?")

I murmured that I didn't speak Twi and that my mother wasn't here with me. What I meant to say was that my mother was not walking the earth any longer, which was why I was there by myself in such a miserable state. I managed to gather what was left of my strength, swallow some saliva, lick my dry lips, and answer her questions.

"What is wrong with you?"

"I have malaria," I said.

"I am the doctor. I'll come up with the diagnosis! Tell me your symptoms," she lectured impatiently.

I listed all of the symptoms that had me feeling like I was going to die right there in her clinic. She went through her checklist and examined my eyes, ears, throat, and skin. I was right. After a few minutes the doctor returned with the diagnosis—malaria—and a prescription.

The huge swamp that lay just beyond our fence was the culprit. Malaria is spread by mosquitoes, and mosquitoes breed in standing water. The words "I told you so" were on my tongue, but this was no time for wittiness or appearing disrespectful. I paid the fee, a few hundred cedis, and pushed the door open, cringing as the heat of the fully risen West African sun embraced me.

As I lumbered through town, it must have been obvious to everyone who saw me that I needed a bed. I made the mandatory stop at the pharmacy, and then I began to walk home. I put one uncoordinated foot in front of the other.

Suddenly I remembered that it was my birthday. My birthday! I was twelve years old and as sick as I have ever been.

The memories of birthdays past—family meals, cake, presents from my parents, my mother's smile—carried me home.

When I finally made it up the tiny hill that led to the guest house, I could hear Rocky the dog barking as I pushed and banged on the gate. Mr. Safo opened it.

"Why are you not in school?" On a second look, he could see the reason.

I collapsed on the living room sofa utterly out of breath and lacking any desire to eat, play, or even speak. The sofa had soft cushions, but they felt like hard metal bars against my body now. Tears rolled down my cheeks and into my ears as I stared at the ceiling, sweat oozed from every pore. I took the medicine, and my thoughts quickly took me back to Liberia. When I was sick, my mother took off work to care for her Jungle Boy. She prepared a bowl of soup and placed a wet towel on my forehead to reduce my temperature. I longed for her. The biting realization that those days were long gone shot me back to reality: I lay here needing all the help I could get, and no one was there to offer it.

I missed school for the rest of the week. Justice filled me in on what was going on. I longed to be there, but I had to get better before I could return. Unfortunately this wasn't the last time I contracted malaria while we lived in Ghana.

* * *

I was well enough to return to school the next Monday. To my surprise, when I returned to school, we had a new teacher. It was as if God had heard my cries.

Mr. Siribour was very unkempt and always very sloppily dressed. His white shirts seemed to be brown, and his brown shirts very dingy, but his gap-toothed smile was very inviting, and his sense of humor was delightful. He was one of the first teachers that openly laughed with us.

Mr. Siribour was especially knowledgeable about world politics and history. He told us all about the ancient Ashanti, Mali, and Songhai empires. I was always engrossed in his history lessons. He was proud of West African history and he brought the ancient Africans to life for me. Mr. Siribour brought an air of intellectual confidence that he soon spread to us, his students. Classmates who had previously performed poorly began doing better. As a result of his calm nature, students were not afraid to raise their hands and answer questions. Best of all, Mr. Siribour did not beat us at all, which was rare among African teachers and a first for me. Sometimes he threatened, and he did bring a cane with him, but he never used it.

Mr. Siribour filled me in on news from Liberia: it was very bleak. There was always some new military offensive taking place. The interim government had been installed. There was a new president of Liberia, and it was not warlord Charles Taylor. But Taylor would not give up his push for unlimited power, so the fighting continued in some parts of the country.

Despite this political instability, Sister Lady decided to return to Liberia.

My brother had found a job in western Ghana. Rather than resettle there in a rural area, Sister Lady chose to head home to be near her family with her newborn son, my nephew Keith.

What remained of my family was fragmenting. I had no idea what would happen to me. I worried as I heard bits and pieces of conversations between my sister-in-law and my brother. Despite my eavesdropping I could not put together what they were going to do with me. As I understood it, there were a few options. This is what I thought they were pondering:

1. I could be put in the refugee camp, where at least I would be fed.

2. I could return to Liberia to my father or the closest responsible family member.

3. I could go to western Ghana with my brother.

I favored the last option.

They chose a fourth option, one that I hadn't even considered. They called me into their room and broke the news to me: I would stay with the Safo family in Achimota indefinitely.

At first I felt abandoned. I was left living in another country with a family that I had known for only a few months. But my feelings of abandonment didn't last. I would be assimilating into a real Ghanaian family, and that felt like a relief after weeks of uncertainty.

I ran into the room that Justice and I shared to tell him the news, but he already knew. I would eat breakfast, lunch, and dinner with the Safos—authentic Ghanaian food. After several months I was mostly fluent in Twi, and I could fumble my way through greetings in basic Ga. The Safos mostly spoke Ewe, however, which was difficult to learn.

The Safo family had a small farm next to the guest house. They had a few pigs, and they grew corn. Justice was excited that he would not have to do all the farm work by himself anymore. I was excited to get to work on the farm.

My brother made the arrangements and left the Safos money for my lunch and supplies. Then my sister-in-law left for Liberia, and my brother left for western Ghana. There was not much fanfare or formality in our goodbyes. The Safo family would take care of me while they were gone. I was given instructions to be obedient and do my best in school. I was alone in the world again.

* * *

My mornings with the Safo family were enjoyable. Justice and I were up early to complete our duties on the farm. We cleaned the pigsty and made sure that the pigs were healthy. After bathing, I greased my skin with Vaseline—at Mrs. Safo's insistence—and put on my uniform. Then Mrs. Safo prepared corn porridge and handed us our lunch money, and off we went. Justice and I would walk together or separately, depending on who finished their chores first, or if he could make it to the bathroom before his siblings, Gloria and Confidence.

Most times I would spend my lunch money on food before I got to school. I just could not bear to walk past all of the food stands without buying something. I was still so happy to have access to food that it was almost impossible to see food and not eat it. At lunch I was too busy playing football to think about eating.

I both looked forward to and despised the time after school: playing football and doing my chores. As soon as I came home from school, Justice and I would get huge buckets made from zinc and walk a mile to get food for the Safos' pigs: leftover hops from a local home brewery. The brewery was in a rather congested area of town called Old Achimota.

Old Achimota was dangerous after dark and had a reputation as a slum. There seemed to be more people per square acre than anywhere I had ever seen. The houses were very close to each other, with a mixture of handmade huts and modern houses. The huts had thatched roofs while the modern houses were roofed with zinc. There were also many herbal healing shops and people who practiced African animism in the neighborhood.

Our classmate Desmond Ofori, who had asked me to join their soccer games, lived in Old Achimota. I would often stop by his house to chat before going to get the hops for the pigs. There was also a girl I liked who lived along the route that we took to carry the goods back to the pigs. That's the main reason why I hated this chore so much—she would see me carrying pig slop. Even so, she went to a different school, so this was my only time to see her. I was torn.

On top of that, to avoid passing her house I would have had to walk along a very busy road. So I bore the embarrassment and walked past her house every day. Sometimes I caught a glimpse of her: this was both the highlight and embarrassment of my day. She would always smile at me and say hello in Twi. I was afraid to say anything but hello. I hoped that one day she would strike up a conversation with me, but she never did. I never even got to know her name.

The brewery itself was exactly opposite the open-air public toilet. The Ghanaian government built these toilets in places that were very congested to deter people from relieving themselves in the bushes or on the streets after dark. The area smelled: a potpourri of human feces mixed with a hint of fermented barley. At the brewery, we scooped the smelly hops from the beer into our buckets and carried them home on our heads. Sometimes these buckets weighed twenty pounds or more.

Barefoot and with the juices of fermented barley and wheat dripping down my face and onto my clothes, I often ran into people that I knew from school. I did my best to avoid eye contact. Justice and I usually made two trips to the brewery a day. After the first trip, I was thoroughly soaked in barley juice, and I smelled terrible. As an adolescent in the hot Ghanaian sun I did not smell like roses to begin with, and when the smell of pigs' food was included, I was incredibly foul.

After finishing the day's haul of wheat and barley leftovers, we grabbed coal bags and went out searching for a plant that the pigs loved to eat that helped them with digestion. This particular weed grew in hard-to-find places, and uprooting the thorny plant sometimes left my hands and forearms scratched and bloody. For a few hours I scoured cemeteries, open grasslands, and sprawling savannahs in my search.

My mind had time to wander during these hours. How had my life turned so drastically upside down? I was the son of the Assistant Director of Administration for the president of Liberia. Not that long ago, I had a maid, a driver, a house-boy who washed my clothes, and a tutor who helped me with my schoolwork. I had begun my education at a prestigious private school in the heart of Monrovia. I had been in the presence of a head of state. In the span of two years, I had lost it all and become a boy who lived on a farm. Here I was collecting stinky hops and wandering Achimota looking for plants to feed to pigs.

My sister-in-law was in Liberia and my brother in western Ghana, hours away from me. My daily reality was still un-imaginable to me: I lived in Ghana, I spoke two new languages and was learning a fourth. I did difficult, thankless farm labor from which I didn't directly profit. Few incidents on the farm deviated from the routine. Still, in the midst of my self-pity I knew that I was fortunate to be fed every day, to go to school, and to play football most days after my chores were done.

On very hot days, we had another chore. Iguanas came out of the swamps during the midday heat and in the cool of the late afternoons, some up to fifteen feet long from tail to nose. Despite their size, they were afraid of humans. Our task was to keep them from harming the pigs by running at them and driving them back into the swamp.

One hot afternoon, I decided to sneak up on one of the creatures and try to frighten it. I climbed over the fence into the swamp, slowly and quietly. I walked up on an unsuspect-ing iguana. I was about five feet away when it spotted me. Feeling threatened, the iguana lashed out with its tail and al-most struck me. The tail was long enough that it could wrap around my leg. I fell to the ground, gripped by panic while the beast walked toward me, tongue slithering in the air. The lizard eventually retreated into the swamp, and I retreated to the house.

Justice and I had many encounters with nature, but nothing compared to our almost weekly encounters with one of the most dangerous snakes in the world: the black mamba. There was a never-ending colony of these incredibly poisonous monsters living in and around the swamp.

They only showed themselves during the quietest moments in the day. Sometimes the snakes managed to slither through the fence and enter the pigsty, threatening the prized possession of the Safo family. When the pigs began their loud, high-pitched, terrified squeals we knew it was time to spring into action. We reacted to their cries for help as a firefighter would react to an alarm.

Justice and I developed a dangerous, rudimentary, yet effective plan to deal with the slithering beasts. The shovels and rakes were too far away—Mr. Safo insisted that we lock the farm tools under the front steps. Instead we climbed into the pigpen. Justice—he was faster—would stand in front of the snake to distract it, dodging the lightning-quick venomous lunges. Meanwhile, I would find something to smash the snake's head. If nothing was found, our plan was for me to grab the snake by the tail and repeatedly fling it to the ground as hard as I could until it died.

We practiced our snake-killing routine often. As dangerous as it was, we liked it. It was sheer misguided adolescent bravery that Justice's parents never found out about.

* * *

Most days were filled with chores, school, homework, and then football—the highlight of my life, as always. We played on the unofficial neighborhood team, all for neighborhood pride. Justice played forward, and I played in the midfield. The team didn't have a name, but we had a coach, and we often played teams from surrounding neighborhoods.

We practiced every day after school and played games on the weekends. Our team grew close, a tight knit family. We all lived within a mile of each other. Most of my teammates came from families that raised livestock or baked bread to sell in order to earn a living. Twice a week we would sacrifice our lunch money to rent jerseys for our games. The hunger was worth feeling like a professional. Many other teams rented these jerseys, usually dirty and smelly from the last team that rented them. I doubt if any of us cared. I always wore number 11. We played barefoot because none of us could afford cleats.

Every Saturday the air was thick with excitement: the football game was almost here. But first Justice and I attended a youth program run by churches, called Awana, in the early afternoon—football didn't start until about 5 p.m. Justice got me involved in Awana because they had a ping-pong table, and we got to participate in the Awana Olympics. We sat through countless sermons just so we could participate in the Olympics when the time came. I knew nothing about the personal relationship with Jesus Christ that the Awana teachers always stressed. They said they could pray and ask God for things, so each week I asked him to take care of my family. I was earnest, though it hurt to open my emotions enough to make the request. Sometimes I felt maybe I wasn't asking God nicely enough, so I said to myself, "maybe next prayer I will ask God nicer."

The teachers ended each gathering with a call to prayer for anyone who wanted "to accept Jesus as their Lord and Savior." I never went up. I never even considered it. It just didn't seem urgent or helpful. When that request was made, I knew Awana was almost over. Then my legs began shaking with anticipation of football. My heart raced, and I could not wait until I was on the field. Once Awana was over, Justice and I ran home, made sure the pigs were fine, and headed to the field.

These were my shining moments. I was a gifted left-footed dribbler and a precise passer. Coaches from the other teams and the adults who came to watch would tell me to keep playing and that maybe someday a professional team would come calling. That was the only future I could see, the only future I could bear to hope for.

The neighborhood team was far less successful than our class team. We rarely won a game. The team we most often played, our biggest rivals, always beat us. The majority of their players were fourteen and fifteen years old, and we were all twelve. Our home field was on a slight hill, which made the coin toss a heavily anticipated event. Whichever team won the toss elected to attack the downhill goal first. That team got a lead and played defense the entire second half. It was almost certain that if our opponents won the toss, they would win the game. At most games we lost the coin toss and had to attack uphill first. Each game, our team would inevitably be down 3–0 or 4–0 at halftime, which in soccer is an almost insurmountable lead. We had good players, but we had trouble playing from behind. Expending our energy trying to attack uphill in the first half left us tired and vulnerable during the second.

I hated losing to the boys from the other neighborhood—they were not humble, and Justice and I had to walk through their neighborhood every day to get the pigs' food, purchase food from the local market, and catch the bus to school. They would sneer and snicker as we walked through with our buckets. We stopped and talked trash in English, Twi, and Ga. Of course, this brought the challenge of another game, which we would lose, continuing the lopsided cycle.

One of the greatest athletic triumphs of my early life was in one of these Saturday games. We were playing our hated rivals, the boys who always rubbed it in our faces when they beat us, the boys we had never beaten. We won the coin toss and chose to attack the downhill goal. We played well, but at the half the score was 2–0 against us. Even with the advantage we had not managed to score a goal. On top of that, one of our key players had to go home, so we had to play the second half one man down. I was sure we would lose this one 7–0.

But something came over us. That half, we passed the ball effectively and with precision. We defended impeccably. We played the best football of our lives.

With about ten minutes left we were still down 2–0. I got a pass, kicked it to Justice, and he beat the goalie: 2–1. Then with just a few minutes left in the game, there was a scramble for the ball about thirty-five yards from the goal. One of their defenders attempted to clear the ball away from their goal, but it bounced into my path. I gathered the ball, touched it away from the defender, and shot from about twenty-five yards away. The goalie dove toward the shot to no avail. The ball snaked its way under the crossbar and just inside the post. It was a goal!

I had never been so jubilant in my life. We tied our hated rivals 2–2, but we celebrated as if we won. We could walk through their neighborhood with pride. That afternoon, as we walked home, I was reminded of the game in Barnersville, when my team was able to break even just at the end of a game. Barnersville now seemed a lifetime ago. The game strangely reconnected me to my prior life, but after this tie I wasn't going home to Ma and Pa and my brothers, but I was going home to a Ghanaian family.

The next time I went to Old Achimota, some players from the other team even congratulated us as we walked through the streets. We decided after that never to play them again.

* * *

The school year came to an end, and I was off to Junior Secondary School, a change in my routines and in the patterns of my life with the Safos.

The closest reputable school was a long bus ride away: Kaneshie North 2 Junior Secondary School (JSS). It seemed like there were a thousand students there from the lowest grades up to the last year of senior high. It was the biggest school I'd ever attended. Each class had three sections based on academic ability, all named after flowers: Rose, Lily, and Marigold. Justice and I were placed in JSS 1 Lily, which meant we were not among the most elite students, but we still had potential.

The same school building also housed the Senior Secondary School. Because of the lack of classroom space, our schedule had to be flexible. The junior and senior high shared most of the teachers as well as the building, so we alternated schedules: for two weeks the junior high attended school from 7:00 a.m. until 12:30 p.m. and the senior high went from 1:00 p.m. until 5:30 p.m., then the schedule was reversed. The afternoon shift was the best because by afternoon, most of the teachers had very little energy to teach or beat us.

In JSS I began to realize my potential as a leader when I was elected class treasurer. My duties included making the schedule for cleaning up the classroom after school each day and collecting dues from everyone of thirty cedis per week, or about half a day's lunch money, for classroom needs. We used the money to buy brooms, paper, extra pencils, and the canes the teachers used to beat us.

I collected the money from all of the students. My friends would sometimes—not jokingly—chastise me for using the money to buy the canes that were used to beat us. We often talked about buying thin canes, so that when we received beatings they would not hurt as much. There was a downside to me buying thin canes. Whenever canes would break as one teacher was beating a student, he would ask for whoever bought the cane and whip that person too for buying such a flimsy tool. I was routinely torn between buying thick canes for everyone including myself or thin canes that saved others but got me beaten.

As the treasurer, I was entrusted with all of the money. I balanced the classroom budget weekly and purchased the supplies that we needed. I had no oversight, so I would sometimes buy fried dough with some of the leftover change to make myself feel better about buying thin canes. The chances of me getting caned by a teacher were high, so I thought I might as well enjoy the fried dough as compensation for the unavoidable beating.

CHAPTER 15

News from Home

I was slowly adjusting to life as a refugee and as an adolescent boy: getting used to changes in my body, a new culture, new languages, and learning to take care of myself.

Ghanaian culture, like many others, centers on food. After about a year and a half, I spoke almost fluent Twi, and I could understand a decent amount of Ga, so cooking instruction from Mrs. Safo made me an almost full-fledged Ghanaian. She taught me the proper way to eat with my hands and how to spot a good yam at the market, but above all she taught me how to make fufu, the Ghanaian staple.

Fufu is made from boiled cassava that's pounded into a sticky paste with a large mortar and pestle. Making it requires two people: one person, typically a man, to handle the ten-pound pestle, and another, typically a woman, to move the cassava around in the three-foot-wide mortar. The routine depends heavily on the pounder's attention to detail and his ability to adhere to a steady rhythm of lifting the heavy pestle as the second member of the team pushes, turns, and flips the fufu into its path.

Teaching someone to pound fufu was very risky. I had to maintain a regular beat with the pestle so as not to crush Mrs. Safo's fingers. In time, Mrs. Safo trusted me enough to start a conversation and turn her back to the fufu while we worked.

As I grew to accept my life in Ghana and my place at the Safos', I could compartmentalize the pain of my past. I bought the local newspaper when the headlines were about Liberia, but other than that I kept busy to stave off thoughts of my family and the tragedy that I had undergone. My life had been turned upside down, but I had miraculously landed on my feet—and I wanted to leave it at that.

But some days the questions and memories came anyway. I'd sit on the roof and wonder: What if the war had not taken place? What if I knew where my family was? What if I still had a mother? In quiet moments between school, football matches, and chores I drifted into my solitary world of internal uncertainty.

After I had been living with the Safos for a few months, Boye came to visit me, and he brought a welcome break in my routine. I was overjoyed to see him. His presence prompted me to evaluate the state of my life and to conclude that I was not doing as well as I thought.

He was surprised at how dark-skinned I had gotten from working outside. I had contracted head lice and needed a haircut. The one pair of shoes that I owned had fallen apart. The soles were barely clinging onto the rest of the shoe—after all, I walked about fifteen miles a week between going to school and feeding the pigs. As a result of my busted shoes, my toes stuck out, so I could not walk as fast. My socks had holes too, so most times I did not wear them, which made my feet sweat and my shoes stink. I used my money on food and football rather than clothing repair.

Boye was good-natured about my newly disheveled ways. Out behind the Safos' house together, he gave me a letter.

"It's for you," he said quickly. He stayed inside as I walked away to read.

Gahien's handwriting was unmistakable. I had not seen him in almost two years. I stood motionless on the back steps.

Justice was watching me, so I sneaked away and sat on the roof to be absolutely alone as I opened the letter.

It was dated only a few weeks prior. My tears began to flow: Gahien was alive! As I read on, those tears of joy turned to sorrow as he told me his current state. He was with Caroline and Mocco, but he was not sure where Molley was. They had lost everything. He said there were rebels driving around in our cars. They were still eating one meal a day—sometimes just rice and salt.

Then he dealt the gut-wrenching blow. "Pa was taken away, and we haven't seen him."

I knew immediately that Pa was dead, that Gahien knew it, but in his longing for his own innocence and desire to protect mine, he did not come right out and say it. By the end of the letter there were details, though Gahien could not bring himself to write the words directly: Pa was killed by rebels. His body was most likely left for dogs to eat, like the other dead bodies I had seen in the war. My father was one of those people who lay on a road somewhere dead. I fell onto my face and cried uncontrollably.

"*Pa died . . . Pa died . . . They killed Pa . . . They killed Pa.*" I repeated it to myself slowly in a whisper. Tears dripped from my face, and I couldn't bring myself to get up.

Eventually I made my way back down to the back steps and read the letter again. Justice crept over, though I barely noticed. In typical teenage bravado, Justice laughed. He didn't know why I was crying. He laughed hysterically. I cried slowly. I walked into our room, sat on the bed and wept. He followed me, growing more serious.

"What's happening?"

I raised my head: "My brothers and sister are in Liberia, and they are eating rice and salt every day."

He smirked and made a snide remark about why they couldn't afford food.

My beloved father was brutally murdered! I wanted to scream, but I could barely speak.

"My father . . . my father . . ." I said.

"What?"

"Gone."

I remembered the last time I saw my pa alive. I recalled the feeling I had when he last walked away from me. I'd refused to believe that it might be the last time I saw him. But somehow I knew. I had held on to hope that he was alive. He was supposed to be immortal. Parents aren't supposed die! Not yet! He always seemed to survive—after all, he had survived the coup of 1980. I preferred to live in my inner world where we all survived the war. In that world, I was reunited with them and we went back to the way it used to be. Ma was alive, and we rode to school in the same car and listened to Pa's stories in traffic. I'd believed it could happen, even though I had seen Ma in a casket, even though I saw that casket buried. Now Pa was dead—killed by someone. Some rebel out there shot a gun that killed my pa. The world I fantasized could exist no more. There was nothing left for the dream to stand on. My hopes of a joyous reunion were demolished. My pa had died. He had been murdered.

I was an orphan, one of the sad children of civil wars whom I'd always read about. Whenever someone asked me, "Where is your pa?" I could no longer say, "We don't know." I would now repeat the response familiar to Liberians: "My pa died in the war. They killed my pa in the war."

In the wake of the news came questions and realizations that I didn't want, that I couldn't stop. Had he been tortured before death? What if I had been there? Who killed him? What man or men made me an orphan at eleven? My heart became dark, as I realized that there might still be men walking the earth who had killed my father, who had orphaned me. *My father died. My father died at the hands of ruthless rebels.*

* * *

As the days went by, my new reality set in, awakening the pain I'd been numbing through the work of assimilating in my new home. I wondered: Where is the God that I learned about at Awana? I prayed to that God to save my family. Where was he now? How could I trust a God who left me with nothing? I tried to pray, but I couldn't muster up the words, the faith. If God existed, he definitely did not like me. What had I done? Maybe I took more than my share of toffees back at the Methodist church, or maybe my mind drifted to football during Awana lessons. Whatever it was, it had made God angry, and as a result I was an orphan. My mind went back to so many bad things I had done, and I tried to be remorseful. I believed God was punishing me.

My religious life had mostly been unsatisfying and confusing, but I'd given God a chance, and he failed me. My sister-in-law had told me about Jesus Christ—but I didn't know what "accepting Christ" and "being saved" meant. I liked the idea of being saved or born again—I needed newness—but I didn't really know what it meant. Honestly, family and football felt like all I needed to be saved. She told me to read the Bible, and I did, but I preferred the stories of the Old Testament to the New Testament. Jesus was just another Bible personality to me, like David or Joshua.

Before the war, my father had taken me to both Methodist and Alladurah churches. The Alladurah people had protected me from witchcraft and kept me alive. But they had failed to keep Ma alive, and some of their practices were strange— bathing in cold water, living by the ocean, and the smell of incense. The toffees were all I could credit to the Methodists.

I'd tried a little bit of something from everyone who had offered me religion, but nothing worked. No God protected my father. No God could bring him back. My belief in God had a faint pulse. The permanence of death was all too familiar. My emptiness and loss would never go away. I knew that no matter how hard I prayed my father would not come back. I would never heal.

I still went to Awana, but only for the ping-pong and the girls. The message from the teachers meant even less to me than it did before. As they spoke, my mind yelled back: *What kind of God would allow a child to suffer like this? God did not hear my prayers. He is absent; he is not listening. God does not really have the "whole world in his hands." He does not really love all children, "red and yellow, black, and white." The one thing I prayed for fervently he did not give me. I obviously am not "precious in his sight." You say God is a source of peace and promise, but God let me down.*

In bed at night, I wondered why God didn't care about me, what he was punishing me for, how he chose which prayers to answer.

I was thirteen, and I hated everything. God couldn't—wouldn't—help me now. I had to do life by myself. My sorrow became anger, and my anger turned into resolve and hatred—deep and unforgiving. If there was a God, the men who killed Pa would meet justice at the muzzle of a gun. I decided to make it happen whether there was a God or not.

Each morning, I wiped my tears and vowed revenge: *I will kill whoever killed my father.*

✱ ✱ ✱

When the initial rush of emotion melted away, I had time to think, and I still wanted to kill. I was certain that killing those who did this and having their families feel the pain that I was feeling would make me feel better.

I began to plan.

I would find the men who humiliated and killed my father and made me into an orphan. I would hunt them, even if I died trying. I daydreamed about how I would go about killing those men.

Having seen how the rebels humiliated men before killing them, I couldn't help but imagine that they had done the same to Pa. I wouldn't shoot them, I decided. Instead, I would cut them to pieces with an ax in front of their families. I would do it slowly and mercilessly. I would let them cry, as I had cried. I would grit my teeth, and I would hurt them. I pictured these men begging for mercy. I would show them none.

I made it my life's goal to return to Liberia as soon as possible.

I would stop at nothing to wage a secret campaign of terror against the rebels. My father taught me how to use guns. I would use those skills to avenge his death. Suddenly I had a purpose: to kill anyone who had anything to do with my father's death.

Every time I thought of revenge, a warmth covered the cold ache of my grief. My life was a tragedy, but I determined not to become a victim. Just the way I triumphed on the soccer field, I would get even.

CHAPTER 16

Going to America

Whenever I closed my eyes to sleep, my world came alive. I saw Ma, Pa, Boye, Mocco, Molley, Gahien and Caroline. I could feel their hands and hear their voices. Their laughter comforted me. But when my eyes were open their struggles saddened me, and my life seemed dark.

I wallowed in great dejection, drowning in a lake of hatred. I could not overcome the stench of death and tragedy. There was no one to talk to, no one who would listen.

Sleep was my only escape. In my dreams I was free. In my dreams I was alive, and so was everyone else. Waking up every morning was an ordeal—I crossed from light to darkness as the sun rose.

Often I found myself silently weeping on the bus rides to and from school. I quietly wiped away my tears as other bus patrons looked on. I would work to crack a brief half-smile, but I did not care what they thought about me. Most people simply glossed over the fact that I was an orphan and alone and hurting.

It hurt when I saw Liberians who knew my family and they asked, "Where are your pa and your brothers?" I had trouble bringing myself to say, "Pa was killed, and my brothers are missing." I could see their shock. Most people could not help but put on their apologetic mask. Some could no longer bear to look at me. I am sure some were genuinely sorry about my condition, but some forgot about me as soon as they left my presence. My story was all too familiar. Most people had heard countless stories like it.

I drifted into my own secluded world during class or as I walked to and from school. My imagination was vivid. Often my daydreams featured revenge, violent and satisfying. At other times I caught myself talking out loud to family members whom I knew were dead or in Liberia. Sometimes my friends noticed me. I refused to accept the fact that my family was gone, that my life was gone. My daily reality felt like a nightmare, and I was powerless to change it.

I no longer looked forward to secondary school, university, or even the next day. I wanted to die and take with me everyone who had hurt me—take them to wherever people go when they die. I felt that my promising future had died with my family. My hope for a life of pleasure and success was replaced by the dark hope of revenge.

* * *

Life on the Safo family farm ended abruptly for me, just as I had adjusted to that life. In the midst of the fog of my hatred and apathy, Sister Lady returned from Liberia, and she brought some unexpected news. We would apply for visas to the United States as refugees.

We would sit for some resettlement interviews, she said, and hopefully be granted visas and permission to relocate to the United States. She had family in the Boston area, so we would aim to move there. She and Boye talked cautiously about our prospects, but I could see that giddiness wasn't too far beneath the surface—the joy of knowing there might be hope for their family.

I was not excited. I had trouble getting excited about anything, but more than that, I didn't want to leave Africa.

Most Africans would be overjoyed to go to America, the land of great opportunity and freedom. But I love Africa. It is my home, the land where my mother and father were born, and

the land where they were killed. I was wary of leaving my brothers on Liberian soil—soil still soaking with our blood. Leaving
Africa felt like deserting my family, giving up on their memory.

Also, leaving Africa put my diabolical scheme for revenge
at risk. I felt sure the lawless men who killed my father would
go free if I left for America.

Further down my list of unvoiced objections was the
weather. Charles Davis had said to me a few years earlier
that it was cold in America. I had seen his photographs of
the snow-covered cars. I had never felt cold weather before.
Would I be able to play football outside? What would I do if
I could not play?

Nevertheless, my brother returned to Accra, and we began
the exhausting process of refugee resettlement. We moved
from the West African Examinations Council compound to
an eastern suburb of Accra. I was glad to leave the hard work
behind, but saying goodbye to the Safo family was hard. They
had done so much to help me assimilate into their culture.
They had accepted me into their family.

The temporary home that I shared with Boye and Sister Lady was a white two-story house just two blocks off the
highway from the Ghanaian port city of Tema in a neighborhood called Teshie-Nungua. The schools in the area were not
very good, according to Sister Lady, and it made very little
sense for me to switch schools, so I continued my education
at Kaneshie North 2 Junior Secondary School—which was
one piece of good news, since Justice and I would still see
each other at school while I was in the application process to
leave Ghana. The bad news was that Teshie-Nungua was two
bus rides away from school. So I'd have to get up at 4 a.m. to
make the two-hour trip to school. I was chronically late, so I
made a habit of wearing two pairs of underwear to bear my
daily beating for tardiness.

Still, without the farm work my morning routine was a bit easier. I woke up, showered, and headed for the bus stop. I caught the earliest bus heading for the city, transfered to another bus that was headed to Kaneshie market, and then walked the rest of the way to school. Sometimes when I was tired, I would use my lunch money and take a third bus to school instead of walking. It was always a tough decision, since sometimes the third bus would make too many stops and leave me both late and out of lunch money.

My chronic lateness could have cost me my job as class treasurer, but I was granted some leniency because the teachers understood that I lived far away. The whippings did not stop, but I kept my office.

The house we stayed in was occupied by about twelve people. They were all Liberian refugees, some of whom I knew. Boye, Sister Lady, and my nephew, Keith, who was almost two years old now, shared a room on the second floor. I shared a room with three guys who were all older than me: Tommy, who was nineteen, and the Bestman brothers, William and Julius, both twenty-one. We all slept on makeshift beds made of cushions on the neatly tiled floors.

Despite the distractions and busyness of my life, I felt the pending separation crushing me during this time: separation from Justice, Africa, my country, my brothers, the memory of my parents. I was leaving my life. A part of me wanted stay, but no one in their right mind would turn down a trip to America to start a new life.

I resigned my post as class treasurer about a week before I left Ghana. My teachers wished me good luck on my last day, and I hugged everyone before I walked out of class for the last time. Justice and I were teary eyed as we walked to the bus station. He had become like a brother to me. I had known him for almost three years and shared hundreds of soccer games, homework sessions, and language lessons. He was happy for me, but we both cried as we promised to keep in touch. My heart broke as I saw Justice for the last time from the window of the bus bound for Teshie-Nungua. My tears flowed all the way home.

＊＊＊

Amidst the sadness of leaving my lifelong home—the continent of Africa—the fresh hope of America was starting to creep into my mind. Having never been on a plane before, I awoke on March 30, 1993, excited and scared at the same time. My brother had shaved my head the day before, and I put on a new set of clothes, leaving behind the threadbare clothes that I had worn for almost three years.

We boarded the plane headed for a brief stop in Kano, Nigeria. I was exhilarated as the plane took off. I wanted to come back to Ghana, and I cried a bit, but unlike the day that I left Liberia, I felt no shame.

From Kano we headed to Amsterdam. I carried a little pocket map of the world so I could follow the route of the plane. We landed in Amsterdam after about seven hours of flying. We had an eight-hour layover in Amsterdam, during which I walked around the entire airport, amazed by the sights and sounds of the industrialized nation.

We boarded another plane for New York City—America!—then from New York, we finally arrived in Boston, Massachusetts.

While I'd gotten a taste of what was to come at the Amsterdam airport, Boston's Logan Airport was huge and overwhelming. I knew we weren't just passing through, so I tried to take everything in—so much mental stimulation. It was late evening when we arrived in Boston, but the airport was still filled with people—and they were white!

Sister Lady's sister, Aunt Steffi, whom I call Aunty SJ, welcomed us to America. I was too distracted to know who we were looking to meet. I had no idea what she looked like, and I was overwhelmed by all the lights and signs in the airport. I was in America!

Suddenly, Aunty SJ was right there handing me a brown jacket made of some kind of material I had never felt before. I slipped it on, not realizing that the coldest temperatures my thirteen-year-old body had ever felt lay beyond the doors. As I put on the coat, I instantly felt American. With the coat I took on that feeling of confidence that Americans all seem to have.

The automatic doors swung open. *Cold* hit me like a slap in the face. My mind whirled. Aunty SJ's future husband, Uncle JE, could see the horror on my face and said, "You can expect it to be cold like this about three-fourths of the year."

It was not just what he said that scared me, but the casual manner in which he said it, as if it was unremarkable. Aunty SJ handed me a wool hat. I slipped it onto my shaved head and zipped up my jacket. There was ice piled up on every corner. I had never seen such a thing. Again I wondered how I would play football here. How would I survive? I knew the sun was shining, and it was hot in Africa—what was I doing here?

I couldn't go back.

We arrived at my new home in Medford, Massachusetts. The apartment buildings were called the Mystic Valley Towers. I could see the tall buildings of Boston from the upper floors of the twelve-story building. We lived on the third floor in Aunty SJ's two-bedroom apartment. There were seven of us: Aunty SJ, Uncle JE, their seven-year-old son Omar, Boye, Sister Lady, an almost two-year-old Keith, and me. Needless to say, the apartment was congested.

I slept on the living room floor, and I was comfortable there. The floor was soft, and I was given a warm blanket. I spent my first few days just staring out of the windows and imagining the seemingly endless possibilities that lay out there somewhere. I decided to forget my past and hope for better things in the future.

In the months that followed, everything intrigued me. I had many firsts: my first meal at McDonald's, my first trip to a place called the mall, my first train ride, my first American bus ride, and my first time seeing skyscrapers. I played tennis, "football" with an oblong ball with laces, and real basketball with nets. I had never seen or used a dishwasher, a washing machine, or a microwave before. Machines fascinated me. I ate pizza (which I didn't like), Chinese food (which I hated), waffles, syrup, cereal, strawberries, and other new foods. My favorite was Aunty SJ's lasagna. I had never heard of lasagna, and I had no idea what was in it, but it was delicious, and that first night in Massachusetts I ate so much that my stomach hurt.

*　*　*

Before long my day came, the day I both looked forward to and dreaded: my first day of school in America. I wanted to make friends—real American friends!

Aunty SJ took me to school on the bus that first day. She showed me where to put the dollar and when to ring the bell to signal a stop. Back in Ghana, I had to scream at the cowboy, the driver's assistant who collected fares, when I needed to get off the bus. Here, I just pushed a button, and the bus driver stopped at the next scheduled stop.

Finally we arrived at Roberts Junior High. I had never been inside such a big school building before. It was a far cry from my open-air classroom in Ghana. My legs wobbled as

I climbed up the steps. Aunty SJ opened the big doors, and I was immediately intimidated. The hallways seemed so big, so full of kids. They were mostly white and spoke English so fast. My new world scared me.

My enthusiasm for learning dripped out with my sweat. Survival would again be my first priority—but this time I wouldn't have a sense of my surroundings or anyone looking out for me. Getting lost in the building was inevitable. As for making friends, I did not know how I would pull that off. I had been dropped on another planet, and I was losing my breath just standing there.

As classes started, I waited in the hall while Aunty SJ went in the office. After a few minutes, she walked out of the office with a woman who would walk me to my class that morning. Aunty SJ said goodbye, and I could barely speak back to her.

"Mr. Stagliano will be your homeroom teacher," the woman said. "You will be in 8-D. He will tell you where your locker is, show you the lunch room, and introduce you to your classmates. It is the fourth quarter, so the kids are antsy."

She was speaking way too fast. I had no idea what homeroom was, not to mention a locker. What does 8-D mean? I played like it was normal despite my confusion.

She did not ask anything about where I was coming from. She assumed I was joining them from another school in the area. I should have grabbed her and said, "Lady, I am not coming from another town, city, county, or state—I am coming from another *continent*." Economically and socially, I was coming from another world. I have never been as nervous in my life as I was in the quiet hallway.

When we reached my classroom, the door swung open and all the commotion in the room stopped. I froze in the doorway. A bearded, balding man stood up from behind a huge table. I assumed he was Mr. Stagliano, but I could hardly pronounce his name. All the kids stared at me, and I did not know what to say. I slowly and clumsily walked to the front of the room. The fast-speaking lady handed Mr. Stagliano some papers. He looked at them and nodded his head in agreement.

"Marcus, I am Mr. Stagliano. I teach science." He stuck out his hand. I shook it.

He was explaining something, but I could not understand because he was speaking too fast. I stared at the faucet and sink that were in his classroom—why would there be a faucet in a classroom?

"Sit in the back by the door. There is an empty chair there," he said as he turned back to his desk. I walked back. The room was still a bit quiet. As I sank into my seat, the kid next to me asked my name. He was a short, chubby boy with dark hair who looked Mediterranean or North African to me.

"Class, we have a new student," Mr. Stagliano announced. "Where did you come from, Marcus?"

Oh, Lord! I thought. I mustered up all of my pubescent bass.

"I am from Africa."

The students' collective gasp of surprise and admiration was audible. Mr. Stagliano seemed surprised too. Twenty different conversations broke out. Questions seemed to be flying at me from everywhere. With my heavy Ghanaian, British-accented, Liberian-punctuated, quivering, nervous English I responded to some of their questions. My Aunty SJ had warned me, "They know very little about Africa, so do not get mad when they ask silly questions."

I took their inquisitiveness in stride: How come you're not dark skinned? Did you live in a mud hut? Did you wear clothes? What type of food did you eat? Did you ever see lions and tigers roaming your village? Do they have cars there? Did you go to school?

The last two questions hurt a little. I tried to answer them as best I could, but I had to repeat myself over and over. Though we were all speaking English, they could not understand me, and I had trouble understanding them. I was glad that they did not ask about my parents and why I had come to America.

From that rocky start, the school days drifted along. I had a hard time adjusting to the learning style in American classes. My grades were terrible. I found out what gym class was and that, at least, I loved. We played basketball, a sport that I had watched my brothers play when I was younger but had never tried. The day the gym teacher took us out to play soccer, everyone saw me in a whole new light.

I made a few friends in school. The girls helped me a lot. There was a girl in my class named Stephanie who lived relatively close to me. She was white, and she had these weird green metal things in her mouth, with rubber bands. I had never seen braces before. I was afraid to ask her why she wore them and lose her friendship. We walked to and from school together sometimes, though I couldn't always find her after school. At times she showed up at the apartment complex, and we played basketball with the other kids. She always wanted to go to the mall, a place that I was not allowed to go without an adult. I was shocked to learn that she was a smoker at age thirteen. In Africa kids didn't dare smoke cigarettes, even though there were no laws against kids buying them—it seemed like the scariest habit in the world.

Stephanie asked me so many questions. She seemed so intrigued by life in Africa. I told her about life there, but I avoided telling her about my family and what I'd seen in the war. It was too raw, too painful, and too precarious to share those parts of me. American schools and children were so different. They were mean toward each other in a strange sort of way. They used words that were considered curses in Liberia and Ghana, words I had only heard in American movies.

I was awash in idiomatic cultural expressions that I didn't understand. After a few weeks I blended in relatively well, I suppose. My teachers did their best to keep tabs on me. I began my habit of drifting away to Africa in my daydreams during class.

* * *

In early June, toward the end of the school year, we moved to my Aunty Penny's, a sister of Sister Lady's. She was younger and more animated than Sister Lady and Aunty SJ. We spent the summer at her place in East Boston, so I had to take the train to Medford for school. It was a long and enjoyable experience. Boston was such a big city, and there were people everywhere. I was starting to feel at home, to feel proud of my new life. I had turned fourteen, and I was living in a new country, a huge city. I knew my way around town, at least my way on the train and bus from East Boston to Medford. Once school was out, the summer was great. I played basketball all the time.

That August we moved to Maryland for some reason that I wasn't sure of. I left Stephanie and the friends I had made in Boston behind.

I was getting used to leaving.

Still, America was becoming home for me. I started to enjoy the food. I was working on my American accent. I played basketball.

I still longed to return to Africa, but the luxuries and conveniences of America were starting to impress me. I loved watching television, and I took a keen interest in American football. High school was my next stop. I had no idea what a different world that would be.

CHAPTER 17

Drifting Alone

Most mornings my stomach was in knots as the school bus approached Paint Branch High School in Burtonsville, Maryland. Life there filled me with a strange mix of emotions. From the first day on the school bus—the first time in my life, at age fourteen—to my last day of classes, I never quite adjusted to American high school culture.

When I first started at Paint Branch in 1993, I was scared and lost. The building was even bigger than Roberts Junior High, and this contributed to my habitual tardiness for classes. It was difficult to understand the teachers—they spoke too fast. Class assignments were complex to me. Though I never admitted it, I had never used a computer, and I didn't know how to type.

As time passed, I fell further and further behind. My grades were abysmal. The first report card had the worst grades I have ever received. My best grades were Cs. Lost and disappointed, I wanted to do better in school, but I lacked motivation to overcome the overwhelming differences of culture and language. Flunking out of school was a real possibility. I could not pass my core classes. I spent my first two years in Algebra—and failed both times, even with the help of Saturday school tutoring.

I tried to fit in during my first two years of high school, and I managed to make a few friends in gym and at lunch, but there were so many social situations and customs that I had to learn on the fly—where to sit on the school bus, for example. Over time I learned that the cool people sat in the back, geeks in the front, and in-betweeners in the middle, but never next to a girl. You don't talk to the bus driver if you're new. A few students sat by themselves, outcast in the halls at school as well. Some kids listened to Walkmans or CD players. I wondered what it would feel like to own one—but I knew Boye and Sister Lady couldn't afford to buy me one, and I didn't have the money.

My wardrobe didn't do me any favors fitting in either. My sister-in-law did all of the family shopping. Needless to say she picked up things that were economically feasible for our growing family. By the fall of 1993, Boye and Sister Lady had a second child, a boy named Michael.

My comfort and style were last on the list. Like most teenage boys I seemed to grow overnight. During one of my growth spurts I sprouted from 5′3″ and 120 pounds to 5′9″ and 160 pounds in a little over a year. I owned and proudly wore a pair of snugly fitting green jeans. I looked like a Christmas tree that was wrapped too tight. It took a lot to dodge the attention of juniors and seniors who loved to make fun of defenseless undersized freshmen.

Fights were a constant reality in the school hallways. Unruly students verbally abused and threatened teachers regularly—something that never happened in Africa. Most teachers in the high school seemed powerless in the face of threatening teenagers who were bigger and taller than they were. Disrespect was rampant.

School was enough for me to deal with, but I was carrying the weight from my past—weight that no one was helping me carry, weight that I wouldn't show to anyone. My brother Boye was the only one I could share this with, but I assumed he was too busy. He was working and trying to support a growing family of his own as a refugee in a new country. Besides, the reason I liked Boye was because of the quiet and simple life he led. He had always worked hard and said very little. It was just who he was. He did not talk much.

On certain days when my emotions overcame me, I would purposely miss the school bus home. I'd slowly, aimlessly walk the empty halls of the school until the janitors asked me to leave. Then I'd walk home. It was about a two-mile walk from Paint Branch to our house on Collingwood Terrace. During those long, cold walks my imagination, loneliness, and sadness came alive. My ambition was kindled as well. On the road, I worked to make faltering sense of my life.

I thought about Ghana, America, and Liberia—my mother and father. It had been three years since I last saw my brothers and sister. Boye kept in touch with them every few months, so I had a little news now and then, but as much as I longed for them, I couldn't bring myself to communicate with them. Too much pain. Last I heard they were still eating one meal a day. How long can a human being keep living on one meal a day? Walking home made me feel like I was back in Ghana again. Life was simple back in Africa. I yearned for that simplicity now.

I felt guilty for being alive and in America, the loneliness of living as an orphan, self-pity at my pathetic academic performance, regret for not saying goodbye to my family properly, anxiety about the future, and sadness at how life had turned out for me.

My most comforting moments were when I imagined fulfilling my long-held desire for revenge. I saw myself murdering the man who killed my father. I rehearsed the fight, scream by scream, blow by blow, until he was dead.

But the warm hollowness that followed was short-lived. The man was still alive, in my daydreams and in the world. I could kill him every day in my mind, but he wouldn't really be dead.

Tears would stream down my face as I walked down Old Columbia Pike. The two-lane road did not have a sidewalk, and I had to keep an eye out for cars. More than once as I walked, drowning in my sad thoughts, I would drift onto the road—only to be jolted back to reality by a honking, speeding car.

As I got close to home, I would prep myself to answer questions about why I was coming back so late. I lied and told whoever asked what they wanted to hear.

"I was staying after school to get help from my teachers."

In reality, my teachers at Paint Branch could barely put my name to my face. I was just another student drifting in and out of classes.

* * *

As the year continued I walked home more and more. On my walks home, at night before sleep overtook me, in class as teachers lectured—I was learning to tune out the world in favor of my own sad memories. From the outside, I was just another normal teenager going through those hectic transitional years. People didn't see who I was or where I'd come from.

Inside I knew that I was far from normal—I was both dead and alive. I played dead to situations I didn't want to deal with, but inside I was alive with memories of my family, stories of the war, my beloved Liberia, my beloved Ghana, my beloved Africa. Each night I let my grief out, alone, on my pillow, a nearly silent weeping. Maybe God could see me. Maybe he understood. But I saw very little reason to think so, and no evidence to believe.

For the first time in my life I was aimless. For the first time, I felt stupid. For the first time, I seemed to be the cause of my own problems. For the first time I saw no help, no solution or hope for escaping my misery.

At home, I felt I was only there for labor. On Fridays I cleaned the entire house. I raked in the fall, mowed the grass in the spring. I felt the gap between me and my brother and his family growing wider.

As my grades fell and my apathy soared, it seemed everyone around me lowered their expectations for me. Boye and Sister Lady had done so much for me, bringing me along to the States. Now I was wasting the opportunity, unable to achieve the kind of academic success they hoped for, seemingly unable to even try. I was angry at myself for not doing well in school, yet I felt incapable of bringing myself to do well. Every morning when I faced the day, in every class when I faced a test, in every interaction I had with adults, I felt paralyzed. The expectations were low. I still could not reach them. I accepted that I would amount to nothing. The circumstances around me echoed the message in my head that it was foolish to aim very high. Deep down I knew I could do better, but something was in my way, and I didn't know how to overcome it.

I could barely see anything positive about myself during those years. I was an obedient boy. I worked hard around the house, and I accepted criticism from everyone with contrition, a smile, and a pledge to do better. Every adult in my life was chiming in on my lack of effort. No matter how much everyone admonished me, every report card was the same: the grades were below average. I was below average.

After two years in Maryland, just as I was getting my bearings at Paint Branch, my brother got a job in Germantown, Maryland. This meant a new neighborhood and a new school: my third school in just over two years, my fifth in five years.

I had to reinvent myself again.

At Seneca Valley High School I wanted to show everyone—my brother, my peers, myself—that I could be a different person. I'd grown significantly taller, and I had taken to lifting weights. I had one friend who had already transferred there from Paint Branch High School a year before I did, Jairo Solano, who was from Colombia. He and I had been friends since ninth grade; we met in gym class and began lifting together. In August of 1995, I joined the football team at Seneca Valley. My brother and sister-in-law were cautious because they feared I'd give even less attention to my schoolwork.

The game allowed me to take out my frustrations on other people, hitting opponents as hard as I could. I often imagined rival schools as mortal enemies, and I did everything to beat them up physically.

I was athletically gifted. At 5´9˝ my vertical leap was over forty inches. I could dunk a basketball, and I had great hands for catching the football. The coaches loved my obedience and willingness to try all the positions. Belonging to a team helped me make friends. I was even popular. Because of my athletic ability, I started to accrue a reputation. Younger students skipped classes to see me play basketball in gym class, just to see me dunk. For the first time I even had a girlfriend.

My African accent had all but disappeared. Of all the friends that I made, none knew that I was African. Not a single person knew that I was an orphan battling loneliness and a horrible past. My friends were consumed by their own survival. They rarely stopped to get into an in-depth conversation. When they did try to find out about me, I changed the subject or lied about my past. It was traumatic for me. I didn't dare to talk about it. I didn't want anyone that close to me. Sarah and I were only together for about three months. I had so many questions, so many out of control emotions. It was best to keep it all to myself. What did it matter anyway?

Instead, I let my outgoing personality shine. I loved going to school for the social aspect—Jairo and I often acted the part of class clowns together—but I remained disconnected academically. My report cards remained the same. I did just enough not to fail classes. Even after several years in America, I had to spend so much mental energy repeating what teachers were asking me before I understood that it took a few seconds for me to respond to questions. My English foundation had been jarred by learning two new languages in Ghana, and my test-taking skills were underdeveloped.

Math had always been my worst subject. For that God sent me an angel: a teacher at Seneca Valley whom few other students liked.

I was a year behind my eleventh-grade peers mathematically, and I hated algebra. Mrs. Federline taught math differently. She was strict, and she had strong classroom rules, which put off the other students, but when she spoke I listened, and I began to like algebra. In her class my confidence brimmed, and my excitement for learning returned. Not since Liberia had I felt that way about math.

Mrs. Federline took an interest in me when no one else did. She often kept me after school. She checked my planner and made sure I wrote down all my assignments. She helped me fill out my agenda and write down the homework I had for other classes.

One day after school, I told Mrs. Federline that my mother had died. I don't know why I said it—I hadn't told anyone since I was in Africa. I shared no other details. Nothing about my father or the war. I began to cry a bit. She didn't press. She was kind, and that comforted me.

All she said was, "I am sorry to hear that." She mentioned something about the funeral, and I quickly responded, "Oh, don't worry about it."

English literature was a different story. Mrs. Monte, my English teacher, was an avid reader and lover of the classics.

Unfortunately, *The Great Gatsby*, Shakespeare, and the *Odyssey* were a total mystery to me—not to mention boring. I didn't read much. I had never set foot in a library until my arrival in Maryland.

Mrs. Monte made a habit of sitting in her chair and reading demonstratively to the class. All the students admired her enthusiasm. Volunteers sprang up around the class to read paragraphs out loud. Some days I even wished I could volunteer to read, but my Ghanaian/Liberian accent, which was barely perceptible in conversation, became very noticeable when I read out loud.

When I was called upon to read, I refused!

This caused me to lose class participation points, which were the easiest way to pass the class. Although I had four languages dangling around my brain, my American English vocabulary languished, and my understanding of cultural norms was limited. As a result, the comprehension quizzes that followed the daily readings were a nightmare. There were many quizzes where I received zeros.

The English Literature requirement to graduate became my biggest obstacle. As the year came to a close, final exams came and went, and I was in jeopardy of not graduating from high school. Failing English, a language I spoke fluently, was a shame that would last a lifetime. Not graduating high school would only confirm what almost everyone close to me already seemed to think about me: I was stupid.

I knew my performance in school wouldn't win the favor of my family, so around Christmas of my junior year, I began applying for after-school jobs. This too was initially a failure. Most of my friends had retail jobs: Giant, Safeway, Sears, J. C. Penney, Blockbuster, and Hallmark. I applied to these places and never once received a call or an interview. The managers at Giant turned me down more than once. I kept trying because Giant would have been a perfect job for me. It was about a quarter of a mile from where we lived, and I walked past it twice a day heading to school and back. All I needed was a chance to prove what a hard worker I was. The whole process was devastating.

Katrina Briggs, a girl in my chemistry class, worked at Burger King. She lived down the street, and we often walked home from school together. She offered to talk to the manager at Burger King about me, and with her help, I got hired!

I ran all the way home and told my sister-in-law the news. She was not as excited as I was: at $4.50 an hour it was not a great job. I still felt it was better than nothing. I was in charge of cleaning the lobby and taking out trash, which I did with pride from four o'clock to eight o'clock three days a week.

Having a job boosted my self-esteem immensely. Receiving my first paycheck was like a dream—$159.01! I could not contain my excitement. I could afford to go to the barbershop. As a result of my pride and diligence in taking out the trash and doing anything the manager asked, I moved up to taking orders. My work ethic was praised by the managers. Most days I came in half an hour early and left late. I walked home stinking of grease and fries, but proud of myself.

* * *

As my high school years came to a close, I fought just to stay afloat in most classes. Many students I knew were anticipating graduation and moving on to college. While some students could lighten their schedules, I was behind, so I had to take almost a full load of required classes—and pass them all—to graduate. As graduation loomed, I was careful not to include myself in many celebratory gatherings.

Classmates were talking about where they were headed for college. I watched college sports and had some idea about the number of colleges in the United States, but I had no idea

how to get there. Casually, I made the mandatory visit to my
school's career center and looked up some colleges.

The academic requirements for college admission were
steep. There were some schools that I had a chance of getting
into with my GPA, but my SAT scores were low. The average
tuition for most schools was tens of thousands of dollars—
while the activity fees for high school were forty dollars, and
my family had a hard time paying that. College was not an
option. I didn't worry too much about that. The challenge I
had to face first was graduation.

On a quiet Friday afternoon, long after all the students
had gone home, I walked up the stairs into Mrs. Monte's room.

"I know why you're here, Marcus," she said before I could
speak. "You want to know if you will graduate, right—if you
passed my class?" She paused.

In that long moment, I thought about all the times I had
fallen asleep in her class because I couldn't understand what
we read, all the times I brought back food from lunch and
sat in the back of the class eating fries from Burger King. I
remembered all the times I played class clown and laughed
to distract everyone from reading. Now I was at her mercy,
needing her to tell me if I would walk across the stage with
my friends—if I had avoided the embarrassment of failing
English and not graduating from high school.

Behind her desk, over huge stacks of paper, Mrs. Monte
looked at me over her glasses. She glared at me.

"By the skin of your teeth." She winked at me and broke
into a smile. "You made it."

"Thank you so much, Mrs. Monte!" I managed to blurt out.

I ran out of her room. On my way down the stairs, I ran into
Jairo Solano, who remained one of my best friends. The look
on his face was the same look I'd had as I walked up the stairs
a few minutes earlier. He was headed to Mrs. Monte's room.

"Can you wait for me, Marcus?" he asked.

"Ok," I replied.

A few minutes later he too emerged smiling, "I'm graduating! Yeah, baby!" he shouted. Together we walked to Burger King and had lunch. We reminisced about our rough days at Paint Branch and looked to the future, discussing our plans (or lack thereof) after high school.

***

That day, and again at graduation, I couldn't contain my smile. I had finally accomplished something that I was proud of.

After the ceremony, I walked out onto the steps of DAR Constitution Hall in Washington, D.C. Friends were all around with their families. My school journey, which had begun in March of 1983 and spanned three countries, was coming to an end on June 2, 1997. I'd just turned eighteen.

I had done nothing to celebrate my birthday. In fact, I commemorated the day by working my first legal eight-hour day. My emotions fluctuated from pride to sadness. Only two people came to see me graduate: Boye and Sister Lady were there. I knew they had lost a lot of confidence in me since we arrived in the United States. I felt like an underachiever who did not deserve to be celebrated. Seneca Valley High School allotted each student eight tickets for family and friends to attend the graduation ceremony. While my friends were asking for extras, I had a surplus. My family was thousands of miles away. My adopted family of newly acquainted aunts and uncles in the United States were all too busy to attend the proudest moment of my life to that point.

The two people whom I would have given anything to see smiling back at me from the balcony of the auditorium were no longer walking the earth.

Still, I was grateful. I had been reluctant to come to the United States. I wanted to remain close to Liberia. My brother and his wife blessed me with one of the greatest gifts I have ever received when they brought me along with them to the United States. They accepted a lot of responsibility when they made the tough choice to bring me with them. They could have sent me back to Liberia to struggle, but they decided to give me a better future.

At graduation, I greeted many of my friends and met their parents, aunts, and uncles. That afternoon I realized how lonely I really was in this life. Once again I became paralyzed by fear, fear of my future.

I wore my green graduation gown all the way home. People on the train congratulated me and asked, "What are you going to do?"

"I am going to college," I responded. That was a lie. I had not applied to a single college or university.

After the graduation ceremony I returned home and sat alone and cried. I'd received exactly one graduation gift, from my boss at Burger King.

∗ ∗ ∗

My future was rarely discussed. Burger King, the library, and home was my routine. I kept to myself. I was a mystery to everyone. To many around me, it seemed I was resigning myself to a life of mediocrity. I had a job that I took very seriously. I had many associates but no true friends. I shared a house with a family but rarely felt at home. My world essentially consisted of me and only me.

Sister Lady and Boye had two young children, and I sometimes felt like a burden. That summer I moved into the unfinished basement with the few things I owned. I had to start paying rent too, now that I was eighteen—which took most of the money I made at Burger King. I slept on a sofa that was too short for me. The bar in the middle of the couch was unforgiving. It hurt my back, my hips hurt, and the cement floor was too cold to sleep on, but at least the room afforded me solitude. What no one knew was that almost every night of the week, when I came home stinking of hamburgers and fries, I cried myself to sleep and plotted my return to Liberia. I covered my face so that no one would hear me weeping. I was struggling with life, and I didn't know what to do.

My steady diet of Burger King meant I did not eat much at home anymore. Dreading coming home to my basement room, I would walk the streets of Germantown until late at night with absolutely nothing to do. Sometimes I would play basketball until two or three o'clock in the morning. Looking back now, I realize I could have gotten involved in some trouble, but I never did drugs, never attended parties, and never drank. I just existed—existed alone.

I wanted to go to college, but my mind drifted back to a more sinister plan from the past: revenge.

Part of me wanted to move on and forget that my father had been murdered. I hadn't spoken of it in years. Part of me cried and held on to the past.

I decided the United States Army was my only way to escape the pain I endured inside and the isolation I felt at home—and it was a pathway to the revenge I wished to exact. When this plan came to me, what I had been planning since I was twelve years old suddenly seemed within my reach. I contacted a recruiter and officially enlisted.

On December 30, 1997, I was to report for Basic Training. In the meantime, I registered at community college and took some remedial reading and math classes.

At night my thoughts drifted off to what life would be like in the army. I was secretly happy that I was finally taking my first steps toward my goal. I would kill anyone who had anything to do with the death of my father.

In the army I'd learn to use a gun well. I'd learn how to interrogate, how to keep my emotions from taking over. Then finally, I'd kill him, whoever he was. He would really, finally be dead.

I would accomplish something that I, and my family, could be proud of.

CHAPTER 18

Jolted Awake

I ended up at Fort Leonard Wood, Missouri, for Basic Training at the end of 1997.

Sleep was a luxury. Nights were short. But life in the army was just right for me. I had the feeling I was doing something with my life, and I was accomplishing my goal of learning military technique and skills that I could use to go back and avenge the death of my father and the innocent people that were killed by the rebels.

Mornings began like this: Drill Sergeant Johnson screaming at the top of his lungs.

"Get your sorry asses up! This barracks smells like shit! You have five minutes minus three to get that buffer going and make up your bunks." He barked out so many instructions in so little time. I jolted out of bed, running around confused. *What should I do first?* I was still fatigued from the day before and my brain filled with cobwebs. *Should I open the window to get the smell out, make my bunk, go brush my teeth, or get the broom and start sweeping so that someone can start buffing the floor?*

All the recruits were thinking the same way I was, so we ran into each other, to the disgust of our drill sergeant. He used every cuss word in the American English vocabulary with alarming regularity and great versatility—in every different part of speech. Mrs. Monte, my English teacher, would have been proud and appalled.

Drill Sergeant Johnson was superhuman. The man never showed an ounce of fatigue or weakness—he never slept! He was there at lights out at 9:30 p.m., and most days he woke us up at 3:30 a.m. His uniform was always crisply ironed—every crease was razor sharp. His face was clean shaven, his boots perfectly polished and shined. He led us through morning exercises and trained us on army drill and ceremony—my favorite part. We marched to his voice in cadence singing army songs.

The eighteen-hour days were busy. We had so little downtime that I forgot what day it was. But day and night, the memory of the people I saw lying in the streets of Monrovia years earlier was fresh. I dreamt of slaughtering hundreds of rebels by myself. I envisioned rebels as we trained, my anger fueling my action.

✳ ✳ ✳

Halfway through Basic Training, my military career slammed to a halt.

I was diagnosed with a severe heart murmur and a liver problem. I went through another sudden shock. I was medically discharged.

One day I was pushing through the extreme stress of training, the next I was dropped from the program and on my way back to Boye's house.

I was totally devastated. How would I avenge my father's death?

I was ashamed when I returned home. I had failed once again. My brother worked all the time to feed his family and the rest of my family back in Liberia whom I had not talked to in years. Back on my unforgiving couch, I plotted my next step in this misery of time between my birth and death.

Why is this happening to me?

I felt like no one in the world cared what was going on with me. *I* didn't even care. Most of my friends were away at college and moving on, while I had been rejected by the Army. I was disappearing.

At this point, God and church were the last topics on my mind. He, above all people, had forgotten me. He had taken away so much from me. I determined that God was just an idea people made up to make themselves feel good, to make them dance in church, to give them a reason to show off their fancy clothes on Sunday. If he was real, he would not have broken my heart and taken my mother away so early or allowed men to kill my father and destroy my country.

I resorted to my routine of working and shooting hoops by myself until the wee hours of the morning. I found comfort in being alone and dealing with my sadness and rejection. I avoided the possibility of failure. My only friends had no aspirations.

To pass the time and try to make something of myself, I enrolled back in Montgomery Community College and went to the library. I read everything I could get my hands on that interested me. Reading helped me pass the time between work and sleep. Rather than coming home after work, I would go to the library and stay until it closed. The library helped me escape my world of pain.

I got a job at a Kohl's department store. It was a better job than working at Burger King because I got to dress up, and customers treated me with a bit more respect. With Christmas fast approaching, the store was busy. I enjoyed working during the Christmas season because I liked being busy, and everyone seemed to be in a light mood. On top of that, it was one of the first Christmases when I could actually afford to get gifts for my nephews, Keith and Michael—a reason to feel proud of myself.

∗ ∗ ∗

I was scheduled for a double shift on Christmas Eve. In a family of five with one bathroom, every morning was a game of "who could make it in there first." That morning my brother beat me to the bathroom. I hurriedly put on my khakis and a decent shirt and tie and ran off to work. Boye was shaving as I ran upstairs, hurriedly said "good-bye," and began my two-mile walk to work. I had given up begging for someone to teach me how to drive so I could get a license and resigned myself to walking everywhere.

At the start of my walk, the day felt filled with possibilities—a now-rare optimism for me. After the double shift ended, I would meet my friend Patrice and hurry over to Lake Forest Mall to do some last minute shopping for my family.

As I expected, the store was busy. I frantically tried to keep pace with impatient last-minute customers and demanding managers.

At about noon our neighbor, Bruce, came to the store looking for me. Bruce and I had a very cordial relationship, solidified by snow shoveling. We had spent about four hours a day together for three consecutive days clearing the snow in the cul-de-sac we all shared. I liked Bruce, but now I was not in the mood to chat. I tried to shrug him off but he was insistent.

Finally he leaned over and whispered to me, "Your brother just had a heart attack!"

My heart sank. I dropped what I was doing and walked right out of Kohl's (I never returned). As he drove me home, he mustered all of his diplomacy, and said, "Your brother was taken to the hospital, he was not breathing, and paramedics are trying to revive him." He went on with more details, but the more he talked, the less I listened. I drifted into my world of hurt once again.

Why is this happening, AGAIN! I thought to myself. During the ride home, I began replaying scenes from the night

Ma died. I replayed scenes from the Methodist church back in Monrovia. I replayed scenes from the day I found out Pa had died. These days and moments all began to run together in my mind as we rode toward the house.

At home, I burst through the door to find the house in disarray and no one home. The couch had been moved, the Christmas tree was lying on its side, and the trash can in the kitchen was filled to the brim with used medical supplies. I told Bruce to head home and leave me to myself.

"Will you be all right?" Bruce asked.

"Yeah, I guess," I mumbled.

Now that I needed to drive, I could not. Alone, I walked through the house and tried to piece together exactly what had occurred. In stunned silence I sat in the kitchen staring at the plastic wrapping of emergency medical supplies in the trash. A gradual sense of helplessness gripped me. My knees shook. After a few minutes of disorientation, I began to ask myself some questions: where were Keith and Michael? Where was Sister Lady? Was my brother going to be all right? How could he have a heart attack? He was thirty-eight years old and skinny!

The doorbell rang. Mr. Togba, from church, came in.

"Let's go!" he said, motioning toward his car. I followed him silently, without question. On our way to the hospital he explained more about what had happened.

"There was no one in the house when he had the heart attack. He is in extremely critical condition. He probably won't make it." Mr. Togba was not known for tact. He looked me in my eyes as the words left his mouth and pierced my fragile heart.

The old familiar feeling of losing someone close to me took over. Tears filled my eyes. *Not again. Not again!* I screamed inside. I gasped for air, leaning my head on the window of the car. I blinked hard. I pinched myself. I had to be having a nightmare.

This was real. I couldn't breathe.

The waiting room at the hospital was as quiet as could be. Aunty SJ was there and explained the situation as she knew it.

My brother had had a massive heart attack while Sister Lady was out grocery shopping, and my nephews were running around the house. He had lost oxygen to his brain—at that point no one knew for how long. He was now in a coma.

As I sat motionless, trying not to break down and scream my lungs out, I overheard someone, maybe a doctor, saying, "Even if he makes it out of the coma, the best we can hope for is an immobile man who will need help to do basic things."

Boye was the only family member whom I'd always known for sure was alive and well. Everyone else was in Liberia, where the political climate was as stable as a ship in a violent storm. Boye kept in touch with our brothers in Liberia periodically, but I never felt sure that bad news wasn't coming when he heard from them.

I began to envision the possibility of living life as the only surviving Doe. What if I was the only one left? I didn't think I could face that future. I wanted to burst into the room and beg my brother to wake up.

Please don't leave me alone in this world!

Hours turned into a day, and I was back at home in the basement. I woke up Christmas morning and cried. I cycled through anger, exhaustion, and despair.

On the night of December 26, 1998, the prognosis was grim. It had been two days, and there were still no signs of life from Boye. I got on my knees, and I asked God *WHY*.

Why had he taken my parents?

Why was my life filled with tragedy?

Why had he forgotten me?

I talked to God as if he was right there in front of me. I listed all of the things that I blamed him for: Ma, Pa, the war, the separation from my family, their suffering, my current state, my rejection, my disappointments—and my brother, my beloved brother.

I had heard people talk about a life-changing experience, letting go of the past and letting God handle the future. I'd never prayed like that before. I decided to try it out for myself, to see if God was real and if he listened to prayers—I was going to try this prayer thing again. I was sincere.

I wept for hours in the complete darkness

Guilt overwhelmed me. Everyone close to me seemed to die, and I was sure that it was because of something I had done that my family was suffering. God shifted my guilt away from my circumstances to my attitude: hatred and anger had been destroying me for years and were still seething in my heart. I had no other response to life than a cycle of lashing out and withdrawing.

I could continue in that life, but I decided instead to move toward belief. I begged God to forgive me. I told him I'd live life his way.

I would let go of revenge and rage. I asked God, from the sincerest and deepest part of my heart, to please save my brother.

✳ ✳ ✳

On the third or fourth day after my brother's heart attack—it is hard to remember—I was sitting in the kitchen when the phone rang.

When I answered Aunty SJ whispered, "Roosevelt woke up today."

Her words were an incredible relief. God had heard my prayers, and he had answered according to my desire. He said "yes" to me. A massive weight lifted from my shoulders.

A few days after that I went back to the hospital, and Boye looked at me as if he didn't recognize me.

"Jungle Boy?" He had not called me by my childhood name for years.

"Yeah, Boye," I replied. I realized he was not yet himself. I sat and watched as Sister Lady showed him pictures of our home. He did not recognize it. The joy of having him alive was dampened by the realization that he had a long road of recovery ahead.

Boye stayed at the hospital for weeks, and then he was transferred to a rehabilitation center in Washington, D.C. He walked normally but very slowly, and he was given a pace-maker. He recognized me, and eventually he began to recall the house and family members, but his mind seemed to be stuck in Ghana. He struggled to remember that we were in the United States.

I rarely went to visit him, and when I did it hurt me to see my brother in such a state. It scared me too. I felt vulnerable for him. He was struggling with the basics of memory, and we rarely talked. He worked with an occupational therapist who stopped by sometimes while I was there. I was scared that he would never recover.

Once he came home from the hospital, I had to take re-sponsibility for myself and the family. I had to step up and do the things that Boye could not. It was now my job to keep the lines of communication open with our family in Africa.

I knew Boye had been keeping in touch with our family in Africa, but as my relationship with Boye had drifted, and my life spiraled into confusion, I had chosen to ignore my past. I had shut out the possibility of communicating with my family. But since my brother's heart attack they called fre-quently, starving for new information about his condition and his recovery. Mocco called, Gahien called, and so did Molley.

These calls and conversations made me realize how far out of touch I was with my brothers. Even though I missed them, I had depended on Boye to connect with them. Talking with them now was as refreshing as it was painful. It opened up my longing for them. I loved hearing their voices.

The next few months crawled by. Boye wasn't allowed to drive, so I got my driver's license, and he became my passenger. I took him to his rehabilitation sessions and doctor appointments. In the past, I had always treasured time alone in a car with him, when I would ride along and ask questions about life.

It was almost like old times, but the roles were reversed. Now I drove, while he asked the questions, and he asked questions about everything. Sometimes he asked the same questions more than once. I didn't mind. I was just happy to have him back. Sometimes he laughed at himself and his situation, letting his failure to recall basic information amuse him. Most days I held back the tears and silently prayed that my brother would regain his memory and his former life.

Boye was my hero when I was seven years old. I'd reached twenty, and he was still my hero. In fact, I looked up to him more than I did when I was a young boy. My brother had brought his entire family to another country and sustained them through the American socio-economic maze, and he had done it well. In those days with Boye, I continued to cry out to God now that his mind, his most precious asset, what I most admired about him, was failing him. I asked that it would be restored.

My relationship with Christ began to guide my life and my decisions, little by little. God answered my prayer, and yet there was still so much to pray for. Rage was still ingrained in me, and my future was unclear. Nevertheless, my life began a slow 180-degree turn. Likening my new life to my newfound ability to drive, I imagined I was in a three-point turn. My life had been heading straight into a dead end, but I had successfully put the car in reverse and with God's guidance turned it around. It had taken several tries, but I pulled it off.

As the months went by, Boye's recall began to come back, and he regained his ability to drive. His health had gotten better, but he was still not completely himself. He was much quieter than he had been in the past. I rarely knew what he was thinking or doing. It was hard for him, but he gradually returned to work. His recovery, though slow, gave me hope, and as he came back into his place in the family, it opened the chance for me to do something new.

I had achieved a little academic success at community college, so I applied and was accepted to Frostburg State University. A new chapter in my life began to unfold.

I was heading two hours away from home to pursue the academic achievement that had always been a dream for me, ever since I was a boy in Liberia admiring the education of men like Boye and Uncle Nat.

Frostburg State University was all I imagined the American college life to be. It was filled with people of different races and nationalities. I quickly made many friends and went out for the school soccer and track and field teams. A sense of pride was beginning to grow in me, and I felt a sense of accomplishment with each passing year as I won a few awards on the athletic fields as a varsity soccer player and made strong friendships with many of my classmates.

Personal independence started to seem within reach for me, but my commitment to God and new life in Christ was still in its infancy. There was still much more God wanted me to learn. In that basement after Christmas I had taken a step toward letting go of my hatred, but God wanted me to take hold of something else. I had not yet come to that realization.

Even with my growing faith, my vengeful fantasies followed me everywhere I went. My imagination and my daydreams grew more gruesome as I got older. What was born in my mind at age twelve had been developing into something I couldn't control: vitriol for the men who killed my father.

Hate was comfortable for me. It helped me cope. I lugged it around, and it became as necessary and as useful as my right arm.

No matter how far I got in life, I still reverted back to my revenge-fantasy when things did not go right. Whenever someone treated me poorly, or I had a rough day, I'd clench my jaw and mentally begin to sharpen the family ax, a long black handle with a sharp black head, the ax that my family had used to kill sheep and goats when we were living in Barnersville.

The scenes appeared whenever my mind went idle: on the bus from school, between bites at a meal, just before I slept at night, even in church. In fact, more often than not, church was where I daydreamed about killing my father's murderer. I sat in the back rows of the sanctuary trying to listen, and he would appear.

In my vision, I would chase him, and I would kill him, sometimes with a gun, other times the ax. I would have my revenge in this life. Again and again, I dreamt of plunging our family ax into the ribs of the faceless man who killed my father. For years, I replayed that scene.

I killed this man over and over and over, but he never died.

CHAPTER 19

Facing Home

The day I graduated from Frostburg State University, all of my uncles and aunts braved the cold mid-December weather and the two-hour drive to western Maryland to see me graduate. After my guests had left, I was alone to pack up my things: a few trash bags full of clothes, a stereo, odds and ends. It wasn't warm, but I wore my graduation gown anyway as I loaded up the car. I was beaming with pride.

As I set off down Interstate 68 in Maryland, lifted with the pride of my graduation, sadness began to creep in. I thought of my parents, and tears began to flow. I continued to drive, ready for my mind to go to its next fantasy—murder—as it always did when I wept like this. Picturing the culmination of my vengeance always made me feel better. So in my mind I sat on a stool and I began to sharpen the ax or load the gun. I waited for the faceless man to appear. It was a familiar routine.

Only this time, he didn't come.

I realized then that I wanted to end my mental relationship with him. I didn't want him to come anymore. This man had been present whenever I was alone. The day I graduated high school, he was there. When I got my first job, he was there. When I talked to my brothers for the first time after many years, he was there.

I made up my mind that I could not let him be there today, the day I finished college. I couldn't let him be there on the day I got married, I couldn't let him be there when I got my first professional job, and I wouldn't let him be there when my children were born. He controlled me. It had to stop.

Letting go of my escape was difficult. I relied on him to get me through bad days. I blamed him for my failures in life. I clung to the gruesome fantasy of ending his life in a worse way than he had ended Pa's. Forgiving him would mean I would have to face my own life, such as it was, and my own shortcomings. I would have to stop blaming this man I'd never even met.

* * *

Forgiveness is a long, seemingly impossible, process. I continued to cry through many nights. I felt like I betrayed my father by giving up on seeking "justice" for the man who took his life. How could I not kill my father's killer? How could I let him live in peace when he had ruined my life? Why not ruin his life and let his children suffer?

That last question was where healing began. I realized that God did not appoint me to enact that kind of vengeful justice. My attempts would only further the pain I felt as a fatherless son. The pain of not having a father is something only the fatherless can understand. Was I the kind of person who wanted to do that to someone else?

After graduation, I set out on a rocky course, spending my summers at camp in Maine and taking teaching work wherever I could find it. I finished at Frostburg in December 2003 and worked as a substitute teacher until the fall of 2004, when I was hired to teach middle school US and World History at Church of the Redeemer Christian School, following the interview with Mrs. Burke that I mentioned when we began this story. I worked there from 2004 to 2006 and spent my summers at camp. I went to France from 2006 to 2007.

In the summer of 2008 I told my story to my friends at camp and then told it again at Cornerstone Gospel Church, opening up my past to others for the first time in years. I struggled to come to grips with my newfound honesty in the midst of my questions about forgiveness. I had fallen into a pattern of reinventing myself for my own purposes. The habit of lying about myself and hiding who I was that began the day I was prepared to save myself by saying *Marcus Davis* was shaken as I faced the idea that God might want to reinvent me. As I considered and spoke about the things I had experienced, I began to reflect on how God had showed his goodness to me in the midst of my painful life, and to consider what purpose God might have for me, where God might want to take me and my story.

I was hired for another teaching job in Denver, Colorado, and arrived there on August 26, 2008. I was settling into adult life, but my path seemed set for a destination that felt both inevitable and unthinkable at the same time: my homeland.

For years I had told myself I would never return to Liberia— and then I told myself I'd only go back to get revenge. Once I turned to Christ and loosened my grip on revenge, I chose not to think about the possibility of returning to Liberia. I would leave it behind me. And yet I wanted to see my brothers, my mother's grave, my home, my cousins, aunts, and uncles.

Still, I was crippled by horrible memories and by fear: there was too much hurt there. *It is too risky. What if you die there? You have a good life in America. Quit living in the past. There is nothing in Liberia worth going back to,* I told myself repeatedly. But I could not leave my family behind. I could not leave my country behind.

More than that, God kept bringing one word to my mind: *forgive.*

But how could I?

Was it truly possible to be untethered from the burden of hate? Was it possible to face my sorrow? Would it be possible for my hate and my forgiveness to meet in a human face? The more I thought about it, the more I became sure: I had to share the good news of what God had done in my life. I had to find the man who killed my father.

I had to forgive him.

* * *

After years of wavering, years of agonizing about the trip at night, I made the decision to go in December 2009.

I was thirty years old. I had been out of college for six years. It had been eleven years since my relationship with God began after Boye's heart attack. Nineteen years since I left Liberia.

I booked my flight home to Liberia in April 2010, after I had saved up enough money and enough courage to make the trip. My anxious anticipation faded. Instead, fear and a strange paralysis seemed to fill my gut. I was actually doing it.

I was actually going back to Liberia.

The trip would take me through Belgium and the Ivory Coast before arriving in Monrovia. I was scheduled to set foot on Liberian soil on June 30, 2010—almost exactly twenty years since I had last seen my siblings on June 4, 1990.

Sitting behind my desk in my quiet classroom in Colorado, a world away from Liberia, I began to imagine a day twenty years in the making, a return to West Africa—something few Liberians living in the States ever do. Fresh memories from the land I left as a child came flooding back. Liberia, the land where my parents and grandparents lay dead, where my brothers lived, and where ten thousand memories that had lain dormant in my brain would come alive.

It was the land where I hoped to find the man who killed my father. At that thought alone, tears filled my eyes, and I had to contain my emotions for fear that someone might barge into my classroom and find me crying.

My main goal became staying alive until June. Paranoid as it may seem, I took every conceivable precaution that spring. I cut down on my hiking and running, even curbed my propensity for excessive speeding on the road. I ate a healthier diet. I hadn't survived this long just to die before my trip. The anticipation had built up in me so much that some days I drove straight past my apartment heading west on Highway 285 in central Colorado, and before I knew it I reached the quaint, scenic town of Conifer, dreaming of all the possibilities of my trip. I often drove for hours at a time, deep in thought. I dreamed about the food. I worried about the dangers. I imagined I could be poisoned and suffer the same fate my mother endured twenty-one years earlier.

As for my family back in Liberia, they had no idea I would soon be in their midst. I tried to make it a surprise.

The internal struggle over the wisdom of going back to Liberia sometimes got the better of me. At times the doubts overcame my faith. Fighting in Liberia had continued until 2003, with brief respites and countless ceasefire agreements during those fourteen years. Even after several years of relative peace, it was still a very broken country. If I were to die during my trip, the blame for my untimely, preventable death would fall squarely on my shoulders. The United States State Department had a long list of travel warnings and recommendations about Liberia. Reading the five-page packet about my safety while in Liberia deepened my panic. By late May, I was in terrible doubt about my trip.

Finally, in June, I started to relax. I had jumped through all the costly legal hoops—immunizations, a visa, and more. The packing process was difficult: I had to anticipate all my needs in Africa, think of helpful items to leave behind, and stay under the airline's fifty-pound weight limit. Soon all that was left was to count down the days until my departure.

✳ ✳ ✳

I faded into my own world, imagining what I was about to do. I could picture myself hugging and kissing my sister and brothers, standing where my mother and father once stood, walking the halls of J. L. Gibson Memorial School where I once ran with moral innocence and youthful bravado. What would Caroline look like? And Gahien, Molley, and Mocco? Had the war scarred them the way it had me? How had they handled Pa's death? Were Liberians accepting of people like me now, people with the last name Doe? I envisioned myself in a world where I understood the language and the culture, a world where I would reconnect with my past, and come face to face with my sorrows—where I would let them go once and for all.

This trip was a practical, tangible part of letting go of my past, handing it over to the Lord Jesus Christ. What a difficult thing to do! Now there would be no more excuses about why I was not able to move forward emotionally and spiritually.

When I read the Bible, forgiveness seemed to jump up and bite me all the time. It was easy to forgive little things in America, but I had this huge burden to forgive. Since college, my faith had become more and more important to me. I read and prayed regularly and I even shared my faith with others. But I held on to this burden, this still-open wound of my past. I wanted to reconnect with my family, face and forgive the man who killed my father, and walk in solitude and comfort on my own soil. I prayed for healing.

The biggest question that loomed over the trip: how would I handle coming face to face with the rebel who took Pa's life? Would I even be able to find him? Finding someone you knew in post-war Liberia was difficult enough, but I was trying to find someone who wouldn't want to be found. If I did find him, how would I handle it if he broke down, cried, and said he was sorry for what he did? How would I handle it if he was belligerent? What if he blew me off and didn't acknowledge my pain and effort to reconcile? Worse yet, what if he attacked me for fear that I had come to seek retribution?

Every so often, I would get so caught up in my thoughts, anticipating various scenarios and responses. I rehearsed the conversation, just as I'd spent years rehearsing revenge. I would sit at my dining room table, pull out a chair opposite me, and begin to talk to the imaginary man. I imagined him dark-skinned, with a wrinkled forehead, bright teeth, perhaps a slight build. I imagined a man once powerful but now limited to the corners of society, living with his past demons. I also imagined an unapologetic man, a man who cussed at me when I approached him, and a man who was unashamed, unremorseful for killing my father.

I practiced my questions, and listened attentively to his responses. There were times when I began to tear up.

I asked him, "So why did you do it? Was my father cooperative? Was he angry? Did he beg you to let him go? Did he tell you about his family? Did he tell you he had a little boy somewhere who would be heartbroken when he found out? How did you kill him? Where did you kill him? Did you treat his body with dignity? What were his last words? Did you know of him before the war? Do you even remember who I am talking about or was my father just another person you humiliated and killed?"

I imagined I would tell him the kind of man my father was, how he was a lover of Latin, of Shakespeare, of African presidential history. How he loved to farm, or how great a storyteller he was. How he loved to exercise, or how he wept uncontrollably on the living room floor the night Ma died.

I would get angry and scream. *Why did you do it?* Over and over and over I would ask him. My voice would rise a few notches, and I would stand up out of my dining room chair as I got louder and angrier. I would walk over to him and stand over him, blocking out the sun with my six-foot, two-hundred-pound frame. I would stick my finger in his face, poking his chest and intimidating him. I would spit in his face while I spoke angrily, on purpose, just as I imagined he had done to my father twenty years earlier. At this point in the conversation, my anger would reach its peak, and I would restrain myself from attacking him. Finally my imagination would relinquish its grip.

I would sit back down in my chair and sob uncontrollably.

Then I practiced saying the words "I forgive you" through the tears. I would compose myself and shake the murderer's hand.

"I understand you were following orders, or not. I understand you were under the influence of cane juice or opium."

I knew I needed to be composed when I finally met the man who killed my father. What would it prove if I went all that way, and waited all these years, just to break down and kill the man? I would be like everyone else, not having truly forgiven him. If I was angry and violent, it would contradict the love that I now possessed. Though it would be hard to walk away from a man who had done so much harm to me and had stolen so many of my memories and dreams, I knew I had to let love take its course and let forgiveness prevail.

＊＊＊

The dawn of June 29, I rolled out of bed knowing that my journey back in time was about to begin. My first thought as I opened my eyes was, *It's my mother's birthday; she would have been sixty-eight years old today!*

Most years I argued with myself about whether I should celebrate her life on her birthday or solemnly go about my

day. Today, I chose to celebrate. I thanked God that she gave
birth to me. I knew I would be at her grave in a matter of days.
Among all the details I anticipated about my trip, this one
moment had come to mind again and again. I had written a
note to her that I planned to bury at her grave. It updated her
on my life, let her know where I was on earth, what my plans
were, and told her that I still missed her terribly. This seemingly futile act brought me a measure of peace. I felt as though
I was in fact communicating as I wrote, even though Ma was
dead and had never been able to read. I carefully packed the
letter along with my Bible and the journal that I received as a
gift from my friends at work.

As the morning went by, I received phone calls from close
friends and family wishing me luck and safe travels. They knew
of my plan to find the man who had murdered my father, so
the calls were laced with an underlying tone of sadness.

"If I do not see you again, it has been nice to know you,"
some said. They'd long since stopped asking why I wanted to
meet this man in the first place.

Many of my friends wanted me to just let it go, but in
my heart I realized that facing this man would bring healing for me, emotionally and spiritually. It would be closure.
As counterintuitive as it seemed, I knew meeting him would
bring me peace.

Now, my only vision was of repentance and admission of
guilt. I pictured myself hugging the man who took my father's
life. Perhaps we'd be under an almond tree in his yard, and the
conversation would eventually work its way to that day twenty
years earlier. I would cry, but I could never quite predict what
his reaction or mood would be. I hoped he'd even agree to be
in a photo with me.

There was one thing I hadn't told anyone: I wanted the
man's life to change because of me. I wanted him to see that

what he meant for evil was in fact part of what God was using to win this man into his kingdom.

I had not shared my plans to find the man with any family members. The last time I had discussed my father's murderer with any of them was when Gahien told me about him eighteen years before in a letter. In our emails Gahien had hinted at talking about the man, but we never did. My emotions—and my life—had changed so much since that time. Instead of wanting to end the murderer's life, I wanted to bring light into his world. I felt he was responsible for my hate-filled teenage years, but Jesus had set me free from that darkness, and he could set my father's killer free as well. A strange sense of excitement filled my being, and I was calm and confident that the meeting would turn out to be positive. I knew justice might take its course in the aftermath of the war, but that wasn't my concern any longer. We both needed healing, and that was why I looked forward to the meeting.

That afternoon, I sat and waited for my brother Boye, who would drive me to the airport to begin my journey. I had flown to Maryland to see them before going on to Liberia. I shook Boye's hand and bid him goodbye at Dulles International Airport, boarded the plane, said a prayer, and faded off to sleep on my way to Brussels. The eight-hour flight seemed endless. Having waited twenty years, I was now mere hours from my family.

* * *

My anticipation of finally being in Liberia hit a fever pitch as the flight from Abidjan, Ivory Coast, touched down at Roberts International Airport at about eight o'clock on the evening of June 30th, 2010. The other travelers were suddenly moving very slowly. The sight of the silhouette of the trees through the airplane windows brought some calm to the screaming within me. The doors finally opened, and the passengers began to descend from the plane.

I was home!

The air smelled of palm trees and sea water. The heat was stifling. It was all so familiar. The bounce in my step was undeniable as I walked onto Liberian soil for the first time in almost twenty years. The long road back to Barnersville was almost complete. I tried to keep my composure, but it was nearly impossible.

I heard the strange and welcoming sound of beautiful Liberian English all around me. These were my people. This was my country. I wanted to hug everyone I saw.

I had my American passport in my right hand and my book bag slung over my right shoulder. I looked at the signs in the immigration area: *Citizens* and *Visitors*. Filing in line with the rest of the visitors I pulled out my passport, absorbing the strangeness of being a visitor in my own land. On paper I was no longer a Liberian, yet I wanted to be a part of a land I had deserted so long ago—or that perhaps had deserted me.

Sweat poured from my forehead as my patience faded in the long line. Finally the immigration officer called me forward. The Liberian flag adorned his shoulder. His uniform was well-ironed, and his shoes were shiny.

"How long you staying, Mr. Doe?"

"One month, chief!" I replied, eager to express myself in my deepest Liberian accent. The officer did not seem to notice. In fact, he barely acknowledged me.

While I was waiting for the officer to send me on, another officer came into the tiny immigration passageway yelling, "Marcus! Marcus! Somebody named Marcus here?"

My old dormant sense of fear and imminent danger crept in. I didn't know whether to respond. The memories of the war, when people were killed for merely responding to their own name, came sharply to my mind. I decided there must be another Marcus here in the airport, so I ignored the officer screaming my name.

After a few more shouts, the officer left the welcome area and headed through the wooden door that led to baggage claim. I later found out someone had sent the security guard to find me and get me through security more quickly.

When I emerged from the immigration room, a strangely familiar face greeted me. It was a woman in her late twenties or perhaps early thirties.

"My husband, here is my husband!" She was staring right at me with her arms wide open, laughter in her eyes. I certainly wasn't married, and only my brothers knew of my visit, so I was taken aback. I'm sure my confusion was evident on my face, and she seemed to be enjoying whatever joke she was making.

I made my way down the hallway, and this familiar-looking woman gave me a hug. Then I realized who she was: my brother Gahien's wife, Evelyn. I apologized for not recognizing her—I had seen pictures of her when she married my brother. She introduced me to her friends as her husband. My Uncle JE was also at the airport to greet me. He drove us to Barnersville.

"I didn't know your husband was out of the country," one of Evelyn's friends said. She laughed and said, "I'm only kidding; this is his brother." The ladies did a double take.

"They look so much alike."

* * *

The drive home was a great test of my memory: Evelyn asked me if I could find my way from the airport to my house. After twenty years, I was able to navigate it perfectly, turn by turn. Despite the fatigue of travel, my brain was active, and my emotions were overflowing. Laughing and joking in the car as we drove closer and closer to my old home, I began to swell with pride, happiness, and sadness simultaneously. We passed the Samuel K. Doe Sports Complex, near my mother's grave. It was dark, so we didn't stop, but her death came crashing over me again. Then, as the gates to my former home opened, a smile overtook my grief. As soon as the car came to a stop in the back yard, I dashed out and walked briskly toward the house. My legs were shaking! Gahien and Mocco waited for me on the porch. I ran, smiling and crying at the same time. Mocco and Gahien had smiles on their faces. They were overjoyed to see me. I felt safe and cared for from the minute I got there. As we hugged, the sense of relief was tangible.

"Where is Caroline?" She was inside getting my room ready—the same room that we all slept in growing up.

The house was a lot smaller than I remembered: had it shrunk? Or had I grown that much? In fact, I was the tallest of my brothers now, but I didn't yet have my bearings.

I unloaded my bags, and then we sat as a family once again. But we were missing four people, two of whom had made our family possible and were gone forever. Boye remained in the United States, and Molley lived a few miles away across the city. The darkness of the streets kept him from joining the reunion.

Before we began to celebrate, I knew I needed some time alone with God just to say "thank you" for answering my prayers. He had answered another prayer—it was the least he deserved. I needed to talk to him, to process everything I was experiencing.

Sitting on the bed, I bowed my head and shut and my eyes, thanking God for a day that was twenty years in the making, a day that had sometimes felt so far away. Below the jubilation was a sense of sadness: *I wish my parents could see me now.* I was standing in the house they had built when I was born because they needed space for one more child. I cried. This, *this*, was my house, my home, the place prepared for me.

When I composed myself, I walked back out of the room. Staring at the walls, memories began to flood my mind, memories of family Bible readings, meals, and homework. This was where life began for me. I felt again the length of my physical and spiritual journey to this point, this place. Then I pushed the screen door and walked out into the late June, rainy-season Liberian heat. The feel reminded me of the hope and cleansing the rain brought to me when I was little. Would it do the same for me now?

There were so many stories to tell, so many memories: where would we start?

As I sat across from Gahien, Mocco, and Caroline, the laughter and stories began to flow. We were together on the same cement porch we shared for years. They were still here. They had aged and changed a bit, but their personalities sure had not. We joked about the habits we all shared. We talked about our parents—not their deaths but their lives—the fond memories and the tendencies that endeared them to us. My siblings' love for me showed. I felt like the little brother again.

The questions began to come. They were frustrated that I had not informed them of my arrival until three days prior. I had worried that word might spread, and I would be overwhelmed by visitors, but really I had no excuse. At first the questions we traded were fairly pedestrian, but as we continued the conversation, they began to increase in emotional intensity. I asked them about the days before and after Pa's death. I asked how they had survived living behind rebel lines. On that first night we didn't talk about Pa's death. But I did find out the exact date he was killed, August 24, 1990.

That night, I slept in my own home. I tossed and turned at first. The unrelenting heat of West Africa kept me awake, but I enjoyed it. The smell of the room reminded me of my childhood. Staring up at the ceiling, one part of me wished my father would push the door open and belt out his usual morning anthem: "School time, school time, school time!" I felt anxious and exhausted at the same time, relieved by the reunion, but anxious about the days ahead—would I really be able to find and forgive the man who murdered my father?

CHAPTER 20

What the Years Took Away

The night was short. I rose at the first sound of the rooster's crow. I opened the back door and sat on the porch, just like my father used to do. As the darkness faded and the horns of passing taxis and buses crushed the serenity of the morning, I sat in awe of my home, my hometown.

I couldn't wait to take to the roads of Barnersville, to fish in the swamps, to be recognized by neighbors. But I knew the neighborhood had changed. The war had scattered most of the people I'd known. Some had been killed in the war. Others had since died from the fear, stress, and worry that come with living in the aftermath of war. And there were those like me who had relocated to other countries.

I also knew I'd changed: being in Liberia as a visitor had risks. Robberies of visitors were common. Even so, I wasn't very worried about walking in Barnersville.

Slipping on my sneakers, I strolled to the front of the house where I ran into two gentlemen in law enforcement uniforms. I knew Mocco hired security guards to help ensure the safety of our home, but I hadn't met them yet. Their presence was a sign of the changes in the city. Security firms became popular in Liberia after the war, with the rise of unemployment and criminal activity. The guards seemed very surprised to see me, so I introduced myself.

"My name is Marcus. I am Caroline's little brother."

We shook hands, and I sat to talk with them. They welcomed me home and asked many questions about America. I tried to downplay the fact that I had just arrived, instead emphasizing the fact that I was born in Liberia and grew up right there in Barnersville. They were courteous and very well-spoken. As I walked toward the front gate, Stephen, the head officer, rushed to open it for me.

"I will walk with you to show you the area," he offered.

"Barnersville was my neighborhood," I said, proudly.

"Chief Marcus, let me walk with you!" he insisted.

I pushed down my pride and obliged. As I stepped out of the fence, Caroline came over quickly.

"Where you going, Jungle Boy?"

"Just going for a walk," I said.

"Wait until Gahien or Molley gets here before you leave."

I was still a little brother who needed to be protected, and now I was a foreigner in my own land. Was it that dangerous in Barnersville?

"There are some things you need to know, Chief Marcus," Stephen assured me.

Sinking into the wooden chair opposite my sister on the back porch, I resigned myself to enjoying the day at home until Molley showed up to see me.

My body had been running on pure adrenaline, so it was nice to just sit and take it all in. I just could not believe my dreams had come true, and my prayers had been answered all at once. My siblings were alive—not only that, they were doing well. I had nieces and nephews who called me uncle—four of whom I'd played with when we were all kids, but now there were nine more. It seemed like a dream, but it was better. It was real. I had prayed for something, and it came true.

By early afternoon, my favorite Liberian meal had been prepared, and Molley was on his way over. He was the only one I had not seen yet. My earliest memories always include Molley; he had taught me to catch ricebirds almost twenty-seven years earlier. As I reminisced about the traps we set and the birds we'd caught and released, his blue Volkswagen Passat pulled into the driveway and made its way to the back yard. I felt a surge of closeness, even after twenty years, as I watched his car pull up. I stepped off the porch. He got out of the car and all I could do was to fight back the tears.

I jogged toward him, and we embraced. We stood back from each other as we quickly examined each other and hugged again.

"Wow, you big and tall, Jungle Head!"

His affectionate nickname was a twist to my usual moniker because, as a child, I was skinny, and my head was disproportionately large. I hadn't seen a picture of Molley in years, but he was exactly how I remembered. I thanked him for coming to see me. He apologized for not being able to come sooner.

We laughed as we walked onto the porch, and he squeezed my shoulders, as if in disbelief. Tears of pride and joy welled in his eyes, and I could not help but feel the same emotions. On that very porch twenty-seven years earlier he taught me to catch ricebirds.

We sat down, laughed, and just looked at each other. We didn't know where to start. We ended up talking about my childhood, family life, our parents—good times. It was so deeply refreshing to laugh together, to so easily transcend the years of trauma. At the same time, I wanted to know more about those years, more about what had happened to my family, my father, but all of that had to wait.

* * *

Later in my visit I was over at Molley's house. We sat out under a tree, our chairs perched on top of his septic tank. I leaned back in the soft plastic, the wind blowing gently.

Molley's backyard was modest: a few chickens roamed the yard, and his kids were milling about. Between the two of us sat a wooden table, and on the table was a plate filled with neatly sliced chunks of sugar cane. The old delicacy was barely familiar to me anymore, and I ate each chunk as if it were the first time I had tasted it.

"I like sitting here," he said. "I come out here to think, and whenever I have company, I bring them out here."

I could tell that Molley was proud of his home and his surroundings. The house was huge, and there were many people living with him—he loves people and he always has. Between bites of sugar cane he told me the story of how he survived the war.

When he was finished, in the silence that lingered, I was left with this: the man who killed my father—whom I will call General X—was dead. He'd been dead for years. It seemed to me that my brothers had designated Molley as the one to tell me the news, just as, years before, Boye had been the one to officially tell me that Ma had passed away.

Later, when I returned to the United States, I found records on the internet indicating that he had been killed in the fighting sometime between 1992 and 1996. General X had been a well-known member of Taylor's inner circle, but he was dead. He probably shared the same fate as my father: no grave. I had been chasing a ghost for most of my life. General X controlled me from half a world away, from beyond life. He was as real as the feelings of hate that consumed me. He was as real to me as my dining room chair where I'd practiced talking to a void. He was as real as my desire to forgive. He was as real to me as the peace I wanted to feel after I spoke with him.

He can't be dead. He can't be dead. I came all the way here to see him. I felt this was unfair. I felt no satisfaction in his death the way I might have years earlier. I wanted him to be alive. I was expecting a trail to find him that would take weeks, perhaps years. Maybe he would be living in a hut in a village that required a day's walk, through mud and dust, from the main road. But the search was already over: it was a dead end. I needed General X to be alive so that I could be free. And I thought he needed me.

Had this news gotten to me ten years earlier I would have rejoiced in his demise. In fact I would have loved to hear the details of his death, but now it seemed so anticlimactic. I grieved at the news, actually. I was anticipating a great Hollywood ending to my story, but now I felt cheated that he had died.

What I was going to do now? I knew I still needed to forgive, but who and how? I started to wonder about my motivation for coming to Liberia. Did I come to do General X a favor? Was I selfish in my so-called forgiveness? Had I really forgiven him at all? And if I had, why did I need to see him? If I had known that he was dead, would I have bothered to say "I forgive you" so many times in my dining room back in Denver? Would I have cried so many tears and screamed so many words? Would I have spent so much energy praying for General X? I am not sure I would have.

Now I had to process the news of his death. I felt a weight had been both lifted from and placed on me at the same time, and I proceeded with my visit unsure of myself and what I would do. I didn't know how to feel, but I had no choice but to accept it and let go of the burden of tracking down a man who had been dead for years.

I had to picture a different moment of forgiveness.

✷ ✷ ✷

Throughout my trip, I met a few young men who lived in and around Molley's neighborhood. I was uncomfortable around them. They had been young men in the war. They'd been part of the armies, part of the fighting, and part of the chaos. Even years later, they seemed perpetually close to violence, ready to act and react. Having been so morally injured, their instincts were almost animalistic; their inhibitions were worn away. These young men are all over Monrovia now, carrying their burdens: a lost childhood and an uncertain future.

They laughed together, jostling each other and carrying on like teenagers. Their camaraderie was clear. Apart from each other, they were kept to the outskirts of society, their guilt too much to bear.

After a time, as my nervousness wore down, I saw these men for what they were: childlike. While they had hurt others in the war, they too were hurt. In the chaos of war the lines of sanity, the lines of who was good or evil, were blurred. In war it is hard to tell who the good guys are. Civilians and soldiers made choices that they would never have made at other times. In the wake of such violence, there was more than enough guilt to go around. No one offered them spiritual and emotional wholeness. They were doomed to live in a country where they couldn't forgive themselves or be forgiven. How could I serve them? What do they need now? How could Liberians walk the path of justice, reconciliation, and forgiveness?

As I prepared to leave Liberia a few weeks later, still coming to terms with General X's death, I realized anew that God was in control—and always had been—and I needed to forgive not just one man but thousands of men. Liberia as a nation has thousands of former combatants. They are walking around cities pushing wheelbarrows, driving taxis, selling goods, hailing cabs for people, and begging. Some are desperate to be welcomed into society again. The conviction started to grow inside me: we need to forgive them; we need to welcome them back. For us to get past the atrocities and the dark memories, we must first be able to forgive those who deeply hurt us. We must forgive even those whom we know will hurt us again if they get the chance.

God was teaching me this improbable, insurmountable reality through the broken, hurting young men that I met. He was showing me that healing isn't a conversation between me and one man—forgiveness is far bigger than I thought.

CHAPTER 21

Jonah to Joseph

On my last night in Liberia, I lay in bed staring at the ceiling and smiling. It was warm and stuffy. The fan was blowing the humid rainy-season air around the room. Then the clouds opened, and the raindrops began to hit the roof above me. Soon the deluge was loud, and I couldn't help thinking of the times as a child when I bathed in the rain. Those were the times when I felt most clean, most full and whole. As I listened, the tears began to flow into my ears and onto my feathery pillow.

I began to think about the individuals who'd impacted my life. I remembered each family member and friend whom I had seen while in Liberia. I thought about the widespread hopelessness that hovered over the nation like the stench of death. Hopelessness was everywhere. I saw it in the bright eyes of the youth, and in the red eyes of the old. I saw it in the eyes of the women selling in the markets. I saw it in the young men playing football.

Forgiveness, though it wasn't what I'd originally pictured, washed over me like rain. I felt clean and whole, like a child, cleaner than I'd ever been. In that moment God showed me forgiveness beyond what I'd imagined, and it wasn't just for me or General X, it was for the whole nation of Liberia. Though it is not fair—revenge feels more fitting—I chose to forgive. Forgiving goes against every fiber of my being, and every instinct I have ever had. My human nature tells me that the former rebels need to pay severely for what they did, but I have to come to terms with the fact that I have been forgiven. I have not earned or worked toward my own forgiveness. Christ gave it to me as a gift.

As a Christ-follower, I am called to extend that same gift to others.

I began my journey of forgiveness in a very familiar place: the Gospel of Matthew, chapter 6, immediately following the Lord's Prayer.

> *For if you forgive men when they sin against you, your heavenly Father will also forgive you. But if you do not forgive men their sins, your Father will not forgive your sins*

The power of forgiveness is reciprocal. God's forgiveness of me is linked to my forgiveness of others. His forgiveness is my example. His forgiveness is my way of being.

In a culture that publicly humiliates people when they make mistakes, I chose to forgive because I need forgiveness. We all need forgiveness. I have done some terrible things to people—to more people than I can count or remember. There are few things more frustrating than when injustice prevails, when unfairness seems to win, when the bad guys seemingly go free. Some days I desperately want justice, and justice does play a huge part here. Then I am reminded that there is a bad guy in me who has been forgiven.

I chose to not to seek revenge because this choice ends a cycle of wrath and angry living. The freedom I feel now that I have stopped chasing revenge is real. When I let go of the shadow of General X, I also had to let go of the vengeful Marcus. It would no longer be him who shows up at parties. He will not be there when I get married. I chose to forgive him, to let him go. I had to let the self-righteous me go too—the me that wanted to be the forgiver without seeing myself as the one who has been forgiven in Christ.

That night, in my mind, I began composing a letter to General X, a letter I composed for years and eventually wrote down:

General X,

I will keep you hidden by using only *General X*, but my name is Marcus Doe. My family calls me Jungle Boy. In the war, in 1990, you killed a man at the displacement camp at Fendell College Campus. Do you remember that?

He was an older man, fifty-one years old. He was short and dark skinned, a Kru man, named Mr. Doe, from Barnersville. He was asked to turn himself in to you. He was told that no one would harm him.

He did turn himself in. You interrogated him. And after August 24, 1990, his family never saw him again.

The man you killed had six children, and I am the last of them. The man you killed looked like me. Some say I talk and walk like him. Do you remember that man? Please say that you do.

That man was my father, my pa. I wished every day for years that he was alive. Sometimes in crowded places I almost imagine that he is there. I follow older men, hoping they are my father. Sometimes I wish he was living in Guinea or Sierra Leone in a small village, still afraid to show himself in Liberia. The man you killed was my father.

General X, I lived my teenage years preparing to kill you. I joined the United States Army and learned to use weapons and how to kill, hoping I would have a chance to kill you.

But I am not here to fight you. I am not here to punch you or spit in your face. I no longer want revenge. I am not here to curse you. I am here to tell you something. I came looking for you to tell you that I forgive you.

You see, I became a follower of Jesus Christ. Jesus Christ forgave me, and once I understood what that meant, I knew I couldn't live the rest of my life not forgiving you. By following Jesus Christ, I was able to cultivate a heart to forgive you.

I don't wish terrible things for you.

I forgive you.

∗ ∗ ∗

As my personal burden lifted—melting my vengeance, my self-loathing—my burden for my homeland increased.

Forgiveness begins in the hearts of individuals, but it's meant to keep spreading from there. The invisible scars of war last a lifetime—even longer. While some lost very little in the war, some lost more than I did. But we all lost something: innocence, educational opportunities, money, family, property, health, and years that we will never get back. We lost hope in human beings.

I'd learned firsthand—over the years and in this very moment—that Christ is the only hope for those who've been so hurt and those who have hurt others. God is the only way I've been healed, in the past and even now. God had given me this gift to pass on to others. I saw such deep hurt in the eyes of some former soldiers I met. I also saw how the country was unable to forgive them, how they were unable to forgive themselves.

That night as the rain poured over my childhood home, I felt like God was asking me to be a messenger of forgiveness right here in this broken country. I'd been hurt like everyone else here, and now that I'd forgiven, I could show others the way to a whole new life.

Sometimes people ask me why I chose to forgive, but I ask myself, "What if I didn't forgive? What if I still carried the burden of chasing a ghost?" It wasn't the end that I envisioned, but it has been a great surprise of internal peace.

I love people again.

*   *   *

At thirty-one, I had finally landed on the path that I believe God wanted me on, a purpose for all of the problems, a path for my passions, and a way for my will. He wanted me to be a minister of forgiveness in Liberia. I didn't know how the path would lead me from here to there, but I realized that I'd been on this path, the path to ministry, for quite a while. The first seed was planted in 1987 in Mr. Montgomery's class, but it took twenty-three years for me to accept.

Mr. Montgomery, my third grade teacher, was the coolest teacher I had growing up. A tall dark-skinned man, he always wore his baggy shirts unbuttoned about halfway down his hairy chest. A gold chain with a cross dangled from his neck, and his glasses were stylish. He had a high top fade, which he emphasized with moist, shiny curls. He always seemed fresh out of the barber shop. All the boys in my class admired Mr. Montgomery. What made him even cooler was that he knew my older brothers; they had been at university together.

"You have a lot to live up to, Doe," he said the first day I met him. "I know your brothers."

One afternoon, after all of our schoolwork was completed, he gathered the class together for a story. Eager to listen and be near Mr. Montgomery, I pushed my way to the front of the group.

"I will tell you the story of Joseph today," he said. I had no idea who he was talking about.

Before long, I was engulfed in the story of Joseph from the book of Genesis. I could identify with Joseph immediately.

The story of Joseph is a story of great forgiveness. Like me, Joseph had many brothers, a big family. He was full of confidence as a young man, and his father loved him. In a dream, Joseph saw himself ruling over his older brothers, and they bowed to him. He shared this dream with his brothers, and they hated him. They eventually got tired of his boasting and sold him into slavery. He was taken to Egypt. While working in the house of his master, he was falsely accused of a horrible crime and sent to jail. Years later, when Joseph interpreted the Egyptian pharaoh's dreams, Pharaoh made Joseph a government official, giving him power over Egypt's great stores of food. When famine hit the land of Canaan, Joseph's brothers came to Egypt looking for food. They came to Joseph.

Joseph recognized his brothers, but they didn't recognize him. They were under his power now.

Mr. Montgomery told the story in a way that made me yearn for more. He was a great storyteller, so he did not finish the story in one afternoon. I could not wait to get to school the next day to hear the next installment of the story. Mr. Montgomery built up the suspense for the next day.

The second day of Joseph's story was more captivating than the first. That afternoon was like high-priced theater. My imagination took me to Egypt as he talked. The severe famine and drought became real to me.

Instead of exacting revenge on them, he saved their lives. Joseph forgave his brothers for selling him into slavery. He was not bitter—in fact, he wept with them. He gave them food, and together they moved to Egypt with their families.

I was captivated by the story. I wanted my life to have the adventure of Joseph's. I admired his resilience. I wanted to be able to interpret dreams. I wanted to have dreams that meant something. I wanted to be Joseph. I daydreamed of saving my brothers from hunger and being a great man of God, forgiving everyone and saving all the nations from starvation.

I knew I had to tell someone about the story of Joseph, so I told one of the few people who listened to me: my mother. As she sat on her favorite wooden chair on the front porch, I began the story, and in the days that followed, I prayed that God would make me like Joseph, even while I recounted the events of his life to Ma.

Twenty-three years later, I lay in the same room that had been the setting of that prayer. I had been seven or eight then. So many things had changed in my life—to say the least—but that old dream was rekindled.

My life ended up taking a long route back to this place, a trek that at times looked more like the story of Jonah, a man on the run, than Joseph. Even so, the seed had been sown, and now the prayer was being answered. Like Joseph, I needed to forgive people who had wronged me. Like Canaan, my nation suffered a famine, a spiritual starvation that was the result of fourteen long years of civil conflict. Now, like the terror of physical starvation, unforgiveness was choking Liberia.

✳ ✳ ✳

I didn't know quite how or when, but I knew I would be back. Knowing this helped the next morning as I prepared to leave. Tears filled my eyes as I said goodbye to Caroline yet again. Mocco helped load my things into his car. The scene was eerily familiar—these same siblings helped me with my belongings twenty years earlier under far different circumstances.

The last time I left them, it was under a cloud of war, sur-rounded by sadness and uncertainty. Now it was under the cleansing rain of forgiveness and anticipation of what the Lord was going to do. I hugged Caroline tightly and walked toward Mocco's car.

Molley came with us on the fifteen-mile journey to the airport. I said goodbye to my brothers. Our faces were tight, our emotions subdued. Grabbing my bags, I began walk-ing toward the only terminal. I knew this time I would see them soon—and speak to them even sooner. My heavy bags contrasted with the emotional release bubbling deep within my heart. My hands and shoulders ached, and my face was dominated by wrinkles that seemed to chronicle my physical weariness with each step.

But I'd never felt so light.

As I walked closer to the security checkpoint, though, I felt torn. Did it really make sense to go back to the United States? Which country was home?

I was heading "home" now, but the month before, while in the States, I told my friends that I was returning "home." Was I homeless?

No, I realized, I'm a man with a unique problem: I have two homes. I love two countries deeply. Tears poured down my face, mixing with sweat from my freshly shaved head.

With my bags checked and a bottle of cold water in hand, I sat down in the tiny waiting area for my flight. I felt caught between my two worlds. In one world, I was a middle-school teacher. In the other, I was the beloved little brother, an un-fortunate orphan.

Above my conflicting emotions rose the truth of God: the purpose of my life transcends the pull of my two worlds.

I am a child of God, not a citizen of a particular country, or even this world. My new priority was sharing the gospel of

Jesus Christ, of his forgiveness, with all nations, including the two that I call home. The burden of unforgiveness had been lifted during my trip, but God had given me a new burden, a new purpose that would be with me the rest of my life. I came to Liberia to forgive one man, but I would leave to start a movement to forgive all of them.

The plane took off, and I caught a last glimpse of the nation that raised me. I knew I would return, next time with a different purpose: preaching the gospel of Jesus Christ and the power and freedom of his forgiveness to Liberians in every village, town, and city.

As the pilot welcomed us and the attendants performed the safety routine, I surrendered my previous career plans to Christ and began planning my return to Liberia.